PRIMITIVE WAR

PRIMITIVE WAR

Its Practices and Concepts

By

HARRY HOLBERT TURNEY-HIGH

with a new introduction by

ALEX ROLAND

UNIVERSITY OF SOUTH CAROLINA PRESS

Second Edition

Third Printing

Published in Columbia, South Carolina, by the
University of South Carolina Press
Manufactured in the United States of America

ISBN: 0-87249-196-X (pbk.)

Library of Congress Catalog Card Number: 70-120919

Contents

Introduction

FOR HARRY HOLBERT TURNEY-HIGH, THE TERM "PRIMITIVE WAR" WAS AN oxymoron. He used the term, but he did not really believe there was such a thing. He was at pains to distinguish it from what he called "true (or civilized) war." This distinction is perhaps the greatest contribution of this important book; the failure to clarify or sustain the distinction is perhaps its greatest weakness.

Turney-High believed that "war, true war, is a matter of social organization." It is measured in terms of tactics, discipline, specialization of labor, conscription, motives, and organization. Military technology, which he believed had received too much attention from archaeologists, anthropologists, and historians, was a mere tool with which to conduct war; it did not determine the nature of the activity. War, for him, was a social phenomenon, shaped by social forces.

To clarify his views he introduced the concept of a "threshold" or "horizon of war" separating primitive combat from true war. On the near or modern side of the threshold, above the horizon, was civilized war. Conscripted, professional soldiers are gathered in trained and disciplined fighting organizations, served by adequate logistics, and maneuvered in combat according to planned and rehearsed tactics.

Beyond the threshold, below the horizon, was primitive war. All the able-bodied male members of a tribe or kin group decided, often individually, if they wanted to go to war. Those who chose to participate engaged in rituals that prepared them for combat, but they proceeded to battle with no more plan nor organization than if they were going on a hunt. Combat might be initiated according to some scheme, but once engaged the battle broke down into an uncoordinated series of individual combats. Each warrior chose for himself when to break off, usually at the first sign of bloodshed. The motives for this activity were visceral and instinctive—revenge or play, for example—seldom economic or political.

The threshold between primitive and civilized war was not uniform, the horizon was not fixed. Cannibalism, for example, seems to have been practiced as much by civilized groups as by primitive. The Zulus under Chaka and Dingiswayo were a primitive tribal culture with a thoroughly modern military system, which included organization, training, tactics, and war to the death. The pre-war rituals of the Zulus bear a striking resemblance to those of classical Sparta, surely a civilized society. The guerilla tactics of the twentieth century are often difficult to distinguish from those of primitive tribes.

At times, then, Turney-High defined primitive war as simply war undertaken by primitives, or as he put it, pre-literate peoples. But even this criterion failed him. He says at one point that "many tribes with a high enough social organization to know better have no more approach order [in combat] than does a lynch mob." But if civilized societies can conduct primitive war, then how high is the threshold, how far is the horizon? Turney-High could never get his model to hold up across the wide spectrum of cases he examined.

His view of primitive war, with all its strengths and weaknesses, can be compared with that of Quincy Wright, developed in his monumental *A Study of War.*[1] Conceived and executed at the University of Chicago in the the years leading up to World War II, this comprehensive volume was an attempt to see war whole, from the complete range of perspectives available within the scholarly community. Wright envisioned four kinds of warfare, each associated with a principal driving force. Animal warfare came first, driven by human instincts, the province of psychology. Next came primitive war, driven by social forces of the tribe or clan, the province of sociology. It was followed in turn by historical or civilized warfare, shaped by the international state system, the province of international law. Finally, with the introduction of gunpowder in the fourteenth century, came modern war, driven by its weapons, the province of technology.

Each kind of warfare had unique characteristics in Wright's view, and each contributed cumulatively to the nature of war at any given time. The characteristics of animal warfare, for example, never disappeared from the human condition. Rather, they were submerged beneath the motives and methods of primitive warfare, which in its turn was submerged within civilized warfare. The warfare of any given period in the evolution of the human race, then, is a composite in which new characteristics have been superimposed upon the characteristics of all previous eras.

Wright was far more precise than Turney-High in describing the characteristics of primitive war. For him it was war of the hunt. Its essential tactic was pounce and flee. Though this hardly amounts to the sophisticated tactics that Turney-High believed essential for "true war," it is a tactic nonetheless and a successful one at that. It allows the primitive to achieve his objective, or at least escape with life and limb should the attack fail. And for all the reasons that Turney-High is wont to emphasize—lack of organization, discipline, plans, etc.—attacks by primitives are as likely to fail as not. Like Turney-High, Wright believes

1. (Chicago: University of Chicago Press, [1942] 1965).

that primitive war is driven by social motives of the tribe or clan, such as revenge and protection of the in-group; these are seldom worth dying for.

Wright's analysis defines primitive war more precisely than Turney-High, but he does not impose upon it a boundary so restrictive as a threshold or horizon. For him it is primitive war to the extent that it embodies the characteristics of his model, but there is a gray area between animal and primitive war and another between primitive and civilized war. He thus places primitive war in a larger contextual framework than Turney-High, and maintains a greater definitional flexibility.

The value of Turney-High's book, then, is not that it is the preeminent analysis of primitive warfare in the English language or even that it is the most precise or internally consistent. Rather it is the most complete analysis, the most thoughtful and informed, the most original, and still the most stimulating. The other books in the same league with this one do not quite achieve the same level. Maurice Davie's *The Evolution of War: A Study of Its Role in Early Societies*[2] is richly ingrained with anecdotes from the primary literature, but it lacks the focus, analysis, and organizational strengths of *Primitive War*. What is worse, its definition of primitive war is even looser than Turney-High's. Stansislav Andreski's *Military Organization and Society*[3] is a more satisfactory and rigorous sociological analysis of war as a social institution, but it is not properly speaking an anthropological study and it is not limited to primitive war. Kenneth Waltz's *Man, the State, and War: A Theoretical Analysis*[4] is an interdisciplinary study by a political scientist; it adopts a scheme similar to Wright's but does not single out primitive war as a unit of analysis.

One of the great mysteries of recent anthropology is that more has not been written on primitive war. R. Brian Ferguson's 1984 bibliography of anthropology, *Warfare, Culture, and Environment,*[5] lists not a single recent book on this topic to compare with Turney-High's. There are a number of good anthologies containing pertinent chapters and the subject continues to receive attention in scholarly articles and monographs on case studies. But no synthesis to compare with *Primitive War* has been published since the second edition of this volume appeared in 1971.

Since this study remains the best book-length introduction to the topic, its reprinting is a welcome event for anthropologists, sociologists, historians, and other scholars interested in early warfare. Needless to say, I heartily endorse and recommend the book. I suggested to the University of South Carolina Press that it be reissued and I welcomed the opportunity to write this introduction. Even a

---

2. (New Haven Conn.: Yale University Press, 1929).

3. (Berkeley: University of California Press, [1954] 1971).

4. (New York: Columbia University Press, 1959).

5. (Orlando, Fla: Academic Press, 1984).

classic study like this one, however, warrants some home truths about its strengths and weaknesses.

Many of the book's weaknesses will reveal themselves in just a brief perusal. The study was begun during World War II and published just four years after the war ended. Harry Holbert Turney-High was a trained and accomplished anthropologist and sociologist, but a good bit of his scholarly detachment and perspective were clouded by his experiences in the war. He served in the military police in Europe during the war, advancing to the rank of colonel by the time of his detachment from active duty in 1946. He returned to an earlier draft of this study filled with his wartime experiences and with stories and worldviews gleaned from extensive conversations with fellow officers. There is an undeniable tone of presentism in the book. He judges primitive war by the standards of World War II. He focuses on operational issues at the expense of broader cultural issues, in part because he felt the latter had received more than their fair share of attention in the literature already, but also in part because he was imbued with the combat officer's notion that battle is the heart of war.

He also imbibed in the military environment an attachment to the principles of war, a set of universal constants that many practitioners of war believe to be the keys to victory. This handful of fundamentals—surprise, concentration, mobility, etc.—determine the outcome of battles. The commander who knows and manipulates them most effectively wins. There is reason to doubt the efficacy of the principles of war, for in the uncritical mind they can too easily become substitutes for thought rather than stimulants. But Turney-High uses them with a reasonably light hand; the discriminating reader can screen this organizational tool from the text with little difficulty. The author's preoccupation with operations is less easy to ignore, but it is largely limited to the first half of the book. Furthermore, Turney-High makes a fair point that operations receive less than their due in the other literature on primitive war.

Modern readers will be put off by the arrogant, pontifical tone of much of the writing. Armed with his World War II experience, Turney-High seemed to believe that he knew far more about war in general and primitive war in particular than any he surveyed. His language can be preachy and didactic, and he does not hesitate to point out the shortcomings of those who do not share his views. More troubling still are the traces of racism, sexism, and anti-Semitism that marble his prose. They are not blatant, but they are there nonetheless. Some are sadly and remarkably a sign of the times in which he wrote; some are no doubt evidence of personal prejudices that have been made more apparent and more distasteful by the passage of time and our growing cultural sensitivity to such issues. No apology for them quite suffices.

On a less serious note, it should be pointed out that Turney-High had little appreciation for the importance of fortification. This is partly because he focused so intensely on combat, which fortification often precludes. And it is partly because of his perception that weapons and other military technology had received more attention in the literature than they deserved. In any case, he slights this important aspect of warfare.

Balancing these weaknesses are a number of strengths that firmly establish the value of this work. Turney-High was deeply immersed in the primary anthropological literature on primitive warfare. His study is rich in anecdote and illustration, aptly chosen and convincingly presented. This book is a department store of information and evidence on primitive warfare, organized intelligently and packaged attractively. It should be read from cover to cover, but it can be browsed profitably by diving into this department or that. It is at once a successful sustained analysis and a copious, reliable reference book.

Because Turney-High saw his subject whole, he organized his material in an interesting and thought-provoking way. As the subtitle suggests, the first half of the book focuses on practices, i.e., actual combat operations. The second half attempts to distill the fundamental concepts of primitive war, including motives, values, attitudes ("the way people tend to behave toward a value"), and social organization. Students of military operations will be most taken by the first half; students of war as a social institution the second half. Turney-High's view, implicit in the organization, that practice drives concepts, will stimulate all who seek to understand the nature of warfare.

Finally, the book is rich in insights. Turney-High held strong opinions and he was not hesitant to venture sweeping generalizations. Some are simply matters of faith, unproven and unprovable in any scholarly sense. Some are now dated, either by the evolution of cultural values or by the development of more recent scholarship. But some are as current as the latest scholarly debate. The role of warfare in state formation is a case in point. Turney-High wrote over forty years ago that "active agriculture and herding not only have provided the economic basis (and cause) of effective warfare, but, linked with metals, have been the great builders of the state. They have contained the seeds of the destruction of kin societies and the building of civil governments." Whether or not one subscribes to that position, it could just as well have been written in 1989 as in 1949. It attests to the continuing relevance and importance of this classic study.

ALEX ROLAND

Durham, North Carolina
April 1991

Preface to the First Edition

TWO CONSIDERATIONS ORIGINALLY LED TO THE STUDY OF WHICH THIS volume is the product. First, considering the importance of war to all peoples, it is surprising that such a small effort has been made to analyze the complex among nonliterate folk. Anthropologists, sociologists, and other social scientists have largely confined their writing to deprecating war rather than attempting to understand this behavior pattern which has played such a tremendous role in human affairs. Second, considering the qualitative and quantitative excellence of the field literature of anthropology, several authors consider that it is time to enter the generalizing phase of the science.

This work represents an effort to help correct the first defect. It will at least raise questions which other students are encouraged to solve, and it is hoped that the field ethnographers will be encouraged to be more explicit in their treatment of their informants' military behavior.

Civilized war will be discussed only briefly in Chapter I. The term "civilization" refers to cultures with writing, metal-smelting, organized commerce, civil government, city-building, tactical warfare, and such complexes. The military practices of such peoples as the Pre-Columbian Peruvians, Maya, and Aztec, then, will not be discussed, as their methods were basically modern and differed too little from our own. This study, therefore, treats of nonurban societies without stone architecture and literate members. The term used here is nonliterate, which actually approaches the popular meaning of "primitive" and "uncivilized" in most instances.

The method of the study has been this: Every effort has been made to forget opinions based on secondary, tertiary, and often quaternary materials. Only descriptive field literature has been used. Every book and monograph discovered by the author and his research staff has been used or at least sampled. The works read exceed those cited many times. If the reader finds that he would have preferred to have included some topics which are not, or to have others discussed with more thoroughness, the author shares his wishes. He had to let the recorded facts scream, whisper, or be silent. The condition of the field literature made the latter necessary in many important phases.

The library research for this study was begun before the late war. As the year 1942 drew on, it became apparent that many of us would have to enter active military service. In order to obtain criticism of a part of the work, and mindful of the uncertainties of war, the author requested the Montana State University to mimeograph and distribute a portion of the work, which was done. The favorable character of the resultant criticism suggested publication of this, the complete study. Again, publication was delayed in light of the possibilities of the theoretical position being weakened by field experience. Study of the manuscript after separation, however, showed that the recent European war only confirmed the original conclusions.

There are three dangers into which this type of study might easily fall, largely because of its limited Twentieth Century tradition. First, it might be said that it tends to ignore the other patterns of culture with which warfare must certainly be linked. This work is meant to be a study of warfare only, and does not pretend to be a general social anthropology. It is hoped that other students will describe these linkages. Second, one might suspect that the materials have been pressed into an arbitrary developmental pattern. The author has, however, only followed where the descriptive literature has led. Warfare is a relatively simple art, even if it has engaged some of the best minds in history. There are only a few ways in which war can be successfully waged. The peoples who have discovered and practiced these simple principles have engaged in war properly so-called; others have failed to do this and have practiced what is called "primitive war," for lack of a better term. Third, one must always be cautious of using value judgments when comparing nonliterate cultures with civilization. Field ethnographers often live so close to their informants that they develop feelings of local patriotism; anthropologists as a whole tend to constitute themselves a corps of sympathetic advocates of all men without writing. Worthy as these sentiments are, they are value judgments themselves which the author gladly renounces. But if any statement of his that a forged steel axe cuts down a given tree more efficiently than does a stone one be considered a value judgment, he must plead guilty, for he has made the experimental test. If his statement that a social group practicing warfare tactically can defeat a nontactical group of the same size and equal armament is also a value judgment, he must also accept that charge. History repeatedly has made this experimental test.

This work uses the term "principles" of war because warfare is man's oldest and most successful social science. War is the first social science to become truly scientific, for it is the first the practice of which has been reduced to a few simple principles which are true without regard to time or place. This is so obvious that it is strange that it has not been said before.

My thanks go to Professors Melville Herskovits and Ralph Linton for their sound criticism of this volume. Professor Garvin Shallenberger brought a physicist's logic to bear upon the evidence. The late Colonel Copley Enos, able cavalier, taught me my basic tactics. And many thanks to the other officers, noncommissioned officers, and enlisted men of the American, British, and French armies who have continued my instruction in the art of war.

Finally, thanks are due to the Montana State University for permission to use the material originally incorporated in the mimeographed study issued by them.

HARRY HOLBERT TURNEY-HIGH

Columbia, South Carolina

April 22, 1949

PRIMITIVE
WAR

PART I

The Practice of Primitive War

Chapter 1

The Form and Function of Weapons

Since armaments are preeminent in civilian thinking, and since there is great virtue in being obvious, material, and familiar, the average man's mind turns to weapons whenever war is mentioned. The advantage of proceeding from the familiar to the unfamiliar suggests using the topic of weapons as an introductory springboard to this primer of primitive war.

The part which weapons play in war is far simpler than appears at first glance. War is war, a social institution fulfilling a variety of motives, ending in many ways, evoking many emotions. The central fact of miltary theory is that war is a sociologic device, and weapons are merely tools used to facilitate its practice. The persistence with which social scientists have confused war with the tools of war would be no less than astounding did not their writing reveal, for the most part, complete ignorance of the simpler aspects of military history and theory, and an almost stubborn unwillingness to conceptualize warfare as the great captains have conceptualized it—and still do. It would be very hard to find a noncommissioned officer in the professional armies of the second rate powers who has been as confused as most analysts of human society.

This civilian attitude has resulted in hundreds of museum cases housing weapons from all over the world, cataloged, marked with accession numbers, and uncomprehended. A digest of what is known of the material culture of war would require a far larger volume than this. Even the briefest catalog of such works would require an impressive pamphlet. A list of monographs and articles dealing with the way such weapons are held, how many fingers are used in arrow-release, which foot is put forward in hurling the javelin, and just which toes are dug into the ground during the process would also require a fair amount of stationery. But what has this to do with war? Very little, for all such questions of the importance have been solved since the opening of the Neolithic Age, and nothing was added except minor improvements until the perfection of powder-driven projectiles.

Placing a discussion of weapons at the forepart of this work, then, does not signify their paramount importance. It reflects a desire to discuss the fundamentals of the primitive armory, relegate them to their proper places, and then to proceed to warfare's more important aspects.

The theoretical summary of weapons can be briefly made: A man wishes to do another bodily harm. Nature has provided the aggressor with teeth, nails, feet, and hands, together with muscles and a will to drive these forcibly against the defender. Since the defender is also equipped with a skin and skull of some toughness, as well as a desire not to be hurt, the aggressor's anatomical equipment is hardly adequate. If the aggressor picks up a stone which is harder than his fist, he can make a considerable impression upon the defender, producing abrasions and contusions upon his surface, and perhaps reducing his resistance and diminishing his will. If the aggressor chooses a sharp stone, he can insert this into the dermal and muscular tissue of the defender and injure him to the point of death.

The defender, unless caught by surprise, is hardly willing to remain and be pommelled. He may back away, or he may fight back. Prudence enters into the aggressor's thinking. He finds it convenient either to avoid the flailing arms of the defender or to overcome the distance between himself and his foe faster and more safely than his legs can carry him. No one has ever stressed the importance of human prudence in the development of weapons, or perhaps it should be said that no one has called enough attention to the aggressor's fear. Should the aggressor put his sharpened stone on a stick, he has a spear which not only will increase the leverage of his man-piercing tool, but will enable him to stand at a safer distance and poke his foe. This spear may also be hurled. Better yet, it may be hurled with a bow as an arrow, the deadliest weapon man was to know until late in the so-called Renaissance. If the aggressor seeks protection by retiring to a safe distance, the range of the arrow (or cannon or airplane) must be increased, while if he stands in a hole the spear must then be made stronger to root him out of his rudimentary engineering work. The projectile—arrow, ballista, catapult, or cannon—must have greater power of demolition. If the defender puts his fortification on his own body in the form of defensive armor, the same process must be carried through. And so goes the circular process.

Biological and social scientists have long called attention to the cyclical nature of events in nature and in human affairs. Nothing illustrates this better than mankind's expenditure of genius on weapons. If the offense becomes strong, the defense replies by becoming strong enough to vitiate the offense's weapons. The offense thinks up new weapons or improves the old ones so that the defense's genius must think up new defenses or be crushed out of existence. There is nothing new nor old in this. The entire history and prehistory of weapons is summarized in this cycle. Once the offense-defense inventive cycle is conceptualized, one has mastered the first and most important principle of armory.

One often encounters statements of this type: In former times fighting was man to man, while today it is with long distance weapons. This is pure nonsense, of course, as any soldier will agree. Fighting has always been man to man, and still is. Fire weapons only prepare for the shock, the closing with the enemy, and that closing is man to man; that contact is the battle. This is standard military doctrine the world over.

The rise and perfection of weapons, then, sprang from man's desire and need to harm his neighbor's body and determination. Whatever created that desire and need, or whenever it arose is no concern of ours at the present. The origin and perfection of weapons had the same origin as the rest of the material culture, pacific or otherwise.

Man had and has deadly weapons provided by nature—the features of his anatomy. The same may be said of peaceful tools. Yet unaided nature would have left man with inadequate tools wherewith to carve himself a career upon this planet and weapons inadequate to carve his will upon his opponents. The economists have long pointed out that there is not enough desirable stuff in the world to satisfy every man's wants, and the appeal to force is an ancient method of distribution. The rise of weapons is the rise of improving on nature, or better, the art of cooperating with nature in order to make natural phenomena serve military motives.

An unaltered rock or simple unimproved stick are still lethal killers, but they are not, strictly speaking, weapons. A true weapon must exhibit purposive human workmanship. It must be a modification of some natural object; in the terminology of anthropology, it must be an artifact. A weapon, like a tool, must be something material, artificial, and purposive. It is likewise a response to human needs, and its chief function is to serve as an intermediary between the intelligence of the warrior and his desires.

The economist says that human needs are indefinitely extensible, that they have never been completely satisfied, nor will they ever be. If material culture, then, is the corpus of the responses to human needs, then might not the material culture also be indefinitely extensible and capable of improvement, the only limit being nature itself? No generation like the present one, which ascribes almost magical power to inventors and engineers, dares say what the limits of invention may be. When one translates this into the specialized field of weapons he meets staggering military potentialities. Should this be so, the future looks black indeed save for this: War is primarily a sociologic art, and the art of war improves so slowly that Alexander's principles of combat are still standard. The art of making weapons changes rapidly—the art of handling the men who use them changes much more slowly.

The other hopeful element has already been introduced. Weapons and other cultural materials are responses to needs, but improved weapons and tools create needs. Certainly we have civilian needs of which our great-grandparents dreamed not. Every civilized family today considers the automobile a definite need. President Washington did not. Every commander today conceives of the tank as a need. General Washington did not. New inventions make man discover a host of needs of which he had hitherto been unaware. One certain need, which is called to mind by a new offensive invention or improvement of an old one, is the need of a parrying defense, material or tactical. Likewise, when the defense thinks out something new, such as the improvement in castle building under Norman genius, the offense has need of improved siege engines, and these responses to needs do occur partially if given time. Therefore in calling attention to the cumulative nature of invention and improvement in weapons, let us also stress again the cyclical nature of offense-defense invention. While the offense-defense cycle is the most hopeful element of war, primitive or modern, it cannot be expected to function perfectly. An offensive weapon completely effective against the ancient helmet has yet to be invented, for it is still worn. A perfect defense against the Upper Paleolithic spear has yet to be devised, for its modern equivalent—the bayonet—is still an article of issue.

Weapons, then, are the intermediaries between the aggressive human intelligence and its desires, and nature has given man powerful weapons in his hands. How the mind helped produce human hands and how the hands in turn established the superiority of the human nervous system is one of the most fascinating problems of physical anthropology. From certain aspects it might be said that the bulk of weapons, ancient and modern, are primarily auxiliaries and extensions of the hands. The hands are the ministers of the mind, but unaided they would have left mankind defenseless in the face of hostile nature and hostile humanity. While hands are quite sufficient to squeeze the throats or gouge the eyes of our ill-wishers, especially the tractable and pliant ones, there could have been no war based on unaided hands. Yet it is well to recall in this machine age—and machine-gun age—that effective weapons can be simple. The bayonet is still one of the most lethal weapons in the world.

Hard materials have always defeated the human hand, hence the first tools observed in archeology are cutting tools. Now the body of an agile opponent is quite hard enough to defeat the unaided hand, so the first problem was to find piercing weapons, which may be looked upon as extension of the primate finger nails and teeth. This was effectively solved as soon as the spear and the arrow were known. The problem was then basically solved as early as the Upper Paleolithic Period. The modern piercing weapons, the bayonet point and the bullet, may be morphologically different from the antique forms, but functionally they are only derivatives of them.

In light of the paramount importance of tactical operations, the form and structure of weapons are too secondary in significance to merit full treatment in so short a volume as this. To all soldiers, primitive and modern, the result is the important consideration. Therefore in a brief discussion of the effectiveness of the armory, the function alone has real validity. A functional classification of all weapons without regard to time or place is very easy. The doctrine of the present military powers has already made such a classification and, fortunately, it is one which is just as applicable to nonliterate warriors as to those in the uniforms of the powers. This system divides weapons into the following categories, those of: (1) fire, (2) shock, (3) mobility, and (4) protection.

Weapons of fire are devices for getting at a distant enemy while at the same time actually or wishfully remaining safe from his striking power. Fire weapons are therefore projectiles. The sling is an ancient and, if one is to judge by the results of David's attack on Goliath, an effective fire weapon. The writers of classical antiquity were well aware of its value in delivering all kinds of fire. Caesar knew how effective the sling was even in prohibitive fire, in keeping the enemy walls cleared of defenders so that the besiegers could come up close to the enceinte.

The greatest fire weapon of all, from the Paleolithic Capsian until well into the age of firearms, was the arrow, a short spear driven by a spring. Since it is definitely known to have existed before the opening of the true New Stone Age, mankind has had adequate fire weapons from that early time onward. This is one more link in the contention that war is a sociologic trait, one which had to await adequate social organization, command, and discipline. The arrow and bow literature is vast and cannot be summarized here, and the use of the device will be mentioned time and again in the succeeding chapters. Our own day is characterized by the great perfection of fire weapons, often to the befuddlement of the laity. One should not forget the part the bow and arrow have played in this. The powder driven projectile is more than the functional successor of the arrow. It is also the morphological descendant, inasmuch as the cross-bow, arlebest, arquebus, and similar derivatives of the simple bow had to come first. The explosive power of powder was known long before the musket became practical. The improved bow had to teach the fire fighter the use of the stock to sustain great recoil, the sight, the trigger, as well as the possibilities of great range and accuracy in firing a projectile along or through a barrel. After that the expansive power of chemicals could be tamed in the musket.

The blowgun would have taught the modernizing infantryman the same lesson, but he was not aware of its existence or effectiveness. This device, more of a hunting tool than a military weapon, consists of a barrel of metal or reed into which a pellet is inserted and blown with the breath against a distant object with great accuracy and range. The power of a gas under pressure with but one outlet has given mankind many useful pacific tools and was known empirically to the natives of the tropical forest of South America, southeastern United States, Malaysia, and elsewhere. These nonliterate peoples could not appreciate the physics of the blowgun, and hence did not develop the weapon as highly as they might have.

The increasing efficiency of fire weapons made infantry the principal arm for several centuries of modern warfare. Infantry's shock power was too feeble to fight mediaeval cavalry. An effective mediaeval infantry would have required too many specialists to be active against the knighthood. Its fire had to be handled by archers who were so busy learning their craft and carrying enough weapons that they could be nothing but fire troops. The same was also true of slingers. When adequate musketry arose, the infantry was able to minimize the cavalry's shock power before it reached the infantry line. When and if it did, the pike infantry could make a fair stand against the armored horseman. It is true that the perfection of the English long bow anticipated effective musketry. When a detachable point was added to the musket in the Eighteenth Century, the bayonet became standard infantry equipment, providing superb shock and fire power in one light weapon. The infantry battle line became the Queen of Battles, although it seems today about to return the crown to the cavalry in a new form.

The spear or javelin hurled from the hand is a fire weapon encountered in many places and times. Its short range, low accuracy, and weight in carrying about in bulk make it infinitely inferior to the arrow. The last disadvantage was overcome by no people. Several devices were invented from time to time to increase the javelin's range and accuracy, such as the atlatl or dart-thrower known to the men of the Upper Old Stone Age, Australia, the Eskimo, Middle America, and elsewhere. Straps and thongs have also been added to the shaft to increase its accuracy and range by imparting a circular motion to its flight. There is a large literature on nonliterate man's attempts to overcome the fire inadequacy of the spear. A summary of such writing has been made by Krause.[1]

A fire weapon of limited value is the throwing-stick or hurled war club. The aboriginal Australians are famous for their manufacture, perhaps too famous, since too much attention has been paid to the boomerang, or throwing-stick which will more or less return to its point of propulsion. This is primarily a hunting tool and one which could not be of any value to fighting men arranged in a line. The Australian throwing-stick which is not curved and will not therefore

[1] F. Krause, "Sling Contrivances for Projectile Missiles," *Annual Report*, Smithsonian Institution, 1904 (Washington: 1905), pp. 619-639.

return to the hurler is a much better weapon. Many people have used a heavier throwing club, a war club light enough to be thrown but heavy enough to crush, the Polynesians being the most successful.

Throwing-sticks or clubs are really poor weapons. Only a powerful man can throw them far. No one can hurl them with the accuracy of the arrow or even the spear. They are too heavy for any fighter to carry many of them into battle. Their manufacture is expensive in time and skill. Worst of all, their slow movement and large bulk make them easy to see, their arc easy to predict, and therefore very easy to dodge. They must rely on the stunning capacity of their weight, for their piercing power is nil.

Fire weapons—arrows, bullets, artillery projectiles, slings, grenades, bombs, javelins, and spears—are all effective auxiliaries, but should never be relied upon by intelligent fighters for the main effort of the battle. They should be used in preparation for the main engagement, which must be definite movement in the direction of the enemy, accompanied by a desire to incapacitate him by assault. Fire *and* movement, as will be seen, constitute a most effective combination, and one which only courageous fighters can resist.

Fire has the prime weakness often overlooked by civilian writers. Fire weapons may be able to drive an enemy from a position, and often do; they may also be used defensively to minimize the strength of an enemy assault before the moment of contact. Prohibitive fire may also prevent an enemy from occupying a locality, but it is costly and of limited effectiveness. In spite of all these virtues, fire troops can take but can hold a position in the open only with difficulty. Fire fighters may hold with effectiveness only behind natural or artificial cover. Fire and fire only is hopeless if the enemy ever makes contact.

Weapons of shock are the crushers and piercers which are held in the hand of the assailant. Shock weapons are the military instruments *par excellence.* They are not only employed by courageous fighters anxious to close with the enemy, deliver him a blow, and win a decision, but they are the truly deadly ones. They win battles. Following chapters will describe actions of some peoples who relied exclusively on fire weapons and lacked the courage or perspicacity to close with the foe in shock. Such actions neither won anything nor settled anything. Perhaps they were not meant to. A fire fight for its own sake is hardly more than an athletic contest. It is not within any true war pattern; it is wastful of life since it is futile; it can scarcely be called fighting. It is shock or the threat of shock which works one's will on the enemy. The victor of a fire fight is a long way from his objective; the victor in a shock fight is right there.

The war club is primarily a shock weapon, a skull crasher, a bruiser, accomplishing its ends by stunning and killing the foe. It is a weapon requiring close contact, and therefore courage on the part of its assailant. The deadliest shock weapons known to military history are the sword and the spear.

The sword is a derivative of the war club; indeed, it is a war club provided with a piercing point and sometimes with a cutting edge. Several peoples who had not discovered the use of metals had war clubs which were to all purposes swords. The Polynesians improved the edges of their hard wooden war clubs with shark's teeth, ray's tails, and other sharp objects provided by nature. Certain Middle Americans enhanced the sharpness of their club edges by insets of obsidian. Other plain wooden clubs and some stone ones on the North Pacific Coast of America were sharpened so that they were to all intents and purposes swords.

The discovery of metal casting in the Bronze Age made the sword the great weapon of both infantry and cavalry until a few years ago when the General Staff took the saber from the cavalry. The older bronze swords were quite short, for the smiths had not learned how to cast a long weapon. It is regrettable that they ever did. A lesson which both nonliterate and civilized soldiers had a hard time learning and retaining is that it is not the edge of a shock weapon which is dangerous but the point. Anyone who tried to train cavalry recruits a few years back knows how hard it was to keep them from slashing. The only good function a cutting edge has is to enable the assailant to withdraw his weapon from the spasmodically grasping tissue of his victim. A slashing blow is easily seen, dodged, or parried. It rarely hits a vital spot and therefore only wounds the enemy without killing him. He may be left not only alive but very angry and vengeful. Any slashing blow leaves the body of the slasher without guard unless he can cover with a shield, a miserable and clumsy substitute for skill.

As the Bronze Age technicians increased their abilities in casting, swords became longer and heavier and were transformed into cutters and crushers, having all the flaws just mentioned. The reply to this was the cast metal helmet, a false reply to a false threat. Many prehistoric European Metal Age swords were so specifically designed as cutters that they developed a flair towards the point end, the so-called pistiliform swords. This carried the typological development of the cutting sword to an absurdity not to be equalled until the heavily armored knight with his ponderous and clumsy war sword, mace, *bec-de-corbin,* axe, etc., arose in the Middle Age. This latter soldier became more of a blacksmith than a swordsman, breeding massive horses to carry him and his equipment about. The only good this did the world was to develop powerful percherons which later were to haul ice and coal through city streets. The ancient Italians continued and developed the folly of increasing the length and weight of the sword, especially over-weighting the weapon towards the point, which threw it out of balance. When they received a few thorough defeats from the Celt-Iberians of Spain who retained the earlier weapon, they readopted the short sword, much to the subsequent discomfiture of the Gauls and the Germans.

While the Metal Age sword has passed out of existence as an effective military instrument, its Stone Age companion, the spear, is still in good favor. Call it spear, lance, pike, or bayoneted rifle, it has perhaps caused more human deaths than any other material invention of man. One occasionally hears veterans of the World War of 1914-1918, especially those from noncombatant units, deprecate the bayonet. Medical officers say that their hospitals were full of bullet-wounded men, while they were seldom called upon to treat a bayonet wound. Such statements are compliments to the bayonet. Its victims did not require the services of the hospital squads but the burying party. It took the second World War to reduce its value, which decline may not be permanent.

Mankind's cowardice, or wish for security if one prefers that, impelled him to lengthen and over-weight the spear, just as he made a similar mistake with the sword. The Greeks made this error with the greatest cost to their liberty. They destroyed the fencing power of the spear; made it a muscular feat to carry and handle it; made the movement of the point very slow and predictable, and therefore immobilized the pikemen. The Romans, of course, won the Battle of Corinth. This point will be recalled in the discussion of African war. One great African war chief, the Zulu King Chaka, saw this flaw in the large spear and rectified it. Only the appearance of the white man saved South Africa from becoming a Zulu empire.

If the motive power of the tribe was adequate, it was possible to combine shock weapons with the mobility principle. Some peoples used the war horse as a weapon, while our automotive civilization has developed the tank. Fire power, mobility, shock, and protection have been sought in one weapon time and again by inventive warriors. The war elephant was a fairly successful effort, but this animal's impulses towards self-preservation and his low confidence in the omniscience of men made him more of a liability than an asset. The modern tank is a similar attempt to combine all elements, and while it is a most useful instrument, perfection in the combination is still far away.

The term mobility has no special meaning here. A mobile weapon's function is to enable the fighting man to get to the enemy, get around him, or get away from him faster than he could accomplish these ends with his own legs. From the Metal Ages onward the horse has been the most notable weapon of mobility in land fighting, combining as he does shock power with mobility. There might be some objection to calling domestic animals weapons, inasmuch as the warrior does not change their morphology. It was said that the element of artificiality must be added to some natural object to make it either a tool or a weapon. While one could hardly call a war horse an artifact, yet an artificiality is involved, albeit a psychological one. A simple horse is not a war horse. Cavalry horses must be meticulously trained in order to make them chargers, beasts that will have sufficient confidence in their riders to plunge into fire, into a hail of projectiles, strike their riders' foes with their forefeet and stamp them, bite the right party with their vicious teeth, and otherwise cooperate intelligently with the cavalier in striking down opposition. When one has learned that the fundamental factor in equine psychology is self-preservation, as it is with all grazing, fleet, gregarious animals, he has gone far in his lessons in equitation, civil or military. When one appreciates that it takes much skill and patience to overcome this equine fear and to instill in the troop mounts a desire to combat the enemy, he will never say that the element of artificiality is absent and that the horse is not a weapon.

The element of protection hardly seems consistent with valor, but valor requiring useless self-sacrifice is hardly military. To be sure, the best protection is to stay away from the enemy and do all of one's military exercise on the parade ground. "He who fights and runs away will live to fight another day," is not entirely stupid, and is also frequently necessary. "Discretion is ever the better part of valor," said one of the world's greatest captains, but discretion is a tactical device, not an armorial one.

Armor is the best known category of defensive weapons. The correct term, however, is defensive armor, for all weapons are armor. The defensive armory has always been a response to improvements in the enemy's fire and shock weapons, and when used moderately, has great value. The Iroquois and the tribes of the American Northwest Coast and Plateau knew the use of wooden or reed armor. Many others understood the value of suits of quilting, linked mail, etc., in eliminating or minimizing the bite of arrow, pike, and sword. Many nonliterates in Middle America, Polynesia, and Africa knew that armor would enable them to keep in the field longer than if dressed simply in their skins. The use of the shield is known to every continent save Australia, where the twirling stick takes its place.

Aside from such disciplined troops as can form a *testudo* with their shields, this instrument's value has been a delusion. Any armor decreases the mobility of the fighting line, makes the warrior particularly visible, and draws fire from bow or cannon. The greatest modern problem of tank warfare is the weight of the armor. Shall the storm-wagon rely on its speed to avoid fire, thus arming itself lightly, or shall it rely on the thickness of its steel plates and thus become slow? We have no perfect solution yet, and nonliterate man never solved the problem. True, the weight of metal is the great immobilizer, and most nonliterate tribes were also non-metallurgical. Some of the European Bronze and Iron Age peoples did manage to weight themselves down to no good end before the dawn of history, and some pre-metallurgical folk managed to encumber themselves with too much wood. Wherever too much armor is observed, one will find that the enemy fights with very effective war clubs, or the war club's derivatives. Among these would be the tribes of the North Pacific Coast who found armor weight of minor disadvantage since they were seafighters and used the canoe instead of legs to carry them to the scene of action.

Like the dinosaurs of old, when man once achieves some success in a protective device, he is apt to carry it beyond the demands of necessity. He is likely to forget the old cavalry maxim, "The best defense is a vigorous offense." Thus it is easy to violate the "Principle of the Offensive," to be discussed later.

One of the surest ways to do this is to rely too much on fortification. This type of protection is known to all continents. Perhaps the natives in question merely choose their defensive sites with care, fighting behind natural protection of trees, boulders, and streams. Some nonliterate people even choose their defensive sites along the true military crest, sites which will make the enemy climb an eminence against withering arrow fire, arranging their line so that there is no dead space uncovered by fire. Such people are very few. Many others improve such sites by engineering. The archeologists particularly have done some remarkably fine work in exploring and describing the fortresses of nonliterate men. Many ethnographers have also made excellent descriptions of defensive works. Perhaps the cleverest, quite aside from the bulk of earth, stone, and adobe involved, are the palisades of the Iroquois and the *pai* of the New Zeland Maori. Both of these people were aggressive fighters and used fortification in the correct manner: the prevention of surprise, the protection of noncombatants, a place of retirement for the defeated, and a source of sortie and pivot of maneuver for troops primarily fighting in the open. Some Polynesians and American Indians understood the art of trench fortification. The Iroquois knew the value of the curtain, the light wall out in front of the principle defensive palisade. The mediaeval castle at its best also had a curtain, the light wall which kept the enemy's siege engines out of effective range of the chief wall. Whether the curtain is of stone, scantling or, as today, of barbed wire, its primary use is to break the enemy rush so that his full shock power will be frittered away under fire before he can extricate himself and bring himself in force against the main works.

I know of no use of a water curtain, that is, a moat, among any nonliterate peoples. I have seen something with the same function in the waterless country of southern Morocco where a belt of terrible cactus is grown around the chief defensive wall. Many people in Malaysia construct very clever pits in front of their rudimentary fortresses, however. These are filled with sharp stakes, often poisoned, and the whole pit cleverly hidden by vegetation. These are sometimes staggered like modern tank traps, so that no enemy could know of their exact location nor pass through the whole line without luck. During the Philippine Insurrection, United States troops learned to approach these native forts with great caution.

Some particularly clever people construct spring traps along the line of approach to their villages. Some of these nonliterate booby-traps, when sprung, will drive a spear through an enemy. One

African tribe, described later, protected the approaches to their strongholds by planting an extremely poisonous plant there, one whose chemical action causes much greater and much quicker pain than poison ivy.

Protective devices are of value when properly used. They can be improperly used, as some peoples forget that the defensive can only win negative victories. The defense merely staves off defeat. Only the offensive can win.

The anthropologists have been given due credit for the scrupulous way in which they have described the weapons of nonliterate peoples. One flaw in the literature, however, cries for correction. With the exception of numerous and fine articles on the use of projectile weapons, there are practically no descriptions of the uses of the arms. Practically no one thinks it necessary to tell of the manual of arms, of the method of fencing and fighting with the weapons. Ordinarily it has been considered quite adequate to report the presence of such and such a weapon and the materials and methods of its manufacture. This is particularly a civilian failing. The important part of a weapon or tool is its method of use. As has been repeatedly said, a clever man with a club can kill an ignorant man armed with a rifle. This actually has been done, so it is not a matter of conjecture. One very fine description of the use of weapons is written by the artist Frances Del Mar.[2] It would be well for the ethnographers to copy this carefulness.

This chapter will not comment on the origin and development of weapons. It will suffice to say that developmental or typological series can and have been made. Many monographs and books of Old World archeologists have much to say about the time of origin of fighting implements, much of which is extremely civilian. It is not difficult to find remarks positively attributing weapons to Neanderthaloid men deep in the Mid- or sometimes in the Early Paleolithic. Reasoning from form to function, there is not one scrap of evidence of the existence of a weapon, a specific man-killer, until the end of the Old Stone Age, and even then such interpretation is extremely dubious. Indeed, even Neolithic weapons are not as clearly distinguishable from hunting tools as one would like.

This does not mean that mankind had to own specific weapons in order to inflict harm on his fellows. An eye can be gouged with a

---

[2] Frances Del Mar, *A Year Among the Maoris* (London: E. Benn, 1924), *passim.*

well-directed thumb, so no weapon at all is needed with which to hurt people. But inflicting pain and doing it in the most effective manner are two different things. A pacific tool can kill, a woodman's axe for instance. So can a shotgun. But a lumberman's axe was designed to cut down trees and is a poor weapon. So is a shotgun. A war arrow differs from a hunting arrow, or should. One can take a scythe to war, as peasants have been known to do, though it is a grass-cutter and a poor man-killer. So, too, one could take a great piece of artillery duck hunting, but what a poor job it would do! A shotgun does well against geese; a machine gun does well against men, and no sensible person would confuse the form or function of the two firearms. So there are weapons, man-killers, quite distinct from peaceful tools of somewhat similar shape. Specialized man-killers did not appear so early in Old World archeology as some people seem to think. There are even tribes, such as the Eskimo, who have never made a distinctive weapon.

Much could be written regarding the interdependence of weapons and tactics, how changes in the tactical method have necessitated changes in the armory, and how changes in the armory have compelled changes in tactics. The discussion of African war relates a clear example of this. The introduction of the white man's musket and rifle in some areas almost always forced a change of tactics on the natives. This change in tactics sometimes followed the white man's methods, but it did not always do so.

The final statement of the theory of armory is that the weapons of a people tend to conform to those of the traditional enemy, to the terrain, and to the mission. In the first place, weapons must be able to excel or at least to meet those of the traditional enemy fighting under his own terms. If the foe relies on shock and fire, the shock must be met with adequate shock weapons, with defensive armor, and with fire weapons as good as or better than his. Anything else spells expulsion or extinction. This is no more than a re-statement of the offense-defense cycle noted before. For example, one finds reliance on the spear and shield in long grass areas of east Africa. The bow has little value there and is not used. Such shock weapons would not be very useful in the heavily forested region of tropical west Africa, however, and there the bow is much commoner than the spear and shield.

This statement by no means indicates that such an adjustment to enemy, terrain, and mission will be automatic. Conservatism and cultural inertia have been well discussed in both ethnology and sociology, and there is no need to summarize such theory here. Conservatism is always the ruler of primitive war, however, and a people can change its weapons. All Europeans, white Americans, Polynesians, and some Melanesians once knew the military use of the bow. Since cultural change necessitated the abandonment of this ancient weapon, they have relegated it to the function of a toy. Conservatism and cultural inertia create many problems in peaceful life, but in war they spell but defeat and destruction.

Chapter 2

The Theory of War and the Military Horizon

It would be simple but definitely misleading to entitle this discussion "Primitive Tactics." As the problem unfolds it will be increasingly apparent that tactical operations are not primitive. The bulk of nonliterate mankind failed to establish certain simple rules. This is what kept nonliterate man a warrior instead of a soldier, despite the fact that he ordinarily valued "war" and the warrior far more than does civilized man.

This work would fail signally in its duty if it did not reveal the neglect of anthropologists in describing the military methods of their informants. Nowhere is this fault more pronounced than for North America, the best reported continent, and nowhere was the opportunity for acceptable work more possible. The typical field report makes a fine description of attitudes, values, ceremonials, personnel, and motives for war. Indeed, the avoirdupois weight of excellent material about all behavior leading up to an engagement and that immediately following a fight would make an impressive recording. Only the actual conduct of the fight is missing. There can be only one explanation of this vast lacuna: The anthropologists failed to inquire or were not alert when the informants were discussing their exploits.

The ethnographer has not hesitated to describe, classify, and coordinate all culture, material and non-material, to the best of his ability. Neither has he hesitated to discuss war at length, for it is one of man's most important non-material complexes. The core alone, "How does this group fight," is excluded. The field researcher has been meticulous regarding the icing and has overlooked the cake, which is not ordinarily the way the typical field ethnographer works. In justice it should be stated that these remarks are more applicable to the American anthropologists than to those of Europe. Often British anthropologists, for example, include an intelligent comment or two on their informants' military methods, and far, far oftener than ever seen in this country, British colonial soldiers have some knowledge of and interest in the simpler people under them. It would be hard to find a more worthless literature than that produced by American army officers writing on the Indians or the Filipinos.

Since soldiering is ordinarily accounted a profession, it might be that there is some profundity in the simpler doctrines of war which the anthropologist could not be expected to master. This is not the case, and any professional soldier will admit it in his franker moments. In an article in the *Militar Wochenblatt,* a German professional journal, a distinguished general admitted in 1935 that war as an art cannot be rated above the minor arts. Some might agree with General Bliss that warfare is even a science.[1] Bliss maintained that a branch of knowledge which is based on inductive investigation, and which has so systematized and correlated its accumulated knowledge into generalizations or "laws" demonstrable as true is a science. Warfare has long done this, more or less.

There is no intention of allowing a general to define science for a scientific audience. The present purpose is to show that professional generals believe that the prosecution of warfare follows such sufficiently well-known rules that they may be transmitted by instruction, as is true of any science. If these rules exist, they could be learned by the anthropologist and sociologist. As for the scientific nature of war, the unpredictable human and terrain elements enter too much into the subject; the unknown factors called "the fog of war" lay the term open to challenge. A man might be defeated though following the principles scrupulously due to the inability of the human mind to grasp all the factors in the engagement.[2]

Thus it appears that certain rules do exist, and have existed without significant change since the beginning of real military operations. They were practiced by the first civilizations of the eastern Mediterranean and, at least in a rudimentary fashion, by all nonliterate social groups of any military ability. They are simple, easily mastered, readily available, and usually ignored by anthropologists writing on the nonmaterial culture of peoples, particularly in America.

---

[1] Tasker H. Bliss, in Oliver L. Spaulding, Hoffman Nickerson, and John W. Wright, *Warfare, A Study of Military Methods from the Earliest Times* (New York: Harcourt Brace, 1925), p. iii.

[2] *Tactics and Technique of Cavalry* (6th ed.; Harrisburg: The Military Service Publishing Company, 1935), p. 4.

It is now necessary to discuss the concept of the "Military Horizon." This means that there are tribes with social control adequate enough for all other purposes, and certainly making such tribes happy enough in their daily relations with their fellows, but which is so ineffective, so lacking in authority, team work, cohesion, and cooperation that they could not indulge in a fight which could be called a battle. It is also stated herewith that there are tribes which have such capacity for military organization. It is furthermore alleged that the tribes lacking in such organization would have been or have been defeated by those who had it. The generalization is also offered that the military horizon is one of social organization and has next to nothing to do with the state of weapons. While this might be shocking both to the professional soldier and the social scientist, let us venture to say that the art, or the art and science of war, if you will, is a social science. It is also the oldest social science, having arrived at its basic principles centuries before any of the other social sciences were conceived. Engineering and material invention are the handmaidens of war and are not war *per se,* except in the minds of those who must win quickly. Organization and tactics are the major foci of a discussion of war.

The military horizon depends, then, not upon the adequacy of weapons but the adequacy of team work, organization, and command working along certain simple principles. Some groups failed to achieve this and, despite their face-painting and sporadic butchery, were not soldiers. Some cultures do contain the rudiments of the art of war. It is also seen that this achievement correlates with success along other lines. The war complex fits with the rest of the pattern of social organization, which in turn seems to have a close correlation with victory in the technological and economic configurations. This may, indeed, seem "evolutionary," but since it is indicated by the published field data, it is going to be the lot of the critic to comb the monographic data in his own turn and make what refutation he can.

The position that a group with the sociologic trait of tactics, though armed with only Neolithic materials, could defeat a non-tactical body equipped with the latest weapons may seem extreme. But the elements of the art of war change slowly if at all, while weapons are constantly trying to correct their own defects according to the offense-defense cycle, attempting to solve special problems of terrain, raw materials, and changes in enemy equipment, thus making the material side of war too unstable for a generalized discussion. No better example of the paramount sociological nature of the war complex can be found than in a comparison of Battles of Mickmash described in First Samuel and later fought by the British against the Turks in almost the same place and under almost identical conditions during the war of 1914-1918. Despite the vast amount of improvement and change in material equipment between King Saul and King George V, each battle was won and lost by application of the same tactical principles.[3]

The present position, made in the face of a possible charge of oversimplification, is that the principles of the art of war are so simple and so rigidly exacting that there should be no surprise that peoples widely separated in space and time should have discovered some or all of them. We are not here speaking of anything so complicated as an explanation of polyandry among separated peoples, nor the similarities or dissimilarities in the ceramic complex of the Americas and New Stone Age Europe. The art of war or the artlessness of fighting are so simple throughout time and over the face of the world that the discussion could be made very monotonous. Since this statement is extreme, the writer is not content to assert it on his own recognizance. The reader is urged to consult the best military authorities on this score. It is predicted that he will find agreement with Spaulding's statement:

> War is war. Its outward forms change, just as the outward forms of peace change. But from the stylus to the typewriter is just as far as from the club to the machinegun—a weapon also known affectionately or otherwise as a "typewriter." And the development of tactics is neither more nor less remarkable than the development of office methods.
>
> Strip any military operation of external, identifying details, and one will find it hard to put a place and date to the story.[4]

Several professional officers with whom I have discussed the project have stood for the non-existence of the military art among nonliterate folk. It was occasionally held that the American Indian, at least, simply had no tactics, no art of war, no system of combat. This is tantamount to saying that he had no cutting instruments because he lacked steel knives. It is suspected that some tribes lacked utterly any system of fighting. Among the majority it is obvious that some

[3] Vivian Gilbert, *The Romance of the Last Crusade* (New York: D. Appleton, 1923), p. 183.

[4] Spaulding, Nickerson, and Wright, *op. cit.*, p. 3.

pattern was followed, although it was often below the military horizon and inadequate from the standpoint of the officers just quoted. Inadequacy is not proof of non-existence. For example, the Menomini had a very poor method of fighting which could succeed only against similarly incompetent warriors, or against the unorganized whites who had been pushed out onto the midwest frontier, but they had a system which had an advantage which ours did not: It was divine.[5] The Thunderers gave the Menomini leaders very explicit directions, as good tactical advice as Jehovah gave the Jews at Jericho, and almost of the same type.[6] It might have been an incomplete system, but it involved the tactical principles of envelopment, surprise, movement, and shock, all that was needed for the kind of action involved.

Furthermore, one cannot avoid the suspicion that primitive societies had more system to their fighting than they are given credit for in field reports. They made some very creditable stands against the white man, in spite of their small populations and simple weapons.

Let us now summarize the principles of tactics so that we may compare the behavior of nonliterate societies with them. The principles are given such descriptive titles that they will only be quoted, postponing explanation and exposition to the descriptive chapters.

> There are a few fundamental truths which have been applicable in war from time immemorial and which will continue to be so in future wars. These truths are known as tactical principles, or principles of war.
>
> Though these principles themselves do not change, their application is different for units of different sizes and varies from time to time for units of the same size.[7]

The principles referred to are entitled:

1. The Principle of the Offensive.
2. The Principle of Combined Employment of All Forces.
3. The Principle of Concerted Effort.
4. The Principle of Concentration of Force at the Critical Point.
5. The Principle of Integrity of Tactical Units.
6. The Principle of Fire and Movement.
7. The Principle of Simplicity of Plan.
8. The Principle of Surprise.

---

5 Alanson B. Skinner, *Social Life and Ceremonial Bundles of the Menomini Indians,* Anthropological Papers, American Museum of Natural History (New York: 1913), XIII, Part 1, p. 97.

6 *Ibid.,* p. 100.

7 *Tactics and Technique of Cavalry,* pp. 3ff.

9. The Principle of Security.
10. The Principle of Utilization of the Terrain.
11. The Principle of Correct Formations.
12. The Principle of Intelligence.
13. The Principle of Mobility.
14. The Principle of Exploitation of Victory.

One cannot say which of these principles is the most important in civilized war. They are all important, and important with respect to each other. They must function in a composite pattern. At times it may be necessary to emphasize one at the apparent relegation of another to a subordinate role, but they must all be observed in every action. When one is speaking of the simpler cultures, the acid test of achievement of the military horizon is the observance of the eleventh, the principle of correct formations.

The use of the proper formations before, during, and after an engagement is hardly the point in primitive warfare. It is difficult enough to find nonliterate warriors using any. There can be no doubt but that the regularization of the participants in a war party into some kind of a team distributed over the scene of action is one of the *sine qua non* elements of tactics. It is true that even today certain types of action may degenerate into unorganized melees as the result of shock action. This is particularly true of cavalry and the descendants of cavalry, armored and air forces. Nevertheless, the engagement is always entered in formation and, whether in defeat or victory, both sides must withdraw from the fight in some semblance of order if the first is to escape slaughter and the second to exploit victory.

In the first place this is essential for command. The leader must have some idea of where his men are in order to exercise any control over their movements. It will soon be seen that the simpler nonliterate societies were defective in command functions. If for no other reason, it would therefore seem that such societies, so lacking in social organization and compulsive institutions in peace, except in certain clearly defined areas, would also be lacking in military organization and command and, therefore, in effective fighting formation. For the most part this is true, although not as much so as might appear on the surface of the discussion.

Reduced to the essence of simplicity, military organization consists of the column and the line. Those people who do not avail themselves of these two simple sociologic devices are below the military horizon without argument. Their fighting can be nothing but a scuffle, regardless of the amount of bloodshed, and cannot be called a war.

The column is not a fighting device. It is an organizational method of getting men to the scene of a fight in the best condition, close enough to be controlled by a chief, or to render each other some support and mutual protection. Fifty men close enough together to act as a unit can defeat a thousand spread over the terrain, each doing what seems good in his own eyes until he must flee for his life or be cut down by cooperators of bloody intent. It is not implied that such columns must be shoulder to shoulder in proximity, nor one after the other like the old convict lock-step. Should the enemy be well-equipped with weapons of fire, or with horses to make a shock attack on the flanks, such formations would be fatal. In our day the column, threatened by aerial attack from above and by weapons of great mobility, fire, and shock power on the flanks, tends to be more dispersed than it was fifty years ago. All that is meant is that the column should be sufficiently compact to perform the functions required of it.

One form of column is familiar to everybody; the so-called Indian file, the placing of men in one file one after the other. In large units this is practical only for arms of great mobility. Cavalry, horsed or mechanized, often rides Indian file, or more frequently by column of twos. Due to the speed with which such troops can maneuver into a fighting line, this is often desirable. It is particularly ineffective for foot commands of any size. It makes for a spread-out—that terror of all professional soldiers, "column attenuation." It covers such space in depth that a determined enemy can defeat the foremost elements before the rear can be brought up. Its maneuverability is practically nil. The classical Greeks marched in this manner, and were often defeated for their clumsiness.

There may be civilians who will object to the simplicity of this generalization concerning basic formations, although it is the opinion of competent military scholars. Lest it be thought that these principles are the author's, please read the article on tactics in the *Encyclopedia Britannica.* The writer of the article is eminent enough. This extremely common source was deliberately chosen to show that basic military doctrine has long been available to anyone who wished to consider it.[8]

A good approach or withdrawal order based on the column may be considered vital, but its importance wanes before a good battle formation. Whether speaking of the simplest warriors or of the modern, this order must be based on some form of a line or echelon of lines. The line is the simplest tactical formation, and a sociologic trait without which there can be no true war. No one need object to this statement as an attempt to judge all people by our standards. The line is dictated by nature. Whether one is speaking of fighting men or animals, whether of one individual or a group of armies, the vulnerable places are the sides and the back. It takes neither logical profundity nor vast experience to appreciate this. A mammal's fighting equipment is to the fore, in the direction of the enemy. Not being equipped with armor or stinging tails, the forward section contains the only means of offense or defense. The predatory animals who hunt in packs appreciate this and have a battle formation of sorts, relying largely on the technique of the envelopment. Physical anthropology and zoology have yet to give us a description of the psychology of our most immediate primate ancestors. Judged by their behavior, it seems that men were a rather solitary though fierce species of carnivorous primates; but it would also seem that the ability to correct this defect in primate anatomy is purely cultural and without instinctive basis among the decendants of those dour *Simiidae*. Many peoples have never made this very simple adjustment.

This adjustment may be found in a line, and there is no other. Even the most advanced military nations have only improved on the basic concept. The adjustment and formation are very simple, requiring no great reasoning, and all successful tribes use it. The scrupulous ethnologist need not be worried on that score. The tactical line provides a means by which each man, save those on the extreme flanks, may protect the sides of his neighbor and be protected by the enlightened self-interest of that neighbor. Once the line is severed, broken into, or smashed, safety is gone.

Given warriors of equal equipment and will to victory, the decision will rarely be made in the front. If the lines are of equal length, victory will go to that which can maneuver enough to deliver

[8] Thomas R. Phillips, *Encyclopedia Britannica* (14th ed.; Chicago 1946), XXI, p. 739ff.

a crumbling, rolling up movement on the flank. Other things being equal, the longer line will surely win by enveloping the weak flanks of the other. To be sure, there are devices whereby a clever commander of a short line may envelop the long on of an unwary leader. One is the "weak center" formation, whereby it is prearranged that the center of the short line will pretend to be weaker than it is and withdraw enough so that the eager but stupid enemy will surge into the gap. Pressure on the ends at the right moment will make the flanks of the less numerous and clever equal to or even longer than the numerous but too-anxious foe. Large numbers of his fighting men are rendered ineffectual in the center and cannot aid their fellow spearmen in the front rank. The outcome of the Punic war depended upon this maneuver. Indeed, it has been successfully used from the wars recorded in the Book of Kings, through the Zulu King Chaka, to Hindenburg's defeat of the Russians at Tannenberg.

It is not geometrical perfection of the line that counts. Often it is irregular or, as in the Zulu wars, bent into a crescent. It is cohesion that makes an armed body strong, as Hilaire Belloc said:

> Every member wishes to separate himself from the band when it is in danger. Indeed, the wish to decamp is always strongest at just that point, the tactically critical point, where the group is in the greatest danger. The prime object of discipline and training is to prevent this.[9]

This primer of tactics has been sketchy, admittedly at the risk of the reader falling into misconception for lack of exposition. Yet this work does not pretend to be a general exposition of the art of war, and must hold to its own course. Elaboration and exposition in part may be found in the descriptive material to follow. Should the reader find that he needs to read further on the subject, he is assured that the art of war has been well and interestingly discussed throughout the ages, while tactical history has engaged some of the greatest captains of all times, many of whom possess literary skill.

Ethnologists frequently report that certain tribes gathered berries and nuts and, like those of California, may have depended upon wild vegetable foods for their principal sustenance. Such a condition did not make them agriculturalists, although they may have eaten no more meat than a farming tribe. There is something more to the agricultural complex than mere diet, as there is more to war than mere killing. To proceed one step further, tribes like the Ojibway of Minnesota even encouraged the wild rice to grow, planted it in swamps

[9] Hilaire Belloc, *Poitiers* (London: 1913), pp. 112.

which had not hitherto borne it, and carefully protected the swamps from birds. To be considered a farming people, however, they would have actually have had to domesticate the food plant, bring its growth under their control, and systematically plant, harvest, and save certain seed for future planting. Wilhelm Schmidt maintains that the horizon of true agriculture consists in altering the life conditions of the plants by disturbing the soil. Unless the soil is worked, therefore, plant-food production cannot be considered true tillage.

The threshold, then, that divides true war from submilitary combat must be taken as the invention of tactics.

It might be stated with somewhat less clarity, that not only must there be tactical movement of combatants but also the ability to conduct a somewhat protracted campaign. A raid is hardly more of a war than is a modern burglary. It might be said, then, that the following conditions are necessary for true war:

1. Tactical operations.

2. Definite command and control. Without definite military authority in control throughout the action, there exists only a bloody brawl.

3. Ability to conduct a campaign for the reduction of enemy resistance if the first battle fails. This is a much higher condition than that of the mere raid, and implies more self-discipline and social organization.

4. The motive must have some clarity. The war must have a group motive rather than an individual one, or even one based on kinship. True war is above the plane of feuds; it is a political device, properly so-called.

5. An adequate supply.

Very few nonliterate tribes have been able to meet these conditions. A most interesting and vital part of the war pattern, however, is to be seen in the fifth point. This linkage with economic success, this ability to provide surplus food for armies in the field, is so important that there is temptation to place it in the center of the whole military complex. Most peoples either could not produce enough food to prosecute a war or did not perceive the importance of this staff function. The supply function will be obvious in following chapters, but it will be seen to be truly primitive or rudimentary in most instances. Consequently the military operations described are also primitive and rudimentary.

An army fights not only on courage but on food. Any discussion of war, then, is extremely artificial unless it describes the social and economic organization of the tribal or national culture. A social organization capable of producing an economic surplus by a high agriculture, and a means of transporting such food, is as necessary for war as the invention of tactics. Without it, war is confined to raids or to single battles. Campaigns are impossible, and therefore the most civilized motive for war is impossible: the subjugation of enemy peoples and the expansion of the group's territory at their expense. A small party may live off the country, but this is not possible for an army, especially one pursuing a fleeing enemy who may be spoiling the available food along their line of retreat.

An invasion in former times was slow unless the mission could be accomplished by a raid. (Some Asiatic exceptions to this will be mentioned later.) Witness the poor conduct of the Trojan war as an example of the folly of inadequate supply. The attack was made by a descent from the sea, which meant that a foreign base had to be established in order that fields to feed the troops might be available. The Greek troops were thus tied to their corn fields and could not move far inland. One might suspect that adequate military supply had a slow development, and hence true war was tardy in appearing in the world.

Lest the civilian reader be confused by this discussion of what is and what is not war, it is desirable that a truly military campaign be described. An example will be chosen of a people who had only recently emerged from primitivity, the Hebrews as revealed in the earlier books of the Old Testament. They had achieved the military horizon, to be sure, but retained several submilitary practices, and were far behind their more powerful neighbors both in weapons and in the art of war.

They occupied what is now known as a buffer state. To the north were the military empires of Mesopotamia, and to the south was Egypt. Both sides were very anxious to hold Judaea, or at least keep it in harmless native hands. It served as too valuable a base of attack for either of the great powers to be content if the other held it. Its foreign relations were, therefore, almost always hostile. The religious attitudes and values of the Hebrews included hatred and fighting of the outgroup as a sacred duty. Their strategy was extremely simple, as it was with other peoples at the dawn of history. Before the kings arose, the two armies set out to find each other, fought, and went home. Seldom were campaigns found before the social organization was strong enough to support the monarchy, and that against Sisera is an exception.[10]

Organization was simple, being merely a levy of tribal manhood militia service. The horn was sounded from village to village, informing the eligible that it was spring, and "the time when kings go out to battle." This time was set for purposes of supply, as a crop had to be in. Furthermore, if the invasion were planned before the enemy had grown his crop, the invader would have nothing to live on while in hostile territory. Ordinarily each man carried "iron rations" on his person sufficient for about three days. When this was eaten it was necessary to live off the country of friend or foe. Organized supply such as in Judges 20 was rare until later.

In contrast with the poor staff work in supply, military intelligence was fairly well organized, which is typical of folk far less civilized than the early Hebrews. A spy system was maintained in hostile territory, and when the armies drew together, scouts were sent out to prevent surprise and to reconnoiter the enemy's strength.[11] Tactics existed but were simple, usually consisting of conflicts between two parallel lines with simple enveloping movements. The forces were frequently divided into three echelons.[12] The tactical retreat was known and employed. More elaborate tactics are to be found in the command of Joab before Rabbathammon.[13]

Keeping this summary in mind, the following description of the short campaign against Gibeah will illustrate every element of true war, even if practiced in a rudimentary way.

Whether there was an economic *casus belli* in this intratribal war is not known. The motive was the ancient one of the purity of womanhood, even though a concubine was concerned.

A certain priest was on a peaceful mission to Bethlehem-Judah to bring back his concubine who had deserted. Passing with her through the friendly allied country of Benjamin, the priest spent the night in the city of Gibeah with an elderly stranger. During the night, however, certain persons, nationals of the place, broke the law of hospitality and killed the young woman by sexual abuse, a grievance hardly to be borne.

---

[10] Judges 4.

[11] Judges 2; I Samuel 26; Maccabees 5; Judges 1; II Samuel 15; Judges 7.

[12] Judges 7; I Samuel 11; II Samuel 18.

[13] II Samuel 10.

Arriving in his own country, the priest complained to the civil authority of his treatment in Gibeah. This was before the rise of kings, and government was vested in a tribal council which was immediately assembled. The priest's complaint was deemed grievous enough for intersib action, and an embassy was sent to the tribe of Benjamin to demand the summary execution of their offending kinsmen. In the meantime diplomacy was backed by preparedness, and the mobilization order for the militia went out to the other tribes of Israel. A force of four hundred thousand swordsmen was nationalized and put on war footing. An adequate supply was organized, for the record states, "We will take ten men of an hundred, throughout the tribes of Israel, and an hundred of a thousand, and a thousand out of ten thousand, to fetch victual for the people . . ." Observe the tribal authoritarianism in this enlistment and staff work in contrast with the submilitary behavior soon to be described.

Diplomatic relations were soon severed. The embassy had gone to offending Benjamin, stated the case of the offended tribes of the rest of Israel, and was allowed to go among the Benjamite villages to conduct its own propaganda campaign. All this came to naught, for Benjamin haughtily refused to surrender the guilty parties. Diplomatic relations therefore failed, and war was declared on both sides.

The mobilization order then went forth in Benjamin and every available man was *authoritatively* ordered to the standard. Remember this when reading the invitation to war of the Plains chiefs in America. Benjamin's fields and villages were depopulated; everyone concentrated within the fenced city of Gibeah as the mobilization point. All noncombatants were ordered within the circumvallation and the defenses were strengthened. The offending city of Gibeah contributed seven hundred picked men, and the other Benjamite elements raised twenty-six thousand good swordsmen of the line. Besides the swordsmen, Benjamin was able to muster an effective fire element. "Among all these people there were seven hundred chosen men, left handed; every one could sling stones at an hair and not miss."

The situation at the opening of hostilities was as follows: Benjamin lay behind its fortifications anticipating a war of position because of its numerical inferiority. It had twenty-six thousand infantry swordsmen, seven hundred able slingers, and strong walls. Having adequate notice, Benjamin could fight from a prepared position.

The confederated sibs of Israel had a superiority of three hundred seventy-four thousand swordsmen, such an overwhelming shock power that the Benjamite line could not hope to meet it in the open. Such a number could easily surround and invest the fortified city of Gibeah and, while lacking engines capable of reducing the works, would have to rely on a war of position and attrition. In such a case, their numerical superiority and the excellence of their service of supply could easily reduce the garrison by starvation. Israel, however, was deficient in fire power, a fact which was to cost them dearly.

Passing to the opening of hostilities and the first engagement, one reads how Israel invaded Benjamin territory. Arriving at the theater of war, the council in which the supreme command was vested convened. It hardly thought the full force of Israel was necessary to defeat Benjamin and, with contempt for the principle of mass, ordered the one division of Judah to assail Gibeah while the remainder rested in reserve.

The division Judah moved against Gibeah at dawn but was dilatory in its attack, taking leisure to pitch its camp under full observation of the enemy. Since even this one division outnumbered the city's total garrison, it was tempted to rely too much on its shock power. The mass of shock was a principle of tactics which had been borrowed from the great neighbors with which Israel was surrounded, and almost never proved as successful as the light mobile methods of the nation's earlier Bedouin history. Thus, instead of making a vigorous attack on the fortifications, or investing the place by siege, it proceeded to tempt the Benjamites outside their own walls in order to crush them. This, of course, would have saved Israel the expense and strain of a long siege.

Gibeah was in a sad plight and was forced to take desperate chances. If the city had been surrounded and the arteries of its food supply from friendly territory cut off, the eventual capitulation of the garrison would have been inevitable. But Israel signified its dislike of a siege as well, and had formed in a heavy line straddling the two important highways, and was slowly moving towards the wall. Gibeah decided on daring, seeing that their numbers were comparable to that of the one division of Judah, and moved out for a sortie.

The Judah division had thus lost the initiative by its clumsy moving forward like a steam roller. Benjamin, on the other hand, had high morale, an almost equal number of swordsmen, and an effective firepower of seven hundred slingers. The fire superiority was apparently aided by a superior mobility. Benjamin then threw forward a line of light-armed slingers, covering by fire a line of swordsmen behind them, a fine combination of fire and movement.

The Benjamin fire superiority soon began to tell. The excellent slingers began to inflict heavy casualties upon the solidly packed Judah for which the latter were unable to retaliate. Soon Judah was immobilized by the hostile fire and was greatly discomfited.

At the proper time, before Judah could recover from this embarrassment, the mobile swordsmen of Benjamin fell ferociously upon the weak spots and flanks of the Judah line and destroyed it then and there. The Israelite casualties were numbered at twenty-two thousand. The main body was so far in the rear that it could not send support forward.

Benjamin, on the other hand, though elated with its victory, did not have the numerical strength to exploit its success by a blow against the main body, and was forced to retire behind its fortifications. Israel was made to suffer for a tactical error which many have made since. She divided her forces in the face of an able and aggressive enemy. Every good commander proceeds on the modest assumption that the enemy troops are the equals of his in equipment, training and *esprit.* Contempt is a fatal luxury. Furthermore, Israel allowed the initiative to pass to the capable Benjamin, and therefore fought on Benjamin's terms—a bit of folly, considering her large manpower. Seemingly Israel's overconfidence allowed them to choose an unfavorable terrain upon which to receive the Benjamite shock.

The second engagement proved no better. Israel's first defeat was a terrific surprise, but despite loud wailing, her morale was still high, as it should have been. Apparently, however, she had learned no lesson, ascribing the defeat to lack of valor on the part of the division of Judah rather than on her own tactical errors.

Consequently, on the second day a similarly numerous body was drawn up before Gibeah in the same formation. When it arrived at the same unfavorable ground, Benjamin delivered an attack, the exact counterpart of the first day's movement. Benjamin had seen from its towers that the main body was again too far in the rear to be of any assistance to the task force, and that Israel had not learned in the dear school of fools. They decided, therefore, to duplicate the same fire-and-movement infantry maneuver, the results of which were again disastrous to Israel. The confederated tribes left eighteen thousand casualties on the field the second day, and Benjamin remained unharmed.

The third engagement showed a change of heart on Israel's part. The confederated sibs had now lost forty thousand of their best men, ten percent of the total effective strength, had suffered two crushing defeats, and had inflicted no appreciable damage on Gibeah. By now they had decided that they had walked into a war instead of engaging in spring maneuvers, and that something had to be done about it.

In the first place, they were wise enough to perceive that the tribal council constituted too loose a command center. This is often a defect found in allied troops. They now thought it wise to centralize the command in one person whom all would obey. The war chiefs had lost confidence in each other, so they elected to high command one Phinehas ben Eleazar ben Aaron, who was not a military man at all. Phinehas was the High Priest of the Lord who had accompanied the command for magico-religious purposes. While he was not a fighting man, he was a scholar and was thoroughly familiar with the successes and reversals in the nation's martial past, and he could appreciate the reasons for both. At first the priest had scruples regarding a man of the ephod actually taking up arms. Furthermore, the rebellious Benjamin was still an integral part of the House of Israel, and he found it distastful to shed the blood of his kin. Nevertheless, the war had been undertaken to avenge one of his minor clergy and, overcoming his scruples in prayer, he took the field.

The literate Phinehas recalled a method of assailing a walled city without recourse to siege which had been successfully used by Joshua in the campaign for the subjugation of Canaan, and decided to employ it. Again, he reasoned that the garrison of Gibeah had been made overconfident by its two easy victories, so he decided to dangle before them a pin-hook baited with the appearance of Israel's persistent stupidity. Even as a priest he saw the folly of dividing the forces in face of an aggressive foe, only to be defeated in detail, therefore he decided to attack in strength.

Under the cover of darkness a sizable force was moved up to occupy the meadows near the two gates of Gibeah. The garrison, gloating behind its strong wall, had neglected its service of security and did not discover the stratagem. By dawn this detail had taken cover in the wheat fields.

The main force was then divided into three bodies, but this time in easy communication with each other. Too much had already been lost by violating the principle of cooperation. The two flank parties were to contain the main strength; the center, which was of no great power, was to be the bait. Those familiar with tactical history will at once recognize this as the "weak center" formation successfully used by Hannibal's inferior force against the Romans at Cannae, by Hindenburg against the Russians at Tannenberg, and by many others in between.

The plan was as follows: The two strong flanks were to be concealed under the cover of the low hills. The central force was to advance slowly down the road as before, leading Gibeah to think that Israel could not learn. But as soon as the Benjamites had attacked the weak center, this center was to become not the main effort but merely a pivot of maneuver and to effect a tactical withdrawal with the appearance of defeat. Benjamin would likely pursue this obviously craven force until it should be drawn within the two strong jaws. The strong flanks would then catch them in a set of pincers and crush them. Once the attack was well under way, and the garrison of Gibeah drawn into the field, the party near the gates would rush into the poorly defended fortifications and set fire to the town, destroying any possible place of refuge for the remnant of which might escape.

Phinehas's estimate of the situation proved correct. The battle proceeded as he had planned it in every detail. Yet when the Benjamites perceived the nature of the stratagem they launched a desperate attack on the weak center, hoping to effect a break-through by which to escape. The center of Israel hardly expected this wild attack and began to give way. Their morale was already sorely tried and they looked towards Gibeah to see it in flames, but the liers-in-wait also encountered a hitch in their plans and Gibeah remained intact. The day was almost lost in spite of Israel's great strength. The field troops looked towards Gibeah and finally it burst into flames as the shrieks of women and children suffering the sword came to encourage the ears of Israel. Heartened thus, Israel set about the job of slaughter with good courage and will, while Benjamin, beholding its citadel of retreat being demolished, lost all hope.

A small portion of the Benjamites managed to break through the Israel line and escape. Israel was exultant over its crushing victory and ably exploited its success. The confederated tribes had no cavalry and the mopping up, while partly successful, did not prevent the Benjamite remnant from fighting a rear guard action. Benjamin had lost twenty-five thousand casualties, but some six hundred men escaped to the rocky passes of Mount Rimon which they could hold Thermopylae-fashion against all comers.

The war was thus terminated by the complete defeat of guilty Benjamin. It was an internecine war, however, and the victors felt a fraternal interest in the Mount Rimon remnant. It seemed unfortunate that the tribal integrity of Israel should be disrupted by the total destruction of one of the sacred sibs. Benjamin was humbled and repentant, but wary enough not to come down from Mount Rimon. Now the victors wished to rebuild "little Benjamin," their sister, but at the sack of Gibeah all the women and children of the latter had been slain. Unfortunately in the confederacy's first rage all had sworn a mighty oath never to give a daughter in marriage to the Benjamites who had such a poor regard for womankind.

In their mercy they recalled that the town of Jabesh-Gilead had been dilatory in the campaign and had not taken the oath. Therefore the victors sent a party of twelve thousand picked men to assail Jabesh-Gilead. They slew every male, and every matron, carrying away four hundred virgins as wives for the ex-enemy, and as a peace-offering. Yet this left two hundred men of Benjamin without wives. The victors again recalled that they had no love for the people of Shiloh, whereat the young girls would come into the vineyards to dance. The victorious confederacy then gave the two hundred Benjamite bachelors and widowers permission to hide and, at the right moment, each to seize himself a wife. This being done, the Benjamite remnant departed to repair its farms, villages, and its strong city of Gibeah, and also its population. The confederated militia was then demobilized, and peace again reigned in Israel.

This chapter has intimated that some kinds of combat are not war. The foregoing analysis of the Gibeah campaign was made to show what true war is, although practiced quite early in mankind's written history. If the Gibeah campaign is kept somewhat in mind while reading the following description of truly primitive war, it will be of some help, for no other descriptions of true war will follow.

Chapter 3

Formations

OVER THE HILL AND ACROSS THE RIVER LIVES AN ENEMY, A FOE BECAUSE he has something we want: farm lands, heads, and other things which stir our envy. Perhaps we own horses, pretty women, storage bins, and other things worth defending. We know he can harm us whether we be on the offensive or defensive. To that foe the world's most beautiful color is the crimson of our blood. We have many things with which to work our will on him or to prevent his prevailing against us. We have all the panoply of war, munitions and supplies. Our chiefs are wise, experienced, and in possession of real authority. Men in plenty we have, and all imbued with a will to win.

Impressive as these things are, they are not enough. Men eager, courageous, and equipped must be shaped, molded into those correct formations which a previous chapter made an indispensable element of true war. The principle of correct formations is a vital constituent of the military horizon. Few professional soldiers would argue with this statement. Formations are the sociologic core of war, and with that core we shall now deal. Intimately surrounding this core, however, are the principles of cooperation, the integrity of tactical units, the combined employment of all forces, and cooperation which consequently must also be treated in this section. By these, men are shaped, and men must be shaped if they are to work as a team in either war or peace.

Thus the horn, conch or bronze, has been sounded and men set forth to war and he who first sets forth already has an advantage. The player who takes the bid tells how the card game is to be played. He who waits also serves, but he usually serves his enemy who has not waited. Even primitive fighters know this, and with the best of reasons. And so the side which hopes to win sets forth to war, or at least to a pleasant exercise in murder.

The approach order is of great importance but, apparently, it is too difficult for the bulk of primitive tribes to appreciate. It requires discipline, planning, and other military elements discussed in this book, hence disorder is the rule of most of the nonliterate world. Many tribes with a high enough social organization to know better have no more approach order than does a lynching mob.

Much of the approach to battle will be discussed under the concepts of intelligence, security, and battle plans. Only a few examples will therefore be given here.

Typical of far too many tribes were those of the Canadian tundra. These simple sub-Arctic hunters practiced warfare only in its rudiments. Each man went forth with two hundred arrows. The warriors got within range of their enemy as best they individually could. They discharged their arrows "like snow" when something like range had been attained. During the approach and the engagement every opportunity was taken to utilize the cover of trees. They were reported as being expert dodgers in this type of warfare, children being taught arrow-dodging from early age.

The approach order of the American Great Plains bison hunters relied too much on scouting, so is discussed under intelligence. The most settled semi-agricultural people used something more, however, although not much. Typical of such groups were the Omaha.[1] They secured intelligence by a line of scouts preceding the war party. Upon reconnoitering the enemy camp, they halted until one of their chief's lieutenants could come up and check their survey. If all seemed well, the Omaha advanced in companies of twenty each, each man holding the hand of his neighbor to prevent dispersion. Just before the attack the chief indulged in tactical magic with his war bundle and exhorted his band in whispers. Each warrior found cover and, at the whistled signal, opened a fire-fight on the enemy's lodges. Unfortunately the Omaha usually bungled a battle well begun. On the march, however, their work was definitely good. There was a hierarchy of command not unlike that used in the advance of a modern small force. The line of scouts marched from two to four miles ahead, providing the service of security. Next came the "captains" and their servants or orderlies, the former carrying the war bundles, since their function was more magical than tactical. The chiefs were careful to rest when they saw their troops were fatigued.

[1] James O. Dorsey, "Omaha Sociology," *Annual Report* 3, Bureau of American Ethnology (Washington: 1881-1882), pp. 321ff.

From the Southeast comes an account by General Milford of an almost perfect approach organization. It must be taken with some caution since it was written by a soldier who may be reading his own training and experience into his account of the Indians. This doubt is bolstered by Swanton's remark that the chiefs of the Creek Confederacy were not generally obeyed. A march order of this kind would have been impossible without authority. The general says that the Muskogee march order was arranged by the chief. The band advanced in column, each family (*sic*) having its specific position. To prevent surprise, the youths and their chiefs formed the van while the old men acted as rear guards. Men in middle life were the flank guards. The women and children marched in the safe center. This order was maintained until contact with the enemy, when the youths advanced to form a line of scouts to cover the approach of the men of middle life. The helpless dropped to the rear to be guarded by the old men.[2]

The doubt cast upon the excellence of this social organization in the approach to battle may be mitigated by recalling that the Creek and their neighbors were socially capable of making widespread confederacies, if not particularly strong ones. The motives for such confederation was to keep the peace among the relatively strong groups and to exploit the less organized neighbors.

Unless a mounted action was sought, the approach to actual battle was often best made afoot, even though the tribe owned horses. This is typical of a modern cavalry fire fight, and it has been observed that even some horsed Plainsmen approached on foot, including the Omaha just mentioned.

In South America the Jibaro entered hostile territory with great caution. Being a riparian people, they made approaches by rafts camouflaged with leaves and branches. Like most primitive warriors, they liked to approach at night. If they came up to an enemy village by day, they surprised and killed anyone found outside the precincts and waited for nightfall. The fire-ring and fire-arrow were used to set the village aflame, and no one could expect mercy from these fierce killers. They did not like open warfare, but if two hostile parties unexpectedly came upon each other in the approach, they would not refuse it. Each side war-danced in full view of the foe, hurling the customary insults and boasts. Whether or not it was con-

[2] Milford, in John R. Swanton, *Creek Social Organization and Uses,* Annual Report 42, Bureau of American Ethnology (Washington: 1924-1925), p. 43.

sidered good form to attack the enemy in the midst of his dancing is not reported.

Negro Africa reveals approach orders varying from the best to the worst. The armies of the kingdoms ordinarily marched in good order. It is said that a Zulu *impi* (regiment) marched very rapidly, soon outstripping the supply train and herds. Miss Krige reports that it could march forty miles by night and forthwith give battle.[3] This record is a bit too remarkable even for the admittedly remarkable Zulu. For the finest modern infantry to be able to march that far in column *at night,* or even by day, and be able to give vigorous battle would be an excellent achievement.

The Ashanti had a well worked out approach order. Some kind is reported for the not distant Ibibio. At the conclusion of the preparatory magic, the men set out in silence in a straight line for the enemy town, and they might not look backward or even take a few steps to the rear on any pretext whatever. They might address no woman on the way.[4]

As the Dahomeans approached a town marked for destruction, the commanders imposed the most stringent march discipline in order to prevent the enemy from being informed of his fate. The Dahomeans relied almost entirely on surprise in battle, and great care had to be exercised to prevent failure of the surprise. Captives from the towns marked for attack had been taken beforehand, and were compelled to accompany the army to show the way. Naturally, these men deserted when possible to give their friends the alarm.[5] Just before the contact the Dahomeans might have surpassed the Zulu. Their preparatory intelligence, immediate approach, and careful reconnoiter were magnificent, but then they relied on the surprise surround while the Zulu liked a stand-up spear action.[6]

Good approach order is not infrequently found in Polynesia, in spite of a statement by Brown that the Samoans observed no formation in camp or on the march. Each man did as he saw fit, save that shelter

---

[3] Eileen J. Krige, *The Social System of the Zulus* (London: Longmans Green, 1936), pp. 273f.

[4] Percy A. Talbot, *In the Shadow of the Bush* (London: Macmillan, 1912), p. 233.

[5] Sir Richard F. Burton, *A Mission to Gelele, King of Dahomey* (New York: Scribners 1893), pp. 15ff.

[6] Sir Richard F. Burton, *The Lake Regions of Central Africa* (New York: Harpers, 1864), pp. 85f.

was consistently used.[7] This seems contradictory to other reports and even to Brown himself in other passages.

The approach of the Kiwai of New Guinea is very fine indeed. It is made on dark nights only, and with the aid of the most excellent scouting service. Should the Kiwai themselves lack scouts with local knowledge, they hire the services of men from neutral towns. It must be said that the control of the chief is surprisingly real and valuable while the men, led by the scouts, accomplish the surround.

The preceding chapter described the line and the column as the chief military formations, all others being derived from them. The column is, of course, the approach formation while the line is for battle. The column in approach is more often lacking than in use, and implied rather than described. The civil states of the American areas of intense cultivation are indicated as marching their troops in columns of several men abreast. Indian file was adequate for the uncivilized tribes of both the northern and southern continents because of the small size of the parties in the field. It was not adequate where many Men were taken on the expedition, and was successful largely because it was the logistical pattern of both sides. Remember that the Greeks had nothing better. Column attenuation was the thing most to be feared both because it exhausted the warriors and because it made them vulnerable. The foremost elements could be defeated before aid could arrive from the rear.

The field evidence regarding logistic formation in America is most scanty, and there is some reason to think that the Indians were wiser than the ethnographers have reported. For example, Denig says that the members of the Soldier Societies of the Assiniboin were detailed to ride the length of the body to prevent straggling, useless noise, and disorderly travel, keeping whatever column there was policed into efficient order.[8] This is just one hint among many of the same kind.

Many people, with the Plains horse-raid in mind, consider that the Indian observed no approach order and did not use the column. The horse-capture was, of course, a theft and as such had no more use for the column than had any other form of robbery. Yet it is rather clear that the device was used in such planned actions as were fought. The

[7] George Brown, *Melanesians and Polynesians* (London: Macmillan, 1910), pp. 167f.

[8] E. T. Denig, "Indian Tribes of the Upper Missouri", ed. J. N. B. Hewitt, *Annual Report 46*, Bureau of American Ethnology (Washington: 1928-1929), p. 549.

common use of the Indian file has been mentioned. This refers to marching in single file, one man after the other, a column with the front of only one human being. There is nothing primitive or stupid in this. It is the way small units often advance to the combat today. A sergeant usually so forms his squad if advancing over dangerous ground. It is most efficient, and was the only practical column in the heavily forested regions in which many Indians fought.

It was definitely attributed to the Omaha a few paragraphs back. It is said that they attempted to prevent column attenuation as a prelude to defeat. One of Wissler's Blackfoot informants gave him an account of training along such lines among those socially simple people. Boys on their first war party were warned by their leader to avoid column attenuation in order to prevent fatigue. Once individuals fell behind the others they were forced continually to maintain a trot to keep up.[9] Karsten implies the single file on land to the Jibaro, which is as good an approach order as the tropical forest would need or permit.[10]

The best use of columns of approach comes from Africa, and the best use of the device in Africa was among the Zulu. The Zulufied Thonga acted in the same manner, as all tribes influenced by Zulu methods largely followed the same march order.[11] Small parties of Zulu marched in single file columns, but larger bodies marched in columns of several men wide. The eyewitnesses are rather vague on the exact front of the column. In Africa, where large infantry hordes were taken into the field, the single or Indian file would have been unforgivable, but the Negroes had learned of the close column.

Useful as the column is, the line of battle is the eventual test of war. Nonliterate men occasionally invented or accepted the device, but not often enough to preserve their liberty.

The statement is often encountered that the American Indian used no tactics and hence no line. This probably means that the writers have fallen into the error of the older explorers who expected the

---

9 Clark Wissler, *The Social Life of the Blackfoot Indians,* Anthropological Papers, American Museum of Natural History (New York: 1911), VII, Part 1, pp. 32f.

10 Rafael Karsten, *Blood Revenge, War, and Victory Feasts Among the Jibaro Indians of Eastern Ecuador,* Bulletin 79, Bureau of American Ethnology (Washington: 1923), p. 24.

11 Henri A. Junod, *The Life of a South African Tribe* (2nd ed.; Neuchatel, 1927), p. 470.

close-order line of the drill field. Because the Indian fought with great interval and distance, taking every opportunity for cover behind boulder and tree, it was assumed that he exercised no battle order at all.

Undoubtedly this was true for many groups, but it certainly was not true for all. Due to the efficacy of modern weapons, our own line soldiers take interval, distance, and use cover, but the line is there even though it be wavy and hard for the enemy machine gunners to estimate. Irregularity is not the significant point, and it never has been since the perfection of fire weapons. Organization, mutual protection, and cohesion are, were, and shall be vital issues. They are the cause and effect of discipline; they are the fighting man's greatest source of safety. The reasons for this were given in Chapter 2.

Actual references to lines of battle are rare. They are less rarely hinted at. Often engagements are described that could be fought in no other way. Just as often, to be sure, it is obvious that the action was a pell-mell of disorder with no one knowing where he belonged or what his function was. On the whole, there is reason to think that this was not universal in America. Witness the fact that Skinner clearly states that the Kansa and Iowa charged in a line, and that one of the functions of the police societies was to keep that line in order.[12] This latter function of battle police is certainly used today. To be sure the Kansa were a small Dhegiha Siouan group closely kin to the Osage and Quapaw. Perhaps as such they had led a better life in the past and this preservation of battle order might be a survival of more integrated society on the Plains which knew so little fighting order. Yet this is a dubious reservation. Eagle Shield, one of Miss Densmore's Teton informants, spoke to her very distinctly of the battle line. Certainly the Teton Sioux must be considered Plains people *par excellence*.

> . . . . The second night a man who had been on the lookout said, "The Crows are after us; they are on our trail."
>
> I said: "We are not cowards. We must stand our ground and not run away." My companions cried, "What shall we do?" I said, "We will go to that little rough ravine and take the horses there." It was a 'draw' in the prairie, and at the end of it were some great rocks. It was a moonlight night, and bright as day. We got the horses into a ravine

[12] Alanson B. Skinner, *Societies of the Iowa, Kansa, and Ponca Indians,* Anthropological Papers, American Museum of Natural History, (New York: 1915), XI, Part 9, p. 690.

> and could hear the voices of the Crows. Evidently there were many of them. I made up my mind that we had a hard time before us, but we had good guns and plenty of bullets. I said: "We will crawl up on top of the ridge land and lie flat in a line far apart. We can see them on the prairie and as soon as they are in range, we will fire."[13]

No small cavalry detachment, finding itself in a position where it had to fight for its life against a large force, could have been better led than this one. Cover was sought for man and beast on the best possible position, apparently at the military crest. The force deployed into a line of battle that, knowing the Crow as one does, must have been impossible to dislodge. Witness the informant's survival to tell the tale!

It is impossible to describe the Plains method of war preceding the introduction of the horse, although the above might contain some hint. Wissler found it impossible to acquire any knowledge on this point when working with the Blackfoot. He assumed that the horse greatly changed such methods, but that is only the usual civilian assumption that foot and horsed tactics differ more radically than they ever have. He made an even more important statement that the Blackfoot charged knee to knee in a line when delivering a mounted shock attack, but deployed over the length of the enemy front to deliver fire. When firing from the ground the Blackfoot used their recumbent mounts for cover. The modernity of such practices suggest the suspicion that the Plains warriors may have been better cavalrymen than they seemed.[14]

As for the Plateau, my own Kutenai and Flathead informants have very specifically stated that they deployed into lines during a fire-fight which, though outnumbered, would cover the entire enemy line in order to prevent envelopment.

Densmore describes the works of a small Ojibway party organized to harrass the Sioux near St. Paul. The leader deployed warriors in a line behind adequate cover near a road the Sioux must travel. He ordered them to hold their fire until the proper moment. But he allowed the main body of the entrapped Sioux merrily to pass by so that they could murder one man who had straggled behind. This feat enabled one Ojibway to wear fancy clothes. As the commander said

[13] Frances Densmore, *Teton Sioux Music*, Bulletin 61, Bureau of American Ethnology (Washington: 1918), p. 380.

[14] Clark Wissler, *Material Culture of the Blackfoot Indians*, Anthropological Papers, American Museum of Natural History (New York: 1910), V. Part 1, *passim*.

they "just killed that man to let the Sioux know that they had been around."[15]

Very little praise can be given the Ojibway commander for such an action. He actually commanded his troops, which few Indian chiefs could say. He exercised all necessary knowledge of surprise, use of terrain, and commanded his fire fighters to form the all important line. Adequate cover was taken and a beautiful trap laid. He had every opportunity of dealing his enemy an effective blow, but he abandoned the use of war to indulge in a ceremonial murder. He refused to fight a battle, so could not exploit the victory which was in his hands. The principle of concerted effort was easy for him, but he threw it away. Since one marauder could have committed this homicide, he violated the principle of economy of force by bringing a whole party afield to indulge in a little exhibitionism for the benefit of one of his *coup*-counters.

If the central Algonkian Ojibway had their troubles, how sad was the fate of their eastern cousins who had the indomitable Iroquois for hereditary foes. These people had at one time been the serfs of the Algonkians and represent the classical example of the worm which turned. Only the white man's interference and their basically small population, constantly reduced by war, prevented the Great League from becoming the masters of northeastern United States.

Our knowledge of Iroquois tactics is not what we would like it to be. The League was abolished before the rise of American ethnology. Our chief sources, tales of travellers and the reports of the Jesuit missionaries, are all of a non-technical nature, and hence are no more than suggestive.

It is reported that the Iroquois fought in a line, or rather two lines in echelon whenever open country presented itself. This follows the principle of correct formations. Indeed, they are the only people north of the Rio Grande who consistently practiced every principle of the art of war at all times, emphasizing those which the mission demanded, as a good general should.

The California area was marked by peoples of simple cultures, small social groups, and great social isolation. Only one California group, the Modoc, had any success against the white man. Most of them were peaceful and were ruthlessly enserfed and slaughtered,

---

[15] Frances Densmore, *Chippewa Customs,* Bulletin 86, Bureau of American Ethnology (Washington: 1929), 71.

the first by the Spanish, the second by the Americans. Tactically they were as incompetent as anything America could show, although Kroeber hints that the Maidu formed a line for fighting.[16] Indeed, Dr. Kroeber implies the line for several California people.

The Indians of South America seem to have used the line, certainly the surround, which is a line of a kind, but the evidence is very dubious. The early missionaries, reporting the tribes of Amazonia, say that "Those of the forest fought dispersed, but in squadrons when in open ground," whatever that means.[17]

The finest use of battle order in Africa was made by the Zulu. Their famous crescent and its operation is discussed in the chapter on battle plans, since its functioning entailed so much thought and team work.

Yet even before Kings Dingiswayo and Chaka, who founded Zulu preeminence, the southeast Bantu had some idea of battle formation. They formerly fought in a straight line, which among nonliterate people is a very fine achievement. The Zulu modified the line into a crescent which proved its superiority by rolling up the enemy into a ball and vitiating all his effectives save those on the margins. Others adopted Zulu tactics. The BaThonga had clear ideas of the attack, forming in an echelon of lines, and of the proper use of reversed and refused lines. Later they adopted the Zulu crescent. These features as well as the principles of combined employment of all forces, concentration of force at the critical point, integrity of tactical units, and economy of force are implied in the crescent line, even for the Thonga. The battalions were ordered to attack by echelons. If the commander observed his men giving way, he followed the principles of economy of force and mass by sending in companies to the critical point until the assault was successful and the pursuit begun.[18] No such leadership and organization will be found in native America save in the central areas, and it is not very clear there.

The principle of correct formations, or of formations at all, is only rudimentarily observed in most of Melanesia. An old missionary source says that Papuans never willingly range a force in front of an

[16] Alfred L. Kroeber, *Handbook of the Indians of California*, Bulletin 78, (Washington: 1923), p. 400.

[17] George E. Church, *The Aborigines of South America*, ed. Clement R. Markham (London: Chapman & Hall, 1912), p. 93.

[18] Junod, *op. cit.*, p. 467

enemy line. When circumstances make this absolutely necessary, neither side suffers much in the engagement.[19]

Humphreys describes only primitive mass actions for the New Hebridean Melanesians, and their use of the line is not clear. The two masses met and indulged in a series of individual combats, so apparently the line was not common. When one man was killed the action stopped so that all might feast and praise the successful warrior, his tribe, and their allies. The next day the enemy sought to get a score in the same way. Casualties were rare in such general skirmishes.[20] Of course such mass duelling, or individual combat of champions is not war at all, any more than duelling is war. It is merely an athletic event, hardly more effective or lethal than football as played a few decades ago.

Melanesians have often been capable of open combat as well as the savagery just mentioned, as Bishop Codrington witnessed. He tells of the individual or mass ambush, the dawn attack, and the athletic events just described for the western Pacific, but he also says that the Floridians can at times do better. He mentions the clash of lines of spearmen as a rarity but also as a possibility. He says that occasionally real masses are used by persuading or buying allies. If the surprise attack fails, the allies may settle down to "something like a siege."[21]

The chapter on battle plans quotes Riley as saying the Kiwai Papuans relied entirely on the dawn attack. Landtman gives a somewhat different version of Kiwai fighting. He says that these Papuans sometimes deliberately threw away their tribal preference for surprise by having scouts shoot a few arrows at individuals and then fly away with their whole war party, which is certainly subtactical. All this accomplished was to make the enemy angry and leave his camp in an uproar. He admits that the night surround and stealthy attack were common and that a general stand-up fight was rare, but some of his description can bear no other interpretation than that the Kiwai could fight like modern infantry. On such occasions a large party advanced in three lines in echelon, first, the old experienced men, next the "strong fighting men" in the prime of life, followed by the young men. The party advanced cautiously to the right and left of the scouts who had

[19] Charles W. Abel, *Savage Life in New Guinea* (London: London Missionary Society 1902), p. 131.

[20] Clarence B. Humphreys, *The Southern New Hebrides* (Cambridge: University Press, 1926), p. 58.

[21] Robert H. Codrington, *The Melanesians* (Oxford: Clarendon Press, 1891), p. 305.

signalled contact. Zulu-like wings were formed by the "strong men" to contain the flanks and assail the enemy's rear. If the enemy became alarmed before the fighting line was formed, the old men engaged them in a fire fight to keep them hotly occupied until the envelopment was completed. Arrows were directed at the enemy's shoulders if at too long a range to kill. This disabled him as an archer, so that he could no longer fire even if but slightly wounded. If the range was short the fatal areas of the armpits or center of the chest were sought.[22]

The missionary Brown takes pains to say that the Samoans observed no battle order, that each man fought as he pleased.[23] Actually, the Samoans, being Polynesians of high grade, exemplified the principle of formations in both the line and the column, as related by many writers, including Brown himself in other passages. The principles of utilization of the terrain, planning, and the integrity of units are clearly implied in their battles as well. The Samoans were really on the military threshold, as the descriptions of their mass duels show. Very probably they would have crossed that threshold had they not forced their battles to conform to ceremonial attitudes and values. The importance of head-taking set up a standard of individuation which prevented the necessary socialization required for true war.

Dr. Buck described a battle between a small party led by Mautara on Mangaia against a large one of Ngariki which was the identical penetrative movement used by Napoleon at Austerlitz and the Germans in the 1940 campaign for France, and by many commanders who believe in mobile war. It shows how civilized the Polynesians could be on occasion.

The common Polynesian formation was the clash of two battle lines in the Homeric fashion, but Mautara knew he had too small a force for this. He therefore told his men that it was victory or the cannibal ovens for them and organized them in a column with depth, not a line, on top of a slope. He then ordered them to charge downhill against the large Ngariki force like a hurled spear. Concentrating at the critical point, this spear split the long enemy line in the center, enabling Mautara's party to defeat their numerous foe in de-

[22] Gunner Landtman, *The Kiwai Papuans of British New Guinea* (London: Macmillan, 1927), pp. 157-159.

[23] Brown, *op. cit.*, p. 167.

tail after a fierce battle.[24] Buck's description shows an aggressive, modern, and sagacious commander with real troops at his back. Many commanders would have stood and been chopped to pieces by the longer line, or would have fled without disgrace. The more civilized might have tried the weak center movement, a device whereby the shorter line seeks to envelop the longer. This Mangaian commander adopted the maxim that the best defense is a vigorous offense. Surely his observation of the principles of the offensive, of simplicity of plan, and of correct formations was good because it was successful against an able, aggressive, and numerous foe.

So far as Eurasia is concerned, there was an appreciation of the value of the line of battle which dictated fair formations from Ireland to India among all Metal Age peoples. The line crops up repeatedly in the songs of the Aryan invasion of India. For example, there are many passages in the *Ramayana* describing the invasion of Ceylon which clearly indicate the battle line. Yet in the last analysis, both sides seemed to put their faith in champions. The ties between Early Hindu and Early Greek cultures are more than linguistic. The culture of the Indic Aryans was in transition at that time, so that the transitional character of their tactics, from championship duel to true war is not surprising. In contrast, it must be admitted that our knowledge of them rests almost entirely on their poetry, the epic nature of which might easily accentuate the value of the hero champions beyond the actual practice of the times.

But what of formations after the battle is over? The victor's worries are moderate, of course. He need not form to escape destruction, although another chapter will show that he had best be systematic if he expects to make the most of his victory. Proper formations are of paramount importance to the defeated, since an aggressive, intelligent foe will surely destroy him if he withdraws from defeat in a disorderly rout. After all, proper formations are organized mutual aid, and a people or nation needs its friends more in defeat than in victory; and who has not suffered defeat at times?

I have been able to find but one hint of a good order of withdrawal among the American field reports. Early explorers say that the Arikara returned by tactical units called "platoons." Each platoon kept perfect step to its field music and held to its own standards or

[24] Peter H. Buck, *Mangaian Society*, Bulletin 75, Bernice P. Bishop Museum (Honolulu: 1930), p. 56.

guidons.[25] By implication they must also have approached in the same way, and perhaps fought in organization, thereby obeying the combat principles of integrity of tactical units. This seems to have been so rare that it might be that the early observers cited by Lowie read civilized warfare into the account. This suspicion is bolstered by the behavior of the culturally similar Omaha. When the Omaha in attack had massacred enough strays and had enjoyed a fine holiday, when individual warriors exhibited their valor by slapping the face of some unwary foe, honor had been satisfied on both sides and the attack withdrew. When the defenders saw that they were no longer smitten, they promptly pursued. The withdrawal on the Omaha attack then invariably became a rout-flight, regardless of whether they won or lost.

Of other continents one can say little. Eye witnesses have told us that the Zulu withdraw from an action as well as the best guard troops, but one has learned to expect that. To the northwest of Africa the Dahomeans organized and planned a war with the finesse of the general staff of a totalitarian state (which they were), advanced in fair order, fought by encirclement, and withdrew as a rabble with the needless loss of hundreds of their troops.

Self-reliance has its part in war, but the keynote of good fighting is cooperation, and the more rugged the better. In order to affect disunity in the enemy ranks there must be unity within one's own. Organized and directed friendship, if you will, is needed to discomfit those to whom we are not friendly. Individual heroes belong to poetry. The battle is a symphony wherein the soloist is seldom significant.

It is necessary, after the battle organizations just described are formed, that they act in unity to accomplish the common end, the destruction of the enemy's will to resist and the imposition of our will upon him. It is therefore part of the shaping of men into workable structures that the mutual aid principles of the combined employment of all forces, of concerted effort, of integrity of tactical units, and concentration at the critical point be employed as intelligently as possible.

There is nothing profound in these principles. Combined employment of all forces means that every man, every unit should have

[25] Robert H. Lowie, *Dances and Societies of the Plains Shoshone,* Anthropological Papers, American Museum of Natural History (New York: 1915), XI, Part 10, pp. 649ff.

a specific job to do. The whole war party should be used sooner or later in the action.

The integrity of tactical units is seldom a part of primitive warfare, although some parties are large enough, specialized enough, and well enough led to employ it. It means simply that if the party is divided into cooperating units, the commander should take care not to split up these units during the action. Each should have its own job. The Zulu are one people who saw this clearly and apparently never violated it.

The above principle is really a function of the greater one, that of concerted effort. War more than any other human occupation requires team work by numerous men. A successful war party ought to respond to the commander's will as the orchestra responds to that of the conductor. All units of the war party should direct their efforts to the common end.

Violation of concentration at the critical point is so prevalent in primitive war as to be one of its features. The warrior, in contrast with the soldier, almost always yields to the temptation to accomplish useless little victories, the slaughter of one man or the crushing of one small party. This fritters away the force's strength so that more often than not no real advantage is acquired by the victor nor permanent injury done to the defeated. Force which is not brought to bear at the right point and the right time is wasted. The enemy's weak point or points should be ascertained and struck with sufficient force to make him regret having entered the contest. Nowhere was this rather obvious principle violated more often than in North America.

The effective use of proper formations is intimately bound up with troop specialization, a fact not often found among primitive warriors. Lack of specialization is just as much a mark of primitivity as is lack of specialized tools in the material culture of peace, or lack of division of labor in social and economic life. Even in small modern units like the squad, so many are riflemen, some are automatic riflemen, another is a grenadier, another is guide, and so on, most men performing specialized functions while working as a team. This coordination in small units is anything but savage. It implies the organization of men and materials into one beautifully coordinated whole, working for the common mission according to a well-understood tactical pattern.

It would seem that such elaboration would be beyond simple nonliterates. Scraps from field reports lead one to think, however, that at times the reporters have not written what they may have seen. Actually, pre-firearm warriors needed such specialization more than modern soldiers, due to the lack of versatility of their weapons. A rifle with a bayonet is both a weapon of fire and shock, but a bow is only a weapon of fire and a spear is ordinarily one of shock. Therefore, the need exists if the culture can rise to the occasion. In answer to the question one finds typically such reports as the following by Gifford regarding the Kamia of the Imperial Valley of California: There were three kinds of warriors: (1) armed with bows and arrows, (2) armed with clubs and shields, (3) armed with stabbing pikes.[26]

Gifford does not affirm or deny the use of these troops as a team. Here was every opportunity, according to the printed page, of having the same tactical organization the Romans used. The archers could have disconcerted the enemy by fire. The heavy clubmen should have led the assault, while the light pikemen could have maneuvered where they pleased to finish off the immobilized enemy. Perhaps that is what the Kamia did. Reasoning from form to function, that is what they should have done with their specialized fighters.

Densmore speaks with more clarity regarding the Papago. Instead of allowing everyone to shoot in a haphazard fire-fight, their chiefs designated certain men to be "killers" beforehand, while others were appointed to protect them.[27]

This work frequently suggests that the warrior and police societies on the Great Plains of America were better organized tacticians than were the rest of the fighting males. Their horse and foot elements were obviously used in combination by the Assiniboin.[28]

Similarly, James Mooney refers to the Ghost Dance association of the Arapaho as consisting of eight degrees. Nearly all men over seventeen belonged, and no one outside it could participate in a public ceremony or join a war-party. The third degree consisted of the Club Men, those in the prime of life. In attack their special duty was to dash ahead and strike the enemy with their clubs which were also the insignia of their degree. After delivering this blow they would ride back and take their places in the *line* for the regular mounted attack. This was dangerous work, but the Club Men were given proportionate honor.

---

[26] Edward W. Gifford, *The Kamia of Imperial Valley*, Bulletin 97, Bureau of American Ethnology (Washington: 1931), p. 31.

[27] Densmore, *Chippewa Customs*, p. 180.

[28] Denig, *op. cit.*, pp. 548f.

Two types of cultures characterize Southwest United States. First were the town-building or pueblo tribes, peaceful, successful farmers, non-aggressive, merely wishing to be left alone. Constantly pressing upon them through the centuries were hordes of wild hunters, attempting to loot the corn which in their savagery they could not grow. The pueblo-building peoples were brave enough, but their chief military efforts were defensive, and hence could not be victorious in the end. Between these two extremes were groups such as the Pima, not advanced enough to erect impressive pueblos but corn-growing and peace-loving, and also beset by such pests as the Apache. The Pima were pacific enough, but unlike the pueblo peoples, they did not object to using the principle of the offensive to carry the war into Apache territory. They had specialized troops for fire and shock designed to advance by fire and movement, according to correct formations, and maintained the integrity of tactical units, a rare observance in America. They were well aware of their true mission, ridding the good earth of their foes.

The Iroquois were described a few pages back as capable of using the tactical line. These lines advanced according to the precept of fire and movement. In the front the archers marched in good order, delivering arrow fire to immobilize and disconcert the enemy. If trees prevented closer action, this fire won the battle. If open country permitted a shock assault, at the proper moment a line of heavily armed shock troops, protected by wooden armor, would rush in front of the archers and assail the discomfited foemen most ferociously with clubs. The archers then became light-armed tomahawk auxiliaries of great mobility, hacking off anyone who got beyond the line of clubmen. Given anything like even numbers, such tactics were bound to win the day against the enemy at hand.

The typical American Indian war party, however, was a force too small and the use of troop specialization was too undeveloped to make the principle of cooperation of much significance. The use of support and reserve was known to some, but to so few that the principle may be passed without discussion. Specialized troops were seen in some of the better Plains tribes, the Iroquois League, on the North Pacific Coast, and possibly among some Californians. Those people who succeeded in achieving the military horizon, Iroquois, North Pacific Coast, and probably some of the Southeast Woodland monarchies, apparently made good use of the principle.

An element of the warfare of barbarian Europe which pointed away from primitivity was the use of specialized troops and the observation of the principles of concerted effort and combined employment of all forces. Julius Caesar said of the Germans under Ariovistus that each horseman went to battle with a foot soldier companion, very brave, highly trained, and very fleet. If the cavalry found it necessary to withdraw, they fell back upon this elite infantry for protection. The infantry could concentrate very speedily upon observing any mischance in the mounted fight and rush to the rescue. These expert runners would cling to the cavalry's manes and aid both in the advance and retreat.[29]

Caesar's trained eye saw in this a remarkable combination and cooperation of trained and disciplined fighting men. Here, too, was the forerunner of the knight-and-squire relationship which the Germanic tribes were to continue through the Middle Age. The combination of infantry fighting in a cavalry line was used by the British in the Napoleonic wars. Such work required training and great courage, whether executed by Germans or Wellington's Highlanders.

Caesar had the highest praise for British chariot troops. They would drive in all directions to confuse the enemy line by the noise of the wheels and showers of arrows. When they had worked themselves into the enemy cavalry's resultant interstices, the fighting men would jump out and fight afoot while the drivers would gradually retire to a distance and dispose the chariots in such a way as to form a quick get-away device for their own troops if needed. "Thus they show in action the mobility of cavalry and the stability of infantry."[30]

Such fine cooperation between the shock and protective elements and the infantry is still a goal to be attained by the combined use of modern infantry and tanks. Caesar admitted that the British cavalrymen were successful against his own legionaries in pursuit and retirement. They never fought in close enough order to please Caesar. Their detachments were posted at wide intervals but in foreordained order. Each party covered the other, and fresh warriors could take the place of tired ones.[31] They should have been defeated in detail for being so bold, but their mobility and cooperation prevented this.

Some experts might consider this British use of mounted infantry bad, but the proof of its excellence lies in its victory over Roman

---

[29] Caius Julius Caesar, *The Gallic War,* i. 48.

[30] *Ibid.*, iv. 3.

[31] *Ibid.*, v. 16.

cavalry. Its sound combination of mobility, cooperation, use of reserves, and concentration at the critical point gave the great dictator cause for worry.

Tacitus reported a similar condition of disciplined cooperation among the Germans. He commented on the inferiority of the mounts, giving most of the credit for cavalry success to the elite corps of infantry which fought with and among the horsemen. These were men apart from the regular line infantry.[32] But if he deprecated the quality of German horses, the discipline and precision of their cavalry maneuver were rare on the modern drill fields, to say nothing of on the battle field. Tacitus might be suspected of puffing up his Germans, as he did more than once.

The Celts in no wise fell below the German standards. They advanced in a close order line of swordsmen whose attack had been prepared by a flight of javelins, adequately observing the principles of fire and movement. The cavalry was subordinated to the infantry attack. They had charioteers before they dared have mounted cavalry, which is probably true of all Aryans. Livy, in reporting the Battle of Cannae, observed that the Celtic people differed in the use of the sword. The Gauls cut and the Iberians thrust.[33] The Romans relearned the value of the short thrusting sword from the Iberians, which is the chief reason why most of the civilized world is governed by the Roman Law. Infantry attacks by swordsmen apparently were typical of all the Celts, for Irish poems describe the same thing. It was not true of the historic Greeks who considered the push of pikes with the long spear the primary infantry effort. They used the sword only as an auxiliary weapon, therefore Roman courage in closing with the enemy resulted in the Romans selling the Greeks as merchandise.

In spite of the subservience of ethnographical and tactical reporting to the demands of poetry, it seems that the early Vedic army utilized similar cooperation between specialized cavalry and infantry troops. The poems mention groups called *sardhocs,* the cavalry of heroes and charioteers supported by the unarmored common people acting as infantry.[34]

The principle of war here under discussion could upon occasion be well observed in America, especially among the Plains warrior associations. There is no doubt but that this particular trait contained

[32] Cornelius Tacitus, *Germania,* 6.
[33] Titus Livy, *The History of Rome* xii, 46.
[34] *The Rig Veda,* i, 8, 11, 53, 71.

the germ of military professionalization which might have blossomed into something effective if given the proper nourishment. Wissler reports an action of the Oglala Teton Blotaunka Society which indicates this. The leader took the party within about three miles of a large enemy camp. A detail of from six to ten men was then sent forward to rush, kill or otherwise excite the enemy into following the advanced party. This type of raiding would content most Indians. In this case the mission was not so trivial. The gadfly element merely stung the foe into accepting an ambush. When they got close enough the Blotaunka lodge launched a vigorous counter-attack which was intended to kill all the effectives participating. This done, they rushed the weakened main camp and wiped it out, returning home in time for the appropriate ceremonies.[35]

In Oceania the superior social organization of Polynesia would lead us to suspect that this area would excel Melanesia in the observance of these principles, and the facts bear this out. Some of the better Melanesians could and did use it in their village raiding, as will be seen.

Buck describes an action between the aggressive Polynesian Tongaiti and the Te-kama on Mangaia which should be read, since it followed the old maxim of aggressive soldiers, "Grab them by the nose and kick them in the pants."[36] The party was divided into two units. One unit formed a pivot of maneuver to immobilize the defensive Te-kama, while the other executed a movement around the Te-kama rear while they were hotly engaged in front. Cavalry and other mobile soldiers prefer to fight this way. It is always a good fools-mate to try on a foe in love with the defensive. The description of this action makes it plain that the Mangaian Polynesians appreciated the value of concerted effort, concentration at the critical point, the integrity of units, and the economy of force.

The same author describes a more typical Polynesian action in another section. It by no means utilized the cooperative principles of mobile troops as did the foregoing, but it did contain the use of cooperation of another type.

The first party to arrive at the designated battle site arranged itself in a line about five files deep. The front line was composed of the

---

[35] Clark Wissler, *Societies and Ceremonial Associations of the Oglala Division of the Teton-Dakota*, Anthropological Papers, American Museum of Natural History, (New York: 1912), XI, Part 1, *passim*.

[36] Buck, *op. cit.*, p. 44.

heads of families armed with the longest weapons. Behind them were their sons in file according to seniority. The other party came up and was allowed to make a similar disposition with no attempt to break up the maneuver by shock. Time was allowed for the various families to be sure that they were ranged opposite ones with whom they had a grudge. The two battle lines then came slowly together and the fight consisted of duels between members of the front ranks, those to the rear cooperating by protecting the heads of families, passing up munitions, dragging the dead and wounded away from the grasp of the cannibalistic foe, and taking the place of those disabled. Even the wives who formed the final rank played an heroic part in the service of supply, even offering their own bodies to protect those of their mates and sons. Naturally such a battle lost its rigid order fairly soon, but so do many modern ones.[37]

While the foregoing action does not exhibit the cleverness of some Polynesian battles, and certainly required but little manipulation on the part of the commander, it is not exactly primitive unless one chooses to call most pre-Roman tactics primitive. It is true that the element of surprise was thrown away. It is also true that the wonderful opportunity for shock action was discarded for a Frederician line action. But in all, this battle sounds very much like Greeks fighting after the invention of the phalanx, only better. And possibly its resemblance to Greek or Aryan line actions might be more than accidental parallelism. There was cooperation between the files organized on a kinship basis. There were echelons of support and reserve, as well as some thought for security and sufficient numbers. It is true that next to no attempt at mobility was made. This was static battle in which the longest line was almost certain to win, given troops of equal hardihood.

Melanesia and Papua were for the most part quite incompetent in the use of these principles. Landtman, however, describes a Kiwai action which clearly used a pivot backed by a mobile unit, exemplifying the principles of cooperation, movement, and the combined employment of all forces. According to Landtman the Kiwai had real battle ability beyond the savage dawn attack which seems to be as much as Riley can credit them with. Riley thought them tacticians of no mean order, however, and with this we may agree within the limits of the type of action they were called upon to fight.[38]

---

[37] Buck, *op. cit.*, pp. 159f.

[38] Landtman, *op. cit.*, pp. 157ff.

This discussion has, I hope, shown that along such lines, and columns, the men of the tribe must be shaped if they are to prevail in the approaching combat. Yet mere formation is not enough. The shaping of men will be no more effective than the pretty figures of a full dress parade of cadets on a grassy drill field unless the formations are handled according to the simple principles herein outlined. Formations are only instruments. They do not work themselves any more than a violin of the finest workmanship can play itself. They require skillful handling, which is the commander's role, and adequate foresight, which will be discussed in the principle of plans.

Chapter 4

Discipline and Command

LEADERSHIP AND OBEDIENCE, SUPERORDINATION AND SUBORDINATION, are essential to any task requiring team work. This may be said categorically. The more important the task, the greater its magnitude and complexity, and the greater the danger involved to the cooperators, the greater must be the element of discipline, administration, and command. Discipline and command are two faces of the same coin, and if this coin be military, are strong forces which make for victory. War is not child's play, even if it be primitive war, and the loss of a worker, protector, or kinsman through military death is serious in all societies.

The reason for this discussion of the command function might be clarified by three citations. Romans said that a Choctaw chief could not pretend to command but could only persuade. Any attempt to command on his part would have brought desertion or even his assassination.[1]

Against this situation let us pose the opinion of a modern professional soldier:

> The question is frequently asked, why do we need discipline in the army? The answer is that there can be no orderly effort of any kind, in the army or out of it, without teamwork, which is merely the ultimate expression of organized discipline.[2]

The fruits of organized, commanded, disciplined group effort is success in achieving the group goal. The reward of such behavior as described by Romans is strikingly enunciated by Denig for the Assiniboin. Their war parties never fully accomplished their missions, and the chief cause of failure was insubordination. No man could

[1] Romans, *The Natural History of East and West Florida* (New York: 1775), p. 25.

[2] Address by General M. B. Stewart.

make plans, carry them out, or actually lead. The nominal Assiniboin head chief was only leader of his own band, which contained many men who considered themselves his equals. Everyone's advice was asked and nobody's taken. A party might look fair on setting forth, but soon old personal grudges cropped up and the party was disrupted by disputes. In the end, a large percentage of the army drifted home in detached parties.[3]

But who is the primitive commander? The choice of a commander for magico-religious reasons could be called primitive when contrasted with the civilized methods of choice on the basis of training, experience, and the qualities of leadership. A dream may have tactical value if one is fighting other dreamers. If not, its value is probably negative, although one must not discount the value of a dream as a creator of morale.

The Assiniboin just mentioned had no permanent war leaders. An individual had a dream, whereupon he went to the young men and tried to recruit them for a party under his leadership. They might, of course, enlist or not according to their own wishes. After the party had departed, they took care to stop four times on the way to the point where the dream had predicted victorious contact with the enemy. At the last spot the leader had to have a dream which would confirm the original one. It is said that such a party was usually successful, which is, of course, the final test of efficacy.[4] This might be taken as the general pattern of the Great Plains command.

Among the Winnebago the sacerdotal element was injected by the inclusion of the war-bundle idea. They thought that no one should lead a large party unless he could prove his possession of some special blessing from the supernaturals guaranteeing every detail of the expedition.[5]

This bundle trait must not be underestimated. The fetish idea, whether one is speaking of sub-Saharan Africans, or the Indians of north central United States, or the palladia of the eastern Mediterranean, has some importance regarding the command function. When the Iowa launched an attack, their commander had strictly ceremonial duties. The sacerdotal idea was introduced when instead of com-

---

[3] Denig, *op. cit.*, p. 548.

[4] Robert H. Lowie, *The Assiniboine,* Anthropological Papers, American Museum of Natural History (New York: 1909), p. 28.

[5] Paul Radin, *The Winnebago Tribe,* Annual Report 37, Bureau of American Ethnology, (Washington: 1915-1916), p. 156.

manding the action he had to stay behind, pray to the bundle, sing, and rattle for success. If the party was successful, the glory went to him and his rattling, not to the fighting men.[6] When the war leader is considered a priest to a fetish or god, the idea is introduced which may, under proper circumstances, lead to the concept of priest-kingship, a concept which has done so much for certain African kingdoms, the civilizations of the American area of intense cultivation of maize, and for the eastern Mediterranean.

LaFlesche, speaking of the reasonably well-organized Osage, plainly indicated that their war leader was considered more the high priest of the expedition than its commander. He was the intermediary between the people and the supernatural *wakanda*. He was too laden with tabus, vigils, and continual supplication to lead the fight. It was just as well to keep him occupied this way, for the warriors would not have obeyed him even had he given any tactical instructions.[7] This might have been very good tactical and organizational procedure if the Osage had not encountered the United States Cavalry, whose tables of organization, command, tactics, and theology were notably different. LaFlesche reported that the songs and ceremonials to be rendered before an Osage attack took more time than the battle itself. To the misfortune of modern armies, there are no more such singing soldiers to vanquish. Cromwell's psalm-singing infantry did not wait until they got to the doxology before they struck. The priest-king idea is most beneficial provided that it does not interfere with tactics, or that the praying be done the night before as Stonewall Jackson did, or that some less holy man should actually command.

The commonest form of acquiring command in America was to elect one's self to the post. Typically, the Assiniboin allowed any chief or brave warrior to raise and lead a war party. He had only to persuade men to follow him.[8] This method was admirably suited to a people who had enlistment by individual preference rather than tribal levy. It is without doubt primitive in nature and is very widespread. It has an unapproved or illegal survival among living historic people in the nature of partisan or guerrilla troops. Despite the

[6] Skinner, *op. cit.*, p. 686.

[7] Francis La Flesche, *The Osage Tribe: Rite of the Chiefs: Sayings of Ancient Men,* Annual Report 36, Bureau of American Ethnology (Washington: 1914-1915), p. 107.

[8] James O. Dorsey, "Siouan Sociology," *Annual Report 15,* Bureau of American Ethnology (Washington: 1893-1894), p. 224.

limitation that the warlike operations of such personal troops shall be confined to the public enemy, this type of leadership and recruiting is primitive because it is essentially private and personal in nature and non-public. Limiting the effort to a tribal enemy is the only modern note. Otherwise it falls into the recruiting and leadership pattern of the Italian renaissance mercenary troops against whom Machiavelli railed.

This type of leadership was really a matter of organization rather than command. Such a person had to have a favorable name for success against the enemy, or no one would volunteer to go with him. Yet he could not attempt to command any of his followers with any ring of authority. A Chickasaw leader was a man famous for having harmed the enemy, but he could do no more than propose or persuade. His party would have deserted in a body had he attempted more.[9]

Often, by contrast, some distinguished man might be asked to lead a war party. This does not mean that he had any official permanent title, rank, or authority. After the expedition he would lapse back into the ranks of distinguished private persons. The Plains-Ojibway and Plains-Cree parties were usually of this semi-private type. If, among the latter, no one was inspired to lead a party, the warriors might organize one themselves and not only request some distinguished warrior to lead it but actually make him substantial gifts to do so.[10]

A more effective method was for the group to decide to go to war, define its objective, make up its party, and then elect a proper chief to head it. This was the method of the Jibaro, a loosely-knit people with no concept of tribal authority. Yet their perception of the utility of choosing a real chief impelled them to do so. On those rare instances when a whole Jibaro tribe, or even a temporary federation of tribes went to war as a unit, a chief over the whole was elected.[11]

The civil chief in America was not necessarily the war chief. More often the reverse was true. Indeed, the term chief itself is more often meaningless than otherwise. Most American societies had not developed authoritative rulers, and the civil state, where it existed,

---

[9] Romans, *op. cit.*, p. 70.

[10] Alanson B. Skinner, *Political Organization, Cults, and Ceremonies of the Plains-Ojibway and Plains-Cree Indians*, Anthropological Papers, American Museum of Natural History (New York: 1914), XI, Part 6, p. 490.

[11] Karsten, *op. cit.*, p. 18.

is out of the scope of this volume. But even when a civil chief of some rank and authority had arisen, he was not necessarily the war commander. This may be for two reasons. First, he may not have acquired sufficient military prestige for him to have the *de jure* right to lead his people in battle. Furthermore, he might hold his chieftainship for reasons other than military. Some of the older writers postulated that all chieftainship and kingship came from the power of some distinguished warrior to persuade or overawe the commonalty into making him governor in all things. This happened time and again, but to trace the civil state to war alone is an oversimplification. It discounts, for instance, the power of the spiritual leader. Among the Southeast United States tribes the most influential chief, often a rudimentary king, was a peace chief and forbidden to shed blood. Even some of the Northeast Woodland peoples had similar ideas. In the second place, the civil chief might not be a war chief because the culture had developed beyond this, as has our own.

Inspection of the literature shows that the American Indians used both methods—the war chief being the general chief, as well as the separation of the peace and war powers. An Assiniboin head chief was leader in all things, including war, thus differing from the neighboring Omaha and Ponca who used the dual civil and war chieftainships.[12] The Yuki, though simple and isolated Californians, had a specialized war chief aside from the civil power. He was a notably brave man, ruling by influence rather than direct command. In a battle he stood in the rear or on one side where he advised and encouraged the fighting men.[13]

The Coeur d'Alene had two kinds of war, public and private. In the second type, these Plateau people used the Plains method of individual organization and command. In the tribal wars, however, the head (civil) chief assembled a council of chiefs, that is, band chiefs and distinguished warriors, wherein the matter was discussed. If the council decided on war, they hoisted a robe on the council lodge. All who wished to join likewise hoisted a robe or blanket on their own tents. The chief or chiefs decided upon going to war but they did not necessarily lead the expedition. They themselves elected the war leader, although they went one step towards the civil state by keeping this suffrage to themselves and not sharing it with the warriors who would make up the bulk of the command.

---

[12] Dorsey, *op. cit.*, p. 224.

[13] Kroeber, *op. cit.*, p. 177.

The nearby Okanagan had two types of chieftainships, that conferred by heredity and that acquired through prestige. The large bands had permanent war chiefs aside from the civil leaders, while such command among small bands was temporary.

The rise of an hereditary chieftainship not vested with war command was not unusual. Miss Densmore reported that any Ojibway warrior might organize a private war party by sending a messenger with tobacco to the men he wished to recruit. These men assembled, the prospective leader gave a speech concerning the objective sought and encouraged the warriors to enlist. He gave a banquet to those who pledged to go and all smoked the pipe. Now the Ojibway did have hereditary war chiefs, so prestige depended upon one's own abilities. Persons of various sibs would leave their own unsuccessful chiefs to enlist under a good one. The hereditary chief was the president of the council, made decisions regarding the general welfare, settled small disputes, and represented his band in tribal councils and in international affairs, but he was by no means an authoritative war chief *de jure*.[14] The man who actually led was accorded considerable obedience and received all the credit if the expedition was successful.

It might be well to summarize this subject. First, the leader might have no authority at all, as in Guiana, hence there could be no discipline. War could be no more than "a disorderly route," and since everyone was his own judge as to when to retire, could be only of brief duration.[15]

Second, several instances have been cited of the titular commander having only sacerdotal functions, so there is no need of multiplying examples. Where his duties consisted of remaining behind the main action to pray to some *wakanda* or bundle it is doubtful if he should be called a commander.

Third, the commonest degree of authority in the Americas was adequate for the type of action fought, and as much as could be imposed upon companions as disorderly and anarchic as most Indian fighters were. The authority of such command was generally advisory only, no matter what title the leader might hold. Therefore, Fletcher and LaFlesche complained that Omaha war parties were not organ-

[14] Frances Densmore, *Chippewa Customs*, p. 135.

[15] Gumilla, in Walter E. Roth, *An Introductory Study of the Arts, Crafts, and Customs of the Guiana Indians*, Annual Report 38, Bureau of American Ethnology (Washington: 1916-1917), p. 582.

ized "into lines, companies, or battalions," each warrior marched and fought independently, and no one awaited anyone else's order to attack (or withdraw).[16]

One should not discount the American Indian's ability to confer real authority on a war chief in certain areas. It has been pointed out that the term " chief" had little or no authoritative meaning among the Plains bison hunters who did not grow corn. On the other hand, these people generally had societies and lodges, most of them involved in problems of war and social control. As a fourth type the councils and heads of these soldier societies were often real commanders vested with real power. Analogous to this was the reversion to primitive war during our own crusading period. Many of the primitive features of command and enlistment observed in this discussion will be recalled for these historic wars. On the other hand there were orders of military monks, the Hospitallers and Templars, who had iron discipline, real tactical training, and true command functions. These voluntary societies constituted the real fighting backbone of the crusading armies.

As a fifth type, the otherwise unorganized Jibaro could confer real power on a chief, called "the old one," during a war of extermination. He alone made plans and dispositions, and the young warriors obliged themselves to obey him implicitly. This absolute authority ceased with peace, and even a successful war chief lapsed to the level of all other Jibaro.[17]

One would expect the socially and economically well-organized tribes of the North Pacific Coast, with their clear-cut caste ideas, to have authoritative commanders. According to Tsimshian mythology, their chiefs had the right of absolute command. They followed the American pattern of having to request recruits, but once anyone had joined up, he was under the very real and great command of his chief. These chiefs apparently could declare a state of war on their own recognizance which bound their people, because they were great chiefs and princes.[18]

War chiefs sometimes became so authoritative that their power increased beyond the functions of war. They were men of such suc-

[16] Alice C. Fletcher and Francis La Flesche, *The Omaha Tribe,* Annual Report 27, Bureau of American Ethnology (Washington: 1905-1906), p. 427.

[17] Karsten, *op. cit.,* p. 7.

[18] Franz Boas, "Tsimshian Mythology," *Annual Report 31,* Bureau of American Ethnology (Washington: 1909-1910), pp. 381f.

cess that they might encroach on the civil chief. This was true in some of the pueblos of the Southwest. The Acoma war chiefs had more than tactical importance. They were "virtually the backbone of the spiritual and institutional life of the pueblo." Since rain is the most important event in pueblo life, the war chiefs had the duty of making it rain. They protected the magico-religious associations and combatted witchcraft. Today they are general overseers of daily life, doing their best to prevent acculturation towards American and Mexican ways. The task is arduous, entailing onerous ritual and routine behavior, demanding sexual continence, and is not rewarded with pay. Acoma has three such war chiefs elected annually without regard to clan affiliation. They are considered the chief heralds of the civil cacique. Indeed, a war chief is analogous to the executive officer of a modern man-of-war. The cacique rules, but through his war chiefs who are obviously the real authority.[19]

The responsibility of the authoritative war chiefs to their civil superiors, or to the society in general, varied in degree as much as did their power. The supreme authority of the group was exerted among the Acoma by giving the war chiefs a thorough if ceremonial whipping upon their assumption and resignation of office. The Plains-Ojibway chief had to run the gauntlet. Weak or incapable Assiniboin chiefs were supposed to resign. Indeed, the council could depose them.[20]

As for successful chiefs, their rewards were likewise manifold. It will be remembered that the Ojibway chiefs got all the glory if the expedition went well. The Iowa chief, as priest to the war-bundle, was so engaged in prayer that he could not command. He could not turn aside nor turn back while marching. He was so tabu that someone had to turn him from straight ahead when this was necessary. He slept alone and had someone feed him. But to this sacred personage went all the credit and loot from a successful party. The property he distributed to the community. Such loot distribution comprises one of the economic roots of kingship. Such advantages given to a commander who could not command reminds one of the South American Mojo. Their caciques could not command, and their greater pres-

[19] Leslie A. White, "The Acoma Indians," *Annual Report 47*, Bureau of American Ethnology (Washington: 1929-1930), pp. 45-50.

[20] Dorsey, *op. cit.*, p. 224.

tige rested only on their individual valor. But they could use other men's women "without repugnance or resistance."[21]

An unsuccessful chief might suffer in many ways. Among those tribes wherein the would-be leader decided himself to go on a party and recruited his own followers, he might lose his own prestige, a very terrible thing. If the society had an aristocratic basis, he might be degraded to the rank of a common person, as among the Choctaw.[22]

Among people with a separate and authoritative civil chief it might go hard with an unsuccessful commander. The head chiefs of the Winnebago were interested in conserving human life and were peace chiefs. Should anyone feel sufficient spiritual vitality for getting up a war party, he was permitted to do so, but he was decidedly responsible to the civil chief for failure.[23]

American war outside the areas of intense cultivation of maize, then, was primitive war because the choice of the commander rested upon reasons which seem whimsical and impermanent when tested by the effectiveness of compelling the other-group to submit to the we-group's will. Because a man has an idea of going to war and being a captain is no sign that he is an able commander. We have people like that today, and if they attempt to put their ideas into practice, we lock them up in prisons or mental hospitals. A dream, too, may be very pleasant if confined to bed, but not as a substitute for tactical planning or a method of military promotion. To go to war under a dreamer against an enemy who plans battles and chooses commanders by utilitarian means is suicidal.

The large forces of Africa were not only well organized but well led. The weak leadership of the American Indian gave his land to the white man without adequate struggle. In Africa this struggle was often very real. Effective command backed by iron discipline existed wherever the kingship or even a good strong chieftainship arose, and this condition was typical of the continent.

The African kings rarely were field commanders themselves. Professional generals often commanded as a matter of course, frequently being responsible to the king for success even with their own lives, as

---

21 Church, *op. cit.*, p. 104.

22 Jean B. Bossu, *Nouveaux Voyage aux Indes Occidentales* (Paris: LeJay, 1768), I, pp. 89-94.

23 Radin, *op. cit.*, p. 156.

in the lake region.[24] In Dahomey the king went to war himself, but was ceremonially degraded at the outset of the campaign and theoretically did none of the tactical direction. He sat on a low stool while the field officers sat on the exalted seats. The commander-in-chief smoked in his presence and ordered him about. This was to deceive the enemy gods as to the reality of the true head and divert their anger from the king.

The emergence of the command function is obscure for Melanesia. Aside from the negritic tribes, who were or are too simply organized for any command at all, there seems to be wide variation. In the Solomons the character of the chief appears to have resembled the *coup*-counting Great Plains dignitary, with the strengthening of some hereditary element. If a man killed a large number of enemies, the existing chiefs decided to make him a chief (*tsunaum*). A raid was made on an enemy village to bring back a live captive. The chiefs then cut the wretch and annointed the candidate for chieftainship with the blood. The prisoner then became food for a feast in front of the village's principle house. The child of the sister of such a *coup*-chief was a chief from birth, so the rank was perpetuated in the family.[25] Other Melanesian peoples had absolute chiefs, and there could be no war unless the chiefs of the constituent villages agreed. This was also true of the Southern New Hebrides.[26]

Miss Powdermaker says that Lesu on New Ireland had two chiefs, a clan head and a war chief. This latter was a rich man with strong war magic. His position was inherited, but only weakly, as his own preference for a successor or some applicant's personal ability were taken into serious consideration.[27] This marks the beginning of the temporal lordship, but what an ineffective one! The pleonarchist and hereditary elements would have cost them their lives if matched against a military people. Melanesian paladins did hold war councils, but one wonders what truly military matters were discussed? In the Solomons they were held in the canoe house or club house, and one suspects that their functions were magical and recreational as well

[24] Sir Harry H. Johnston, *The Uganda Protectorate* (London: Hutchinson, 1902) *passim.*

[25] Beatrice Blackwood, *Both Sides of Buka Passage* (Oxford: Oxford University Press), p. 47.

[26] Humphreys, op. cit., p. 35.

[27] Hortense Powdermaker, *Life on Lesu* (New York: W. W. Norton, 1933), p. 41.

as of staff nature.[28] Apparently little could be expected from such war commands as in the Loyalties where emotional instability is so much in evidence. Shouting, frightful gestures, and screaming were more important than discipline, order, and the subordination of the individual.[29]

The speech-loving Polynesians had war councils and authoritative chiefs, but in many cases these commanders could not overcome their jealousy enough to have a chief of party. War councils were composed of the heads of all families, each sitting in his appointed place. When the proper time came each village was heard from through one speaker only, chosen in order of precedence. Yet there was often no central commander. Each head commanded his own kin only. The older chiefs sat in council and determined the policy.[30] The principle of plan seems to have been observed thereby, but the weakness of not having a definite executive for the plan must have caused much trouble.

We are well informed of the close-knit character of many Polynesian societies. The war function improved tremendously among those peoples who frankly admitted that their chief noble was too tabu to be an effective commander and shifted the martial command to a war lord, or had it shifted for them.

Something like real leadership obtruded among the martial Mangaians. Buck cites more than one instance of true commanders exhibiting a very enviable military skill.[31] One must remind himself that the recent tendency is to think that the earlier reporters may have overemphasized the chiefly character of Polynesian society in contrast with that of Melanesia. It is certain that all Polynesians did not have the tactical and command ability of the Mangaians, or of Kamahameha I. It may have been that this truly military method diffused to just a few island from some unknown place outside Polynesia.

Miss Meade tends to play down the importance of war for Samoan Manua. She implies that the war myths were inspired by but few and insignificant squabbles, that they had no real war gods, war priests, or great respect for the warrior. They had professional spies

---

28 Florence Coombe, *Islands of Enchantment* (London: Macmillan, 1911), pp. 57f.

29 Emma Hadfield, *Among Natives of the Loyalty Group* (London: Mamillan, 1920), p. 169.

30 Brown, *op. cit.*, p. 165.

31 Buck, *op. cit.*, p. 161.

and scouts who sat in the town assembly, and they held war councils, but there were no commanders.[32] This would indicate that they were outside the stream of Polynesian military diffusion, for they would have lived but a short while if confronted by Polynesians inspired by the god Rongo or led by the Mangaian war-lord. No one has ever been able to point to a success of a debating society over a commander in battle. Remember the campaign against Gibeah.

A few theorists have tried to derive the field commander from the champion, the individual warrior of note who met his foe in Sohrab-Rustum, David-Goliath fashion and compelled his followers to come to the field mainly to furnish a cheering section. This does seem to have some validity for Eurasia, but it breaks down so completely for the rest of the world that it may be dismissed as phantasy.

The hangover from primitivity of many Eurasiatics is seen in the persistence of the championship duel. True, such stupidity is not reported in any amount for the warlike Germans and most Celts, but the Aryans of India, the early Persians, and the Teutonic Viking certainly enjoyed it. Instead of this being a common practice of all tribes all over the world, it is probably an integral part of the war pattern of all the Aryans, and since so much of our tradition is derived from these peoples, this led at least one writer to consider such conduct a universal stage.

The duel of champions seems too idealized in Book I of the Hindu epic of the *Maha-Bharata,* although it is obvious that the incident described was more of a tournament than a battle. On the other hand, Books VIII, IX, and X were written to glorify individual combat between the two principals Indeed, the high light of the *Maha-Bharata* is a duel with the retainers used only as spectators, as the chief incident of the Iliad is the combat between Hector and Achilles. Book VII, *Drona-Badha* (the Fall of Drona) tells of some good tactical war, although its chief incident is the championship duel between the rebel Brahman Drona and Salya, the Panchala king allied to the hero of the book. In startling contrast is Book VI, *Bhishma-Badha* (the Fall of Bhishma) which shows that during the time of the composition of the Maha-Bharata (the Twelfth to Tenth Centuries, B. C.), the Aryans could abandon this childish exhibitionism and indulge in war with

[32] Margaret Mead, *Social Organization of Manua* (Honolulu: Bernice P. Bishop Museum, 1930), p. 168.

few if any primitive elements. This date antedates any such excellence in Europe.[33]

The championship duel is quite common in the Norse lays. One of them relates how King Agantyr of the Goths offered to fight King Humli of the Huns who was overrunning the land.[34] Humli could not be bothered.

The method certainly survived in Roman tradition long enough to be written down. Dion Cassius describes such a duel in the struggle for supreme power between the Albans and the early Romans. The Albans and Romans fell into a wrangle about the sovereignty upon the death of King Numa. They did not wish to slaughter each other by a clash of armies, nor did they want the outcome of a single combat to decide the issue. It happened that each side had a group of triplet brothers—mighty men at arms—so a contest was arranged between them. The three Alban brothers very quickly killed two of the Roman triplets, but the third was not content to stand and be valiantly chopped down. He started running around for all he was worth, making the Alban brothers pursue him, and thus separated them. This enabled him to slay each one as he came up.[35]

Eurasia varied as much as America in the more practical part of the command function. The authority varied directly with the rest of social organization and cohesion, from the rudimentary kingships of the Metal Age folk, through the fairly well-organized cattle and horse nomads of Central Asia, to the simple democratic societies of the reindeer Arctic. The response of the social pattern to war necessity is remarked by Bogoraz. The Chuckchee wars with the Tannit tended to develop the war chieftainship, but it did not go far and ceased with the wars. The "conditions of Chuckchee life are too simple for such an institution," but had the wars continued a strong civil chieftainship might have prevailed.[36]

Miss Czaplicka reported a situation among the Chuckchee which is from reminiscent to almost identical with that of the American Es-

---

[33] Romesh C. Dutt, trans., *The Mahabharata* (London: Macmillan, 1899), i, vi, vii, viii, ix, x.

[34] Lee M. Hollander, ed. and trans., *Old Norse Poems: The Most Important Non-Skaldic Verse Not Included in the Poetic Edda* (New York: Columbia University Press, 1936), p. 44.

[35] Cassius Dio, "Fragment of Zonoras," *Roman History*, iii. 6, 7.

[36] Waldemar Bogoraz, "The Chuckchee—Social Organization," *American Museum of Natural History Memoirs* (New York: 1904-1909), XI, Part 3, p. 647.

kimo town bully, who may or may not constitute a rudimentary war leader. He was the war hero during the struggles with the Koryak, Eskimo, and Cossacks but he did not develop much beyond the Eskimo level.[37] Among the Siberian Yukaghir the strongmanship's military importance was more clearly defined as real leadership. It was the strong man's duty to lead his warriors in defense of the clan, although he might not be a member of the consanguineous group himself.[38]

The Ainu culture of Northeast Asia and adjacent islands is very poorly documented. From the available sources it seems that their chiefs had some war authority but were held in check by a council of elders. In strong contrast with other Siberian peoples, the Ostyak chiefs and their families formed an aristocratic military caste whose duty was to defend the tribe against foreign aggression. Like the mediaeval knightly class they occupied themselves in peace times with tournaments and hunting.[39]

The Siberian peoples illustrate the danger of too close a generalization about culture areas. Undoubtedly every one of these tribes should be heaped into one great Arctic culture area, but they seem to exhibit almost every possible degree of war-chieftainship.

Tacitus points out the emergence of the commander from the champion among the Germans. German kings were chosen on the grounds of birth, but generals were appointed for their courage and conspicuous behavior in the front line. Yet these generals could not command, but led by example and through the admiration of their followers.[40] For the retainers to surpass the chief was his disgrace; to be surpassed by him was theirs. To have survived one's chief in battle brought infamy and shame. To defend him with one's own life was glory, the essence of allegiance. The chief fought to win the battle, "but the retainers fought for the chief."[41]

To go a step higher in the authority of command, perhaps as high as one can go, Caesar says that the common people of some tribes were almost enslaved by the knightly aristocracy. These chiefs kept the barbarians in perpetual uproar, and were ranked according to

---

[37] Marie A. Czaplicka, *Aboriginal Siberia* (Oxford: Clarendon Press, 1914), pp. 25f.

[38] *Ibid.*, p. 38.

[39] *Ibid.*, p. 69.

[40] Cornelius Tacitus, *Germania*, 7.

[41] *Ibid.*, 14.

birth, wealth, and number of retainers. "This is the one form of influence and power known to them."[42]

The command problem is by no means solved with the appointment of one commander. In modern war even the smallest unit needs more than one chief. Even in a squad, the smallest modern tactical unit with its own permanent integrity, some man must be designated as leader in event the sergeant becomes a casualty. Furthermore, in working out the combat functions of even so small a unit, good team work often requires that the men working at some distance from the squad leader shall be supervised by someone. In large commands the subordinate commander is even more indispensable. No human can direct more than just so many other men; no master mind can care for all details of supervision. A hierarchy of junior commanders is essential. So likewise is some type of staff to care for details. It is necessary that there be another officer or officers to take the organizational details from the shoulders of the tactical or strategic commander and to act in his name.

A mark of primitivity in war, as has been noted, is a weak command function. This being so, any elaboration of command into a hierarchy, or chain, or channel of command is hardly expectable, and the field literature shows that this is very poorly developed. This does not mean that the hierarchy of command is entirely absent, even in relatively unled America.

The organization of command in an Omaha war party was thus: A young man seeking to organize an expedition with himself as commander discussed the matter with a good friend. If this one approved, he became junior commander and the two set about enlisting others in the banqueting fashion which will be discussed presently. The proper fasting and feasting done, they slipped away in the night and went against the enemy. The hierarchy of command was observed by the two leaders insofar as they chose a lieutenant apiece. The only staff functions were exercised by the commander's messengers, who wore plumes and women's pack straps as insignia.[43] This sort of organization was common to the entire Plains and Plateau.

Some acumen was occasionally introduced into the bundle priest-commander combination. The Osage, while considering the head chief too sacred and too prayerful to direct operations, gave him eight

---

[42] Caesar, *op. cit.,* vi. 15.

[43] James O. Dorsey, "Omaha Sociology," *Annual Report 15,* Bureau of American Ethnology (Washington: 1881-1882), p. 318.

subordinates to take over the bother of directing a large party. Four of these were chosen from each moiety.[44]

The management of Wyandot military affairs resided in a military council which consisted of a chief and all able-bodied men. The war chief was chosen by the council from the Porcupine gens. There were usually several potential military chiefs in the gens who acted as companions and assistants to the war chief, and in case of his death, took over command in order of seniority.[45]

Although the Choctaw were not a particularly well-disciplined group of warriors, their ideas of the hierarchy of command were strangely well developed. Each village had a civil chief and a war chief, the latter having two lieutenants and a staff functionary who attended to all military ceremonials. Below them all fighting men were formally ranked according to achievement.[46]

In the United States Army units large enough to have staffs divide the work into the following departments: the Executive and second in command, Chief of Staff, Administration, the Intelligence Section, the Operations and Training Section, and the Supply Section.

The intelligence function will be discussed later, so will not be dealt with here.

An Ojibway leader appointed four aides before setting out. Theirs were what we call staff functions, since they superintended all preparations, including the requisite ceremonial. They arranged for camps on the march. One carried the leader's pipe and another the drum. Every party carried a supply of magical objects and materials for making moccasins. The leader himself furnished part of the supplies. This is an important point which will be discussed separately in a few paragraphs. If a fight was expected, the Ojibway prepared for the care of the wounded ahead of time. Litters of poles were made for their transportation, as the hereditary Siouan enemy always pursued, hoping to destroy some of the wounded. An old man was appointed to carry extra medical supplies and water. He took no part in the fight but ran to the aid of those

[44] Francis La Flesche, *The Osage Tribe: Rite of Wa-xo-be,* Annual Report 45, Bureau of American Ethnology (Washington: 1927-1928), p. 593.

[45] J. W. Powell, "Wyandot Government," *Annual Report 1,* Bureau of American Ethnology (Washington: 1879-1886), pp. 59ff.

[46] Anonymous French Memoir, in John R. Swanton, *Source Material for the Social and Ceremonial Life of the Choctaw Indians,* Bulletin 103, Bureau of American Ethnology (Washington: 1931), p. 90.

who needed him.[47] This carefulness is consistent with the ability of the Ojibway shown in later tactical discussion.

Even a small Omaha party observed certain staff functions. It had two war chiefs, each of whom had a lieutenant-adjutant through whom he issued his orders. The chain of command was clear in a large party wherein the men were divided into units of twenties, each with its subordinate commander. Obedience was obtained among the Omaha by means of battle police. These men kept order and flogged the laggard or disobedient. Each warrior carried about fifteen pairs of moccasins, some sewing sinew, and a supply of parched corn provided by the women.[48] Note, again, this supply function.

The supply function, the moving of men and materials to the places needed is so important that it is considered a separate branch of the art of war. Logistics is considered almost as important today as are the other branches, Tactics and Strategy. There is no need to emphasize the Napoleonic truism about fighting on one's stomach.

Lack of adequate supply is one sure mark of primitive war. Without food "wars" had to be short. Ordinarily they were confined to one battle. Consequently, campaigns were out of the question. Hence primitive man-killing ordinarily came to no real end, aside from the joy of slaughter. Because of lack of food as much as anything else, the status quo was rarely changed. Nowhere was this inadequacy more apparent than among the American Indians. Neither was this lacuna necessary, except for the poorest people. It was simply a lack of foresight, lack of planning and care, truly a mirror of real primitivity in social practice.

Anthropology has commented on the American Indian's lack of siege methods and wondered why this should be, since several tribes erected fortifications. Some students cannot understand why such works were not invested and reduced by siege, assault, or starvation. The reader must see the reason immediately. It is true that the siege was not part of Indian war. The assault was starved out before the defense, which was living at home within its pallisaded village. This genuine mark of primitivity in war ought to mystify no one.

The people who built forts generally supplied them with rations, but was this in anticipation of siege or just for general food purposes?

---

[47] Frances Densmore, *Chippewa Music*, Bulletin 53, Bureau of American Ethnology (Washington: 1913), pp. 84f.

[48] Dorsey, "Omaha Sociology," pp. 318-326.

Verendrye remarked that the Mandan fortified villages were very well supplied to endure investiture.[49] Were they ever invested, or was the food supply mentioned for this purpose? There is no reason to think that any enemy ever encompassed an Indian work with the intention of waging a war of attrition.

The gentle Papago of Arizona and Sonora were typical of the Indian's treatment of field supplies. They reduced the supply function to a minimum, which is surprising among an agricultural people. They wished to travel light and literally lived off the country, carrying only a little *pinole* individually. In the late afternoon the warriors divided into groups and hunted for the evening meal. They had to catch game with their bare hands, as the use of weapons on the warpath for hunting was forbidden. They ate very poorly because they had to, but they uselessly decreased their fighting efficiency by eating only raw meat "to make men fierce."[50]

The procurement of food and clothing in America was usually performed by women, and it was done poorly enough.

The South American Indians of Bahia Blanca were even more Spartan than the Papago. Each warrior hung a horse or cow lung full of salt on his mount's mane before setting out. This mess was to satisfy hunger on the long march.[51]

Africa has a different story to tell. Sudanese men, for example, had to work for grain, but work they did and grain they had. Economically successful Sudan chiefs could put really effective forces in the field on the surplus, and soldiers always live on someone's surplus. The presence of beasts of burden not only made food production easier but simplified the supply function of the armies. Furthermore, the Sudan wars sometimes included campaigning and they sometimes altered the status quo.

Snelgrave said that he saw a Dahomean army of about three thousand regulars accompanied by about ten thousand "rabble" to porter the baggage, supplies, and captive heads. All this sounds very well on the surface, but Burton reported that Dahomean supplies were most inadequate and that even a victorious army returned home under conditions of great privation. They even lacked adequate drinking

---

[49] Chevalier de la Verendrye, *Journal*, Report on Canadian Archives 1889 (Ottawa: 1890), p. 21.

[50] Frances Densmore, *Papago Music*, Bulletin 90, Bureau of American Ethnology (Washington: 1929), p. 180.

[51] Church, *op. cit.*, p. 284.

water. He estimated that they lost two hundred men for every hundred slaves captured due to privation, starvation, and the filth occasioned by their military ceremonial uncleanliness.[52] Such ineptitude could be forgiven the culturally retarded and socially simple Papago, but hardly the great totalitarian state of Dahomey.

Zulu supply was somewhat better organized. A troop of girls carried food and beer for the expedition until their burdens were exhausted, whereupon they returned home. Male porters were provided for the principal men, otherwise the troops carried their own supplies. They were allowed to help themselves to food found in friendly villages *en route* providing they broke the cooking vessels they had used. A herd of cattle was marched two miles on the flank both for food and in hope that they would assist in finding the enemy cattle.[53]

The staff planning section was poorly developed. Lack of planning will be seen later as one of the things which kept primitive war primitive. Several heads are better than one in making plans. In the most primitive war no head at all was preferred. Not every tribe was completely incompetent on this point, however. The Teton Dakota made plans in council, working out the problem on a skin map or one drawn on the earth like a modern sand table problem. One such map was left behind so that other parties could find the main body when necessary.

The corollary of the plans section, the training section, rarely existed. Teaching youths and children to handle weapons was considered enough. Mature warriors were not trained, nor would they have submitted to such instruction with its implication of their ignorance.

Those groups who did train their recruits were successful against those who did not, as one would expect. The South African tribes, for example, did not leave training to chance but started conditioning the boys as soon as they had been enrolled into a regiment. They had to live in temporary huts used normally only on a campaign, which they had to build themselves under an *induna's* (regimental-commander's) direction. They were sent on difficult missions to gather kraal-building material. They took no food, having to live on the country. They were drilled and daily taught how to run. They were taught arduous singing and dancing exercises which were thought of as military drill. Rigid obedience was exacted.[54]

---

[52] Burton, *op. cit.*, II, pp. 85f.

[53] Krige, *op. cit.*, pp. 273f.

[54] *Ibid.*, pp. 109f.

The classical writers are rather silent about troop training in old Eurasia. Bogoraz says of the Chuckchee, however, that they and the Yukaghir warriors voluntarily went through hard individual training: running with heavy weights, jumping, fencing with the spear, archery, dodging, and general nimbleness. Such exercise occupied their entire spare time.[55] The ideal Chuckchee training fitted the warrior adequately for the type of combat he was called upon to fight, the mass duel and the duel of champions. Observations of a similar kind could be made of the large amount of time devoted to sports among the American Indians. Informants maintain that athletics were practiced only secondarily for recreation and primarily for military training.

Caesar says that the Suebi had a method of training not unlike the individualistic Chuckchee. They would tolerate no battle discipline or direction, but strove by exercise, proper feeding and fasting, going naked in winter, and bathing in streams to make each individual a physical giant.[56]

But let us return to a more general discussion of the command organization. A rudimentary state such as Zululand could be expected to organize its command hierarchy as well as its tactical units. The Zulu, like the Israelites, waited until the harvest for kings to go forth to war. The king summoned his councillors, usually the regimental commanders, to advise him in deciding for war at the Feast of First-Fruits, the opening of winter. Even the despotic Zulu king could not act without his councillors' concurrence, but he could summon a new and more pliable council if need be. The general council was a very common phenomenon, and should have been the seed of a general staff and a council of state. Apparently the Zulu were able to go some little distance down that path.[57]

The actual emergence of staff functions was backward in Africa, but it is amazing that they are at all apparent. It is best observed in the kingdom of Uganda.[58] The neighboring Banyoro and Banyankole developed it almost as well.[59] In this the Zulu were not particularly efficient. Their supply functions were fair. They no doubt

55 Bogoraz, *op. cit.*, p. 646.

56 Caesar, *op. cit.*, iv. 1.

57 Krige, *op. cit.*, p. 267.

58 Johnston, *op. cit.*, passim.

59 John Roscoe, *The Banyankole* (Cambridge: Cambridge University Press, 1924), *passim.*

excelled in peace-time intelligence, and on this much of their success hinged. Chaka maintained spies all over the region. He left nothing to chance. The intelligence was reported to the whole aforementioned war council, but Chaka made and kept his own plans to himself, describing the mission to the commanding general only at the moment of departure.[60] Formulating war plans in peace is a good staff principle, but Chaka's distrust of his council and the general officer commanding mirrors his own egoism and was, of course, essentially stupid.

We have observed that no one man can command every element of a large unit. The hierarchy of command is essential. Now in Ashanti each local chief had a force of brave men. He took these into the field in the king's service when called upon, he himself falling into the capacity of a subordinate leader. The commander-in-chief marched in the rear of the host surrounded by his guard. This guard also acted as military police, chopping down anyone who broke the march order.[61] Observe that the Dahomean and Ashanti commanders were not the kings but were royal appointees. This was also true of the kingdoms of the Kitwara Empire of the Great Lakes region. The king of Uganda expected his general to win. If he lost a campaign, he was liable to the king for his life.[62]

The Zulu Dingiswayo shaped his regiments according to recognizable tables of organization with a real chain of command. At the head of each regiment he placed a colonel, or *induna*. Though only the king could send a regiment into national war, the *induna* could put down local disturbances on his own recognizance, could see that every fit male in his district rendered adequate annual service, from two to three months, and had the power of life and death over his soldiers. Chaka's successor, Dingane, limited the power of death to three chief *indunas*. Only the *induna* could keep his wives with him. Ranking below him was a second in command. Below him were the commanders of the two wings, or battalions. Below him were company (*amaviyo*) commanders, assisted by from one to three junior officers.[63]

The hierarchy of command was seemingly unknown to the bulk of Eurasiatic warriors. This was not because the better tribes could not

60 Dudley Kidd, *The Essential Kaffir* (London: Macmillan, 1904), pp. 302f.
61 Robert S. Rattray, *Ashanti* (Oxford: Clarendon Press, 1923), *passim.*
62 Johnston, *op. cit., passim.*
63 Krige, *op. cit.*, p. 265.

bring enough men to the field to make the subdivision of command useful. The apparent reason was that they could not develop or borrow the idea. It ran cross-grain to their pattern. Remember that this was the great defect in the so-called Age of Chivalry, practiced by these Teutonic barbarians with a gilding of civilization. The Byzantine Emperor Leo the Wise showed that the Teutons were incapable of really superior warfare despite their several centuries of historic contact with the best of the Greeks and the Romans. Years after the fall of the Western Empire and after the barbarians had been blessed with centuries of historic existence, the great Byzantine general and one of the last Roman emperors, spoke worse of them than did Caesar, the first of the imperial list.[64]

Marco Polo is often suspected of being a monstrous liar, yet the tradition of the conquest of Russia by the Tartars he described substantiates him; the fact of that conquest is real enough. Polo conceived a Tartar army to be one hundred thousand horse. There was an officer over every ten men, another over every hundred, another over every thousand, and one over every ten thousand. The prince, therefore, gave his orders to ten men only, and expected them to flow down to each human by a clear-cut channel of command and responsibility.[65] This decimal channel of command might be simple but it is not primitive. From this fact alone, if fact it be, one can see why nothing or no one could stand in face of the Tartar horde.

The concept of superordination and command contains that of subordination and discipline. A social group endeavoring to accomplish some purpose must work like the body of a man. Some must be muscles and nerves; others must, like the higher nerve centers, coordinate and command. No one with a social-science attitude will need to have this viewpoint expanded for him. I have spoken to many old Indian warriors who would admit that their reason for defeat at the hands of white troops was their lack of discipline. And all effective discipline is self-discipline.

Civilized behavior, pacific or martial, requires this virtue. The primitive warrior remained primitive largely because he refused to submit to discipline. The Eighteenth Century doctrine that discipline is "the art of making soldiers fear their officers more than the enemy" is nonsense. Good civilized troops, whether Sumerian or Saracen, Chaldean or Canadian, will carry on the battle even after their officers and non-

---

[64] Leo the Wise, in Spaulding, Nickerson, and Wright, *op. cit.*, p. 291.
[65] Marco Polo, *The Book*, H. Yules, trans. (London: 1903), p. 261.

commissioned officers are killed. This does not affirm that punishment is always unnecessary, for in what walk of life is it not found? But good discipline means the willing cooperation of the soldier with the officer, not the lash.

Nonliterate Africa was not primitive in this feature. It maintained a troop discipline which not even the best organized American groups could have understood. The responsibility of the Baganda general to his king even to the point of execution is a case in point. To be sure, the harshest discipline known on that continent was that of the later Zulu and their pupils, so needlessly harsh that one suspects deliberate cruelty if not sadism.

The Zulu kings had no use for the humanitarian United States Army doctrine that good discipline comes from within the soldier. They preferred the old Prussian doctrine. Even so, the high *esprit* of the Zulu *impis* showed that even this unquestioned obedience did come from within; they suffered Chaka's tyrannies gladly. Chaka said that all cowards must die, and the officers designated some persons as cowards after each battle whether there had been any or not. King Chaka understood the system of rewards and punishments. While his punishments were stern, his rewards for the valiant were lavish.

As Ferguson has pointed out, the Zulu paralleled the Spartans remarkably.[66] The Spartan soldier dared not return without his shield; the Zulu soldier who returned without his assegai was killed. The king hardened his men by making no provision for the return march. Troops who retreated or who were defeated were killed *en masse* by some veteran regiment. Old men were put out of the way. Soldiers were taught from youth to bear pain without flinching. Units or individuals were taught to obey unthinkingly and without delay, even to tackling a lion unarmed and alone. To test loyalty the soldier was sometimes ordered to kill his son or brother.

Would it be unkindness to ask what would have happened to any American Indian group four thousand strong confronted by a Zulu *impi* of a thousand strength? Had one been at the Little Big Horn, commanded by a veteran *induna*, armed as well as Custer's men, would it have lost its standards and collective life? What would an American group, red or white, have thought of a commander who

[66] W. S. Ferguson, "The Zulus and the Spartans: A Comparison of their Military Systems," *Harvard African Studies, Varia Africana II* (Cambridge: Harvard University Press, 1918), II, *passim.*

wished to test the merits of two rival weapons by ordering a fight wherein lives were lost?[67]

The neighboring south Bantu tribes might not have been as severe as the Zulu in the punishment of unsuccessful regiments but they were as harsh as need be. When the Maputju *yimpis* were decimated by the Nondwane in 1876, their chief ordered the survivors back to battle. When they refused, he ordered them to fetch water like women, only on their knees, crying, "It is the result of our cowardice." Afterward he ordered them to put out a brush fire with their bare hands.[68]

In west Africa, all the authorities on Dahomey emphasize the severity of the discipline. Burton says that almost fatal floggings were common for minor military offenses.[69] Skertchly said that each soldier could expect the utmost in punishment if he did not bring back an enemy head to the king.[70]

Much more wholesome was the condition of the Germanic Chatti. German discipline on the whole was not too well praised by its Roman foes. While one telling test must be cited against the Romans for being unable to penetrate the Rhine frontier, yet it must be said that the Germans generally wore the Romans down far from their bases by a nuisance technique rather than defeat in the field. In contrast, Tacitus loudly praises the Chatti, who may or may not have been the ancestors of the modern Hessians:

> They elect magistrates and listen to the man elected; know their place in the ranks and recognize opportunities; reserve their attack; have time for everything; entrench at night; distrust luck, but rely on courage; and—rarest thing of all, which only Roman discipline has been permitted to attain—depend on the initiative of the general rather than on that of the soldier. Their whole strength lies in the infantry, whom they load with iron tools and baggage, in addition to their arms: other Germans may be seen going to battle, but the Chatti go to war. Forays and casual fighting are rare with them; the latter no doubt is part of the strength of cavalry—to win suddenly, that is, and as suddenly to retire; for the speed of cavalry is near allied to panic, but the deliberate action of infantry is more likely to be resolute.[71]

It makes no difference whether or not the Chatti tattooed themselves or indulged in any other primitive trait. If Tacitus is not

---

[67] Kidd, *op. cit.*, p. 290.

[68] Junod, *op. cit.*, p. 475.

[69] Burton, *op. cit.*, p. 42.

[70] Melville J. Herskovits, *Dahomey* (New York: J. J. Augustin, 1938), II, p. 84.

[71] Tacitus, *op. cit.*, 30.

stretching the truth, they had achieved the military horizon. This passage is perhaps the most ringing praise ever written by a civilized man about nonliterate warriors. Had the Britons or the American Indians "gone to war" rather than to battle, how different history might have been!

Nothing could be more important to a fighting group than "how Grant got his army." Who shall be the fighters, who shall stay at home, how shall the fighting men be enlisted, are the paramount questions of socio-military organization. It is in the militia character of the fighters among most tribes that we see another characteristic of primitive war. The following statement might be taken as a type example for all nonliterate folk until, under some inspiration, they achieve civilized war practices.

> Like most Indian tribes of North America, the Menomini did not carry on their campaigns after the manner of nations of the Old World. A standing army was unknown, but a sort of militia existed, for every man above the age of puberty was a potential warrior. In his earliest youth every male looked forward to the day when he could take his place among the fighting men, and devoted much of his spare time to acquiring dexterity in the use of weapons, and endurance on the warpath.[72]

But let no one think that this primitive militia constituted an obligatory *levee en masse.* It was characteristic of primitive fighters that if a warrior did not choose to go to war, at least offensively, he did not have to. Like Achilles of old, he could sulk in his tent and no one had the authority to compel him to enter the campaign. Some kind of a party, banquet, or dance was common in America, whereat either the chief or some private party requested recruits. Recall the common American practice of permitting any private individual to organize a party against the traditional foe without waiting for public action. This is not denying the existence of publicly levied parties, for they did exist among the better organized groups. For example, the Teton tolerated private parties enlisted by self-appointed chiefs who recruited by sending gifts of tobacco to able warriors, but they also could make war as a tribe.[73]

Even the fairly well-organized Omaha society tolerated these privately organized aggressive parties, permitting an individual to invite the owner of a war bundle to a feast whereat volunteers were re-

---

[72] Alanson B. Skinner, *Social Life and Ceremonial Bundles of the Menomini Indians,* p. 97.

[73] Frances Densmore, *Yuman and Yaqui Music,* Bulletin 110, Bureau of American Ethnology (Washington: 1923), p. 144.

quested. When a Pima chief thought there was a chance to wreak revenge on the Apache, he issued an invitation to a meal, during which he besought the guests to enlist. He could exert no authority to compel them to do so.[74] When the warriors of one west Eskimo village wished to go to war, they sent a singer to the friendly villages to sing a song about their wrongs.[75] One would expect better things of the Southeast United States tribes, but Hewat says that a Creek warrior might refuse to join a war party or might desert at will, even if the campaign had been ordered by the chief and council. Only his own desire for prestige and fear of public censure kept him in line, but these were very strong.[76]

A new note is hereby introduced. Desire for prestige and social pressure may serve almost as effectively as positive punishment for failure to enlist for chief and country. This will be discussed at length later. But for the time being, let us observe the enlistment practices of the Indians of Surinam. Whenever the head of the community wished to go to war, he saw that the guests were in a favorable state and all somewhat intoxicated with "Dutch courage"; he had an old woman come into the circle and expound the tribe's wrongs at the hands of the Arawak. People felt ashamed not to volunteer in such a situation. The tribe was then put on a war footing. Everyone responded to the drums and to signals left on the principal paths. An emisary was sent to all friendly villages without saying a word but indicating by a sign that the "nation" was at war.[77]

The young Plains recruit had to be hard driven by his desire for prestige to enlist, for all sorts of hazing awaited him on the warpath. The older Crow warriors considered him fit for any type of humiliating practical joke. Further east his lot was hardly better. The Ojibway treated beginners as animals. They had to camp apart, sleeping in the rudest of shelters, and eating hardly enough to keep them alive. A series of irritating tabus was likewise laid upon them.[78]

---

[74] Frank Russell, "The Pima Indians," *Annual Report 26,* Bureau of American Ethnology (Washington: 1904-1905), p. 202.

[75] Nelson, Edward W., "The Eskimo About Bering Strait," *Annual Report 18,* Bureau of American Ethnology (Washington: 1896-1897), Part I, p. 327.

[76] Hewat, in John R. Swanton, *Early History of the Creek Indians and Their Neighbors,* Bulletin 73, Bureau of American Ethnology (Washington: 1922), p. 77.

[77] Roth, *op. cit.,* p. 579.

[78] Densmore, *Chippewa Music,* p. 144.

Primitive war properly designated, then, was fought by a militia of manpower of the group. Perhaps the term militia should not be used, because the problem as to whether or not to join a war party was so often left to the individual himself. He would not be forced.

The existence of some military caste or class which is permanently on a war footing was one of the avenues out of primitivity. The Plains soldier societies constituted one of the methods by which modernity might have been reached through professionalism. A similar rudimentary military establishment or standing army existed in those secret societies of Melanesia and sub-Saharan Africa which had a military bias. The employment of some age class, such as the Lion Soldiers of the Masai, is a step beyond this.

The ability to choose to go into the field or not is certainly a mark of primitive war. More primitive still, and probably more disastrous, was the fact that in truly primitive war the soldier could leave the campaign whenever he saw fit. Among many of the people cited, a man was permitted to join the party on his own free will, but once in he was in for duration. Nevertheless, the greater majority of them were like the Choctaw among whom it was no disgrace to desert providing one could cite an unfavorable dream. Even a chief could return a whole party to his village on the basis of a bad dream.[79] With all due regard for the value of the magico-religious in primitive or civilized societies, behavior of this type could lead to nothing but defeat for a tribe unless it was fighting against people with similar attitudes. A good stiff jolt of punishment should have directed dreaming into disciplined channels.

The fighting of nonliterate societies, then, can often be called primitive because of its ineffective or defective recruiting technique. This is inherent in the lack of authority to compel men to take the field. There are indeed few links which run through the whole of American Indian societies, but one of them is certainly compounded of the volunteer militia, the constant banqueting and feasting, the reliance on ceremonial, the power of those too proud to fight to stay away, or those too scared to fight to run away without penalty. The private organization of a dinner party with RSVPs regarding attendance does not fit into an adequate war pattern.

Many African chieftains already had the basis for their troop organization and mobilization in the formalized age-groups. Thus, when

---

[79] Bossu, in Swanton, *Source Material for the Social and Ceremonial Life of the Choctaw Indians,* p. 163.

an age-group attained maturity among the Ibo of Nigeria, between fifteen and eighteen, it took some elder as its captain and, after it had performed some fine deed, was allowed to take a name. It formed a coherent unit and could take the field as such.[80]

Kings Dingiswayo and Chaka observed the fine organizational framework of these old African age societies and bathed them in the cauldron of real war. They were regimented (*ukubuthwa*) and were glad to be. The kings gave them real meaning.

Soon after a boy had passed through his puberty ceremonial he ran off to the military kraal having jurisdiction over his father's district. There he ostentatiously drank milk direct from the udder as a sign of his desire to enlist. For a time he cared for the royal cattle and learned the use of the spear. When the *induna* observed that a sufficiently large number of these boys was hanging about, he informed the king, who summoned them to the royal kraal to be "grouped up" into a regiment. Only the king had the power to form new regiments. This he would do as soon as the weather was dry and cool and the harvests were in. Sometimes to prevent the name of some famous old regiment from disappearing, he would send the boys to it as replacements for the casualties or dotards. In any event, a youth had to be a member of a regiment to attain full manhood status and to know his place in the age hierarchy, which was the core of Zulu social life. Furthermore, the king would summon at will the reserve as well as active regiments to the royal kraal for training, ceremonial, or war. The summons he sent through the *indunas* was binding.[81]

This Zulu mobilization method was borrowed by other South Africans. It seems a long way from the American dream-hunting and party-giving system. The soldier could not pick up and go home whenever he saw fit. The warrior was not only in for duration, he was in the regulars until he was too old to be of use. After that he had to serve in the reserve, subject to the king's call. Should he desert, the king did not kill him. His own regiment took care of that.

The Dahomean king was not one whit behind Zululand, and was even more systematic about his conscription. He had a very exacting and efficient form of census-taking. This managed to conscript every useful human for the king's wars. The census was but little behind

---

[80] Charles K. Meek, *Law and Authority in a Nigerian Tribe, A Study in Indirect Rule* (London: Oxford University Press, 1937), p. 113.

[81] Krige, *op. cit.*, pp. 106ff.

our own in complexity, so cannot be discussed.[82] The king always knew his M-Day strength, and always understood just what munitions of war he could expect. Every Dahomean was a soldier and was subject to the king's call at any time.[83]

Meek reports a system of enlistment at the behest of wealthy men among the Ibo which surpasses the power of the rich on the North Pacific Coast of North America. These Ibo magnificos could exert such influence by gifts and protection that they actually became the political heads of the villages. If they were rich enough, they could extend their sway over several otherwise autonomous towns by putting them under financial obligation. They could purchase the sinews of war whereby they could protect themselves and their kin, and offer protection to other kindreds, thus reducing the latter to dependency. The decisions of war and peace rested with them, for only they could purchase the munitions needed for successful war. The conditions of enlistment were also in their hands.[84] They could then become richer by demanding shares of the resultant slaves and loot as interest on capital expended in the munitions business. No doubt this method of building a chieftainship or kingship by purchase and thus organizing society on a basis other than by blood kin has been used in other areas.

Once in the saddle, the magnate's power was bound to grow if his military exploits were successful. He was in a position to solidify his status by economic means, always a strong and useful method of gaining control. The heads of slain enemies were hung on a tree outside his house to increase his prestige. If one of his clients was slain, he would order an age-grade out against the murderer's town and, if the slayers were brought back, the age-grade received a bounty in money or goats. Should one of his own people die in the action, he would compensate his kin out of the sale of the slaves taken.[85]

The technique of muster in Oceania was the *levee en masse.* If a social unit when to war, its members were supposed to go, even in Melanesia, and the moral pressure on them to do so was considerable. Brown says that in New Britain every male was supposed to take up

82 Herskovits, *op. cit.,* II, pp. 72ff.

83 Burton, *op. cit.,* p. 444.

84 Meek, *op. cit.,* p. 111.

85 *Ibid.,* p. 113.

his position at the boundary as soon as war was determined. "If he failed to do so, the people would be very angry with him."[86]

The *levee en masse* was even more compulsive in Polynesia. That region had no regularly enlisted warriors, for every male adult who had been through the puberty ceremonial was expected to participate without reserve. Each village kept watch for slackers, but this was largely uncalled for as every man wished to fight. They had no permanent war establishment in peace times, for its foundation would in itself have been considered a declaration of war by potential enemies.[87] The subsidiary or allied social units, on the other hand, were allowed much discretion as to whether or not they would take the field. In the Northwest Solomons a messenger was sent around to the villages with a branch of areca nuts as a request for them to join a fight.[88] This was likewise common to the New Hebrides.

Caesar records the method of the Suabians. Messengers were sent to all quarters, but not to hold a banquet, or to beat a blanket, but authoritatively to assemble all military effectives.[89] The great general records a similar practice among the Gauls. Teeth were put in the invitation to war which would have astounded the heroes of the Plains. The Gallic chief or king Indutiomarus threatened the Romans with a general uprising which by law all grown men had to attend. The last man to arrive was elaborately tortured to death before the entire host as a matter of routine.[90] This was recruiting with a vengeance!

---

[86] Brown, *op. cit.*, p. 152.
[87] *Ibid.*, p. 164.
[88] Blackwood, *op. cit.*, p. 33.
[89] Caesar, *op. cit.*, iv. 9.
[90] *Ibid*, v. 56.

Chapter 5

The Functional Desiderata

Students of tactics often introduce their texts by definitions of the functions of the particular arm under discussion. One reads in an infantry work that the arms function is fire, mobility, and shock. These three are repeated in the cavalry texts with greater emphasis on mobility and shock. Again, the tank experts say that the functions of the armored force are fire, mobility, shock, and protection. The job of the combat elements of the air force is obviously mobility and fire, while the artillery is reduced to fire, with some mobility. These, then, seem to be the functions of battle units. These functions are accomplished through use of the principles of war and combat. No real difference can be discerned between successful civilized soldiers and successful nonliterate warriors in this regard.

Let us first regard the Eskimo tactically. For the most part they were too pacific to have any battle practices worthy of the name. Their groups were too small for combat effectiveness. Their social organization made no provision for real chieftainships with authority in the other walks of life, and they were practically without motives for making war on anyone. They were capable of effective and fierce resistance when attacked, as the Indians who tried to persecute them generally found out. The Eskimo were, therefore, practical pacifists.

They did not relish an open fight, but would stand up to one if necessary. In such cases they relied on fire *without* movement. They could deliver arrow fire in great volume and, a phenomenon far from common in America, by volleys. Anyone venturing within range of this mass of fire would almost certainly be hit. It is reported that often a man resembled a pin cushion when he finally fell. Since they did not rush an enemy discomfited by fire, the winning side would be that which delivered the best fire and the most of it, had the largest number of archers and stores of ammunition. If one side became weary or wished to eat, it would hoist a fur coat on a stick as a signal for an armistice. If agreeable, both sides would then rest, posting guards to see that the truce was kept. After all had enjoyed their leisure, they went at the fire-fight again.[1] Such behavior was obviously unmilitary and was more of an athletic event.

The pure fire-fight, or archery contest, seems to be typical of the socially simplest people. To call the Eskimo socially simple is no reflection on their material culture, which was rich, nor on their cleverness, but simply says that their social organization was well nigh anarchical. A people almost as simple in organization and much less expert in manufacture were the Californians. People like the Maidu liked to attack at dawn, a fact common among nonliterate tacticians, as will be seen. They relied exclusively on the fire-fight, taking care not to get too close. Most Californians likewise delivered mass fire, but the extreme range made it notably bloodless. They even went so far as to take poorer arrows to war than they used in economic hunting.[2]

Most Californians were too cowardly to make fighting men. They really loved a fire-fight on the athletic level, practiced while well encased in armor. This is well enough as far as it goes, but they needed to advance by movement to dislodge or destroy an enemy by shock to alter the status quo. Kroeber says that the bow was their chief weapon. Spears were "employed only sporadically in hand-to-hand fighting and not for hurling from the ranks." The probable use of the spears was to impale unsuspecting sleepers, for "In a set fight the spear could not be used against a row of bowmen by unarmored and unorganized warriors."[3]

Kroeber should have stressed the term "unorganized," for otherwise his assumptions are unwarranted. He assumes that unarmored spearmen could not attack a line of bowmen. They could and should. Modern bayonet-men consistently attack lines of men firing with rifles and machine guns, weapons far more lethal than the bow. He seems to assume that the proper use of a spear was as a weapon of fire to be hurled from the ranks. Nothing could be farther from the truth, especially since the warriors owned a much better fire weapon in the arrow. The Californians, too, failed to appreciate the function of fire, which was explained in the chapter on weapons. Occasionally one

[1] Nelson, *op. cit.*, p. 329.

[2] Kroeber, *op. cit.*, p. 152.

[3] *Ibid.*, p. 844.

of their brave men would run up and slay an enemy to get his head, but this was considered quite a deed.

One now turns to Oceania to examine the use of fire in the South Seas. Melanesia used fire better than Polynesia, and for reasons easy to appreciate. The Melanesians, being good archers, surpassed the Polynesians in fire weapons. There is evidence that the Polynesians, like ourselves, formerly handled the bow quite well. Its chief use has been as a child's toy in more recent times. The chief Polynesian fire weapons were expertly made and handled throwing-clubs, but no club can have the range, accuracy, and selectivity of the arrow. This does not mean that the Melanesians relied entirely on the arrow for fire, for many of them trusted its less competent prototype, the thrown spear. Brown said that the men of New Britain rarely came to grips but generally fought by hurling spears at a distance, the method of all military cowards, the harmless tossing of weapons at an enemy trained in dodging.[4] This is reminiscent of the tactically incompetent Eskimo and Californians. Some Africans were no better.

Bishop Codrington likewise comments on this over-reliance on fire tactics in the Banks Islands. These people had bows, but the real fight was "shouting of defiance, cursing, abuse and boasting," and stamping the ground with little bloodshed. He makes the interesting comment that the Banks men protected themselves from surprise at night by casting stones with slings from time to time down paths a marauding enemy might use.[5] This is one of the few quotable examples of the use of prohibitive fire by a nonliterate folk, albeit an ineffective and wasteful one. The use of prohibitive fire is very common in modern war, especially at night, as in this case. The Banks men would have done much better, however, if they had exercised the principle of security a little more instead of slinging random stones down suspect paths. A few scouts and sentries would have protected them much better.

The counterpart of fire is mobility, the power to move effectively towards an enemy in the attack, or to get away from him if things should not be as favorable as one had hoped. Simple mobility alone is of little more tactical value than simple fire, unless one is defeated. King Richard the Third's prayer for a horse at Bosworth was anything but foolish.

---

[4] Brown, *op. cit.*, p. 153.

[5] Robert H. Codrington, *The Melanesians* (Oxford: Clarendon Press, 1891), p. 305.

The mention of mobile fighters immediately calls to mind the American Plains Indians. Mobility they had, although as fighters they might be subject to a very conservative estimate. It takes more than a bow and a spear to make a savage an infantryman, and a dolt on horseback is no cavalryman. It is true that the Plains Indians learned to be horsemen of no mean ability. Indeed, one frequently encounters statements that at the end of their culture as a going concern, they constituted the finest light cavalry ever known. Such a statement is pure romance. It is true that they were known to defeat the regular United States Cavalry; witness the Battle of the Big Horn. The reasons for such a rare success is to be found in the large numbers of Indians involved, in the wretched leadership of the post-Civil War Federal Cavalry under men like Custer, and the superior armaments put into the Indians' hands by politics. Remember that the Confederates whipped Custer almost at will, and he never joined Lincoln's victory parade down Pennsylvania Avenue because his horse ran away in the wrong direction. So much for the Seventh Cavalry's leadership! It will be sufficient to observe that the Plains Indians did not prevent their country from becoming the property of the white man. This the Indians strove to prevent, and they had the numbers and equipment to do so. The test of military excellence is the accomplishment of the mission.

With the introduction of the horse (*circa* 1750) they became cavaliers, and if they used any tactics successfully against the whites, it is because they adopted those of their opponents. This is the simple process of ethnological diffusion. As cavalry they inherited all the weaknesses of that arm. They did not have to learn the civilized cavalryman's inherent psychological defect, the galloping away on spectacular, flashy military rides to the abandonment of the principle of objective. Regardless of the preference of flash for discipline still observed in horse cavalry or its more modern derivatives, tank and air fighters, they had the unavoidable weakness of all cavalry, horsed, mechanized, or winged. There is an old maxim that cavalry can take but cannot hold. Even the mediaeval knights knew that. The Plains Indians did not effectually *want* to hold, even their own land, their own bison herds, their own lives, and their own self-respect. They merely resented the white man. They could not or would not submit to enough discipline to keep the cowboy and the farmer off the short-grass lands. They preferred actions which would not interfere with the child's play of *coup*-counting. Hence, they lost all.

Despite all that was at stake, they were not only less capable of aggressive cohesion and team fighting than a successful gang of underprivileged slum children, but even comprehended that their mounted action was futile. All the old Plainsmen I have ever talked with realized that Indians could not fight "walking-soldiers." Infantry can both take and hold, yet the Indians rarely dismounted to fight the white man, although they frequently did in their internecine wars. Who with any historic feeling or ethnological information would dare say that, as cavalry, they could have made any respectable showing against the horsed nomads who poured out of Asia — Magyars, Kazak, Seljuk, Tartars? The great khans would have destroyed them sooner, for they had no reason to quibble with a puritan conscience.

As for Africa, very few people on that continent could be accused of static warfare. The mobility element was enormously increased among some Sudanic peoples when the desert men introduced the horse to them. Much of the Sudan resembles the American Great Plains geographically, and the results of the introduction of the horse should be comparable. Comparable they were, but the Sudanese were culturally in advance of the Plains hunters, so the results were superior. The Mandingo, among others, had to develop their empire without the aid of the horse, for the animal did not flourish everywhere.

Our Eurasiatic ancestors retained a praiseworthy respect for mobility from their manhunting days. It took civilization to bog them down into immobile masses, especially civilization as known to Greece, Egypt, and pre-Persian Mesopotamia. It is true that the civilized soldier most often defeated the mobile barbarian, but this was through better observance of a combination of the principles of combat, and even more often through superiority of organization and command. But civilization was all but overwhelmed by the mobile Magyars and Seljuks when its organized effectiveness declined.

No one used mobility better than the pastoral nomads. Herodotus speaks respectfully of the terrible and able Scyths, praising not only their superiority in tactical mobility but also their appreciation of the cavalry maxim that mobile troops must live off the country. No enemy invading their lands punitively could ever reach them. Their tactics were Fabian, while the nature of their country and its intersecting rivers favored their type of warfare. They had neither cities nor forts; their only dwellings were their wagons. They scorned agriculture and lived on their flocks. As horsed nomads, they were expert mounted archers.[6]

The excellent mobility of the cavalry and mounted infantry of the west of Europe is praised elsewhere in this work. If more be needed, observe Caesar's praise of the Suebi. In cavalry combats they often dismounted to fight afoot. Their horses were trained to stand in the same spot so that their riders could retire quickly if they needed to mount and fly. They considered the use of a saddle a mark of indolence.[7] The repetition of the American Plains Indian's attitude regarding the saddle is interesting. Speaking of the Gaulish cavalry, Caesar said that they charged the Roman cavalry on sight. Having thrown them off balance by shock, they dismounted and fought afoot, stabbing the horses and bringing down the riders.[8] Dismounting in a cavalry melee requires the highest kind of courage. It would be folly today, of course, or at any time since the invention of the stirrup, but it will be remembered that the Welsh kept their freedom in face of the English knighthood for a long time by the same old Celtic method.

Fire is all very well, and so is mobility but, like many things in cookery and chemistry, they are better, or even something entirely else when used in combination. The effective use of fire alone is in the defensive. Used by itself on the offensive it constitutes a marksmanship contest which can effect little. Some tribes just mentioned tried it, however, and we are not far from wrong in ascribing cowardice to them as well as failure. Used offensively, it immobilizes the enemy, disconcerts him, and overcomes his ground advantage if he uses the terrain or fortification skilfully. Mobility alone will produce only a shock action. Shock actions are often praiseworthy; indeed, they indicate able and brave troops. Good troops always want to close with the enemy. But to attempt shock alone on a brave and healthy foe, anxious to see you coming in order to make a blow at you while you are off balance through mobility, is to lead with the chin. The enemy ought to be "softened" by fire before the shock action begins.

Fire and movement ought to be used in combination, then, whenever the situation permits. This is so important that it is considered a tactical principle.

---

[6] Herodotus, *History* iv. 46-47.
[7] Caesar, *op. cit.*, iv. 2.
[8] *Ibid.*, iv. 11.

> It is said that more battles have been won by strength of leg than force of arms. We have seen that a rapid concentration of superior force at the critical point is the secret of victory. To effect such concentrations, troops must be mobile, that is they must have the power of prompt, rapid and sustained movement. Mobility, so far as the troops themselves are concerned, is chiefly a matter of training, and it is the characteristic which especially distinguishes well-trained troops. It is the outstanding characteristic of cavalry.[9]

Good infantry, too, must be mobile. It was not flippancy that dubbed Stonewall Jackson's infantry "foot cavalry." The type of mobility described in the foregoing quotation is not only important tactically but strategically and logistically as well. But with all of mobility's virtues, it must be employed in combat in conjunction with fire. As the United States Cavalry says:

> Combat consists essentially in the advance of the attacker against the defender. The defender will oppose this movement by fire. Accordingly, in order to advance, the attacker must beat down the fire of the defense by a superior fire in which all available fire weapons will take part. The attack, then, has two elements, *fire and movement.* The intelligent combination of these two elements of battle is the aim of all training.[10]

The value of fire and movement in cavalry attacks could be grasped by some nonliterate warriors. The Patagonian tribes normally flung bolas expertly before themselves in mounted attacks, which was most disconcerting, even to the Spanish regulars.

Later pages will describe the Indians of Southeast United States as relying largely on the dawn attack. In addition, they could use fire and movement. Swanton quotes an early report on the Choctaw which describes their clubmen as rushing in to finish an enemy which had been immobilized by the first flight of arrows.[11]

The fire and movement principle seems to have been observed in Surinam. Each warrior carried seven poisoned arrows. A cloud was discharged by each side in the opening of the engagement. The ammunition expended, each side fell upon the other with war clubs, and from then on it was man for man. If one side was forced to retire, it attempted to gather up its dead, knowing the cannibalistic end of the slain and wounded. This function was the chief job of the women. These people are now known to have spread their population and

---

[9] *Tactics and Technique of Cavalry*, p. 6.

[10] *Ibid.*, p. 5.

[11] Bossu, in Swanton, *Source Material for the Social and Ceremonial Life of the Choctaw Indians*, p. 162.

culture into North America as far as southern Florida, using island-hopping seamanship thither from South America.[12]

It seems that even some of the simplest African tribes appreciated the principle of combined fire and movement, as witness the behavior of the Nigerian Ibibio. As soon as the action began they chewed magical herbs for invulnerability and began their fire fight. When the smoke from their antiquated muskets got too dense for good vision, they dropped their fire arms and rushed the foe with machete and sword, sincere in the belief that the gods would make them bullet-proof.[13]

Later pages will describe the Melanesians as preferring a relatively immobile dawn attack in the American manner. Yet fire with movement was far from unknown to them. The courageous men of Alu first attacked their enemy with a shower of arrows. When the critical moment came they dropped the bow and, grasping the spear and axe, assailed the enemy with such vigor that their shields were of slight value.[14]

A naval battle offers the supreme opportunity for the use of fire and movement. Indeed, it is hard to see how a marine action can be fought otherwise. With the exception of the Indians of the North Pacific Coast, the Americans lacked naval war. The African negroid is a poor canoe builder, so one finds no African marine war, even on the rivers. Water-borne African war is no more than a descent upon the shore. Both Melanesians and Polynesians were and are great seafarers. It is unfortunate that we have so few descriptions of their sea fights from competent sources.

One might consider Riley's description of the Fly River natives of New Guinea. Like all island negroids they preferred descents upon the shore, but they could use their fine canoes for actual marine engagements as well as for purely logistical purposes. When, for example, the men of Waduba saw canoes from Kiwai passing over to the mainland, they put forth to capture both the canoes and the occupants. They attemped to maneuver into a position commanding the enemy's escape. A shower of arrows was then directed at the enemy helmsman. The maneuverability of an enemy canoe thus being destroyed, they promptly attacked it at close range with a greater force,

[12] Roth, *op. cit.*, pp. 582f.

[13] Percy A. Talbot, *Life in Southern Nigeria* (London: Macmillan, 1923), p. 234.

[14] Brown, *op. cit.*, p. 161.

and generally succeeded in destroying the Kiwai.[15] Fire and movement were apparently well observed. The use of maneuver and fire to impede the enemy's steering and mobility was used in our own naval engagements right up to the present; now sea fights are normally at such ranges that it is useless to aim for the enemy's rudder. The use of specialists, cooperation, the combined use of forces, and coordination were also well portrayed in the Waduba actions. Riley's chapter on battle plans also illustrates the ability of the Papuan to fight on land according to fire and movement when called upon to do so.

The principal of fire and movement seems to have been known to all the Metal Age Eurasiatic peoples. Such reports as we have, assuming for the moment that they are trustworthy, are somewhat disappointing in their descriptions of the principle. The fire element seemed to rely more on such inefficient weapons as sling shots and hurled javelines rather than on the arrow, which archeology shows to have been developed to a high degree of perfection. The combination of fire *and* movement, though, was well understood. Caesar recounts instances of the able use of the combination against prepared positions. The Gauls and the Belgae assailed a fortified place by raining stones on the ramparts. When the defenders did not show themselves, the attack assailed the place with an infantry "tortoise," firing the gates and under-cutting the wall. The slingers and archers kept the wall stripped at the point the assault was made.[16] Workmanship of this kind also illustrates a knowledge of the use of mass and concentration of force at the critical point.

The object of fire and movement is, of course, shock. At least one can say that shock is one of the goals of mobility. Mobility also has uses in the retreat after defeat, but since few informants will ever admit that their people were defeated, we have little knowledge of that most useful device, the tactical withdrawal. Fire, mobility, and shock imply aggression, the great principle of the offensive.

> Decisive results cannot be achieved by passive measures: The defensive may evade defeat, for a time, but it can never gain victory. In war it is best to retain the initiative and to force the enemy to adapt his plan to ours. This means that we should prefer the offensive to the

[15] E. Baxter Riley, *Among Papuan Headhunters* (Philadelphia: Lippincott, 1925), p. 273.

[16] Caesar, *op. cit.*, ii. 6.

defensive. "If in doubt, attack," is a good rule, especially applicable to cavalry.[17]

Although there were exceptions, such as the Eskimo and Californians, the principle of the offensive was generally well observed in America. The Indian was generally aggressive and good in the attack. The Yuma, to choose an extreme example, scorned a fire-fight. Like all aggressive and successful fighters, they liked close-up shock work, delivering crushing blows against the foeman's chin with clubs shaped like potato mashers.[18] They alone in their general area seem to have had any method of defense against a shock attack delivered against themselves. They would bunch up, apparently like a ring of mediaeval infantry attacked by horsemen, and die there to a man if necessary. The enemy charging against such a ring would do well to be cautious, since they strove to grab individuals from the attack, drag them into the ring, and chop them to pieces with long knives.[19]

The principle of the offensive was well observed all over Africa, only the little people of the forest, the Kalahari desert, and a few Negroes being shy. The greatest masterpiece in the utilization of the principle was, of course, instituted by the Zulu king Chaka when he saw the futility of a fire fight with spears. (The east Bantu were not archers.) He is reported to have made his troops destroy their throwing spears, which forced them to come to grips with short thrusting ones.[20] This is reminiscent of the doctrine of another great warrior-king. One day Frederick the Great's cavalry commander complained to him that the enemy had sabers six inches longer than those of the Prussians. The king replied, "Ach, let our cavalry get six inches closer to the enemy cavalry." Chaka was too intelligent entirely to forego the advantage of combined fire and movement. Actually, "Every Zulu warrior was armed with a shield, one or more throwing assegais, and one stabbing one . . ."[21]

The shock line action was the Polynesian ideal, but it was used with too little fire preparation to be entirely effective. They did know the charge, however, as will be shown later.

Protection, the last of the great desiderata, will not be discussed, because it is hard enough to keep the civilian reader from thinking

[17] *Tactics and Technique of Cavalry,* p. 4.
[18] Densmore, *Yuman and Yaqui Music,* p. 10.
[19] *Ibid.,* pp. 10ff.
[20] Kidd, *op. cit.,* p. 302.
[21] Krige, *op. cit.,* p. 262.

too highly of it even without emphasizing it. It is also too grave a temptation for the nonliterate and civilized soldiers who have grasped it to overuse it. Protection by materials, which is the commonest, also lies entirely within the realm of material culture, which this book has so largely foresworn for reasons which seem good. A certain amount of armor, a device well-known to some nonliterate tribes, is all very well, but there is such a strong tendency springing from the cowardly nature of mankind to destroy any offensive ability with weight, to slow down mobility, and to make the soldier think too much of his own hide's value that it would have been well if it had never been discovered.

This might also be said of fortification. True, the typical American Indian used it far too little, considering that his foe dealt in surprise. But we will let the archeologist discant upon primitive fortresses. War is an extrovert activity, and too much effort expended on fortification is a sign of military introversion. This is not said flippantly.

It should not, however, be inferred that all use of protection is bad. Just because the mediaeval knight used too much armor towards the end does not mean that a certain amount is not good, even on modern tanks. Just because the pueblo-building tribes of Southwest United States tended to wall themselves up from the facts of life, certain Americanists to the contrary, is no sign that a reasonable amount of fortification is not useful. The Iroquois and the Maori were certainly aggressive fighters, but they made adequate use both of fortification and of armor. But the temptation to consider protection too important leads us to avoid discussing it here. The best protection is tactical and lies in the intelligence of the warrior, not in materials.

The principle of mass (or of sufficient numbers), a combat principle, is a device by which the tactical desiderata are brought about. This means, in brief, that one should not send a boy out to do a man's work. Quality must be sought, certainly, but quantity has meaning, too. The commander ought always to dispatch enough men to accomplish the mission. Otherwise they might not only be defeated but exterminated as well. The final situation would then be worse than if no effort at all had been made. This by no means indicates that enormous bodies must be sent forth, as the principle of economy of force will show. These principles are functions of social organization.

The principle of mass was not well developed in Indian America. First, the population was too small outside the civilized culture areas to take large forces afield. Yet the principle does not depend on mere size, but varies with the mission and the condition of the enemy. If the foe has two squads in the field and the commander sends three squads against them, the principle of mass has been observed, even though the chief has thousands at his disposal.

Sufficient numbers were always available to Indian chiefs for the accomplishment of sensible missions. Rather than suffering from paucity of man power, the Indians were defective in the social cohesion which would demand that one band inevitably come to the aid of their kin, or that tribes should confederate to repel or attack different types of peoples. The concept of social and therefore military leadership was too vague for the principle to operate in all its possibilities. Consequently, the sociological patterns demanded that the raid and the ambuscade remain the chief types of operations.

Africa had a denser population. The kings had people wherewith to make war. Sub-Saharan Africa is a land blessed with good geographical features. This, coupled with farming and herding cultures, produced a surplus of food on which masses of soldiers could be supported and a population from which they could be recruited. The King of Dahomey, for example, could take enough troops afield to accomplish almost any imaginable mission, although he handled them only fairly well when he got there.

The large number of troops the Iron and Bronze Age peoples of Eurasia could bring into the field is surprising. There can be no doubt that they could muster sufficient masses to accomplish any mission they had in mind. This is a tribute to their economics.

The principle of economy of force, which says that it is likewise reprehensible to send a man to do a boy's work, was necessarily used by some fighting groups. Few men were taken to the field because more were not available. A Great Plains horse-stealing party observed it, if it can be called military. When the gathering of a *coup* or a few horses constituted the mission, just the right number of men was sent. Large numbers were avoided because they would have been in the way and their approach would have been detected. In spite of all this, the impression remains that the principle was generally honored in the breach by most primitive warriors. The very common practice was to bring along all the manpower willing to enlist, even if the killing of one person, the acquisition of one scalp or head would fulfill the mission.

The question may now be asked, why should all this military activity be exercised at all? The answer lies in the principles of objective and exploitation. These might almost be called the first principles of war and combat. Objective means that one must consider why the battle is fought at all. This in part lies in the motive for the war, but the modern tactical reason is the defeat of the enemy and victory for ourselves. This is done only by the destruction of the enemy army, although few nonliterate warriors grasp the point. Some civilized chieftains also grasp it poorly. The objective of the Union Army in the War Between the States was the destruction of the Confederate Army. McClellan never grasped this. He thought the objective was the capture of Richmond, and had a walk around Virginia for his pains. Neither did the German General Staff grasp the point sufficiently in 1914, or a second world war would have been unnecessary. They thought the proper objective was the capture of Paris, not the destruction of allied resistance. The objective of the battle may be a place, but the objective of the war must be the defeat of a people.

Victory alone is of slight value, except to a militarist properly so-called. A victory must be exploited, if it is not a Pyrrhic one.

> The mere defeat of the opposing force is not the sole aim of the attacker. He is not like the boxer who is content to win a technical decision "on points," but seeks to administer a knockout. The purpose of war is to impose our will upon the enemy, and this must be accomplished by completely breaking down his resistance by capturing or destroying his armed forces. Accordingly, the attacker, having driven the enemy from his position, must *exploit his success* by inflicting all possible damage upon his defeated opponent. Local successes are promptly followed by utilizing the supports and reserves to press the defeated enemy.[22]

The principle of objective, then, represents the art of war reduced to its essence. Without its proper exercise, fighting must be called something else besides war. The civilian is often confused about this in reading accounts of wars. It is difficult for him to comprehend that a defeat along one line means nothing if the enemy's resistance is destroyed at the main point. He finds it hard to understand how an army may win all the battles and lose the war.

It is in the disregard for this first principle that the American Indian showed his major defect as a soldier. People like the Iroquois understood it and were successful, yet the great majority of American tribes behaved towards their enemies like modern game laws regard deer: If you kill them all now, what fun will there be in the future? They

[22] *Tactics and Technique of Cavalry*, p. 6.

consistently failed to pursue and exploit a victory, removing forever an hereditary enemy.

Since they apparently needed the presence of an enemy to fulfill their social pattern, they saw the principle with different eyes. The end of the enemy would have meant the end of manhood society, the *raison d'etre* for the male population. The pattern overdeveloped the war honor concept almost everywhere. It is valuable always, but the practice of war for its own sake rather than the achievement of some socio-economic end is militarism. The Americas were, paradoxically, continents rife with militarism but with little war.

Perhaps we might say that with few exceptions the American Indians had motives different from those of a truly military people rather than having none. The objective was often gained by vindicating honor, or slapping someone in the face with a quirt rather than killing him.

The Omaha, for example, were superior fighters as Plains Indians went. They made fairly intelligent preparations and began their fights with some system. But when the fight opened and the enemy was thoroughly discomfited by fire, they should have rushed in to finish him off by the use of fire and movement. Yet only the very bravest warriors rushed into the beleaguered camp, far too few to accomplish any good. Again, they retreated when one of the leaders had been killed or wounded, even though they were victorious.[23] Thus they utterly ignored the principle of exploitation. From the standpoint of any truly military people they failed in the objective and mission.

If this was true of the better Plains tribes, it was much more so of the simpler. If but one enemy was killed, the party often returned home. This was the mission. *Coup* had been counted, which was eminently more honorable (and safer) than a pitched battle of great success wherein several of the attacking side would be killed.[24]

The Ecuadorian Jibaro, in contrast, observed the principle of objective scrupulously. They had strong honor and trophy ideas, as found in North America, but the real mission of an engagement was the extermination of the enemy. Their foes disregarded the principle of security and paid dearly for it. Reliance was put on the strength of fortified houses and the sentry duty of chickens. The refusal of the inhabitants of one house to come to the aid of those of the besieged

[23] Dorsey, *Omaha Sociology*, p. 237.

[24] Skinner, *Political Organization, Cults, and Ceremonies of the Plains-Ojibway and Plains-Cree Indians*, p. 492.

dwelling was cowardly and unintelligent. A telling counter-attack by the dwellers of the other houses would spoil the Jibaro's game, but such poltroons preferred to lock themselves up and await death, which was sure to follow, for after the victory the Jibaro destroyed every life, human and animal, in the enemy village.

Africa contained both competent and inefficient observance of the principle. The mighty kingdom of Dahomey observed it poorly, though they took huge masses into the field. The Dahomean objective was slave raiding, however, and not the destruction of the enemy. So, like the Plains horse thieves, they should not be blamed too heartily.

The fact that the principle of objective changes warriors into soldiers was well illustrated in South Africa. Observe the before-and-after-taking Zulufication situation in southeast Africa. Formerly invasions into the land of the Thonga were relatively peaceful. Conquerors and conquered intermingled, and there was no memory of real bloodiness. They thought they had performed feats of great valor if they killed two or three of the enemy. The arrival of the Zulu in 1820 changed all that. The Zulu or the Ngoni taught the tribes of the plains to spare no one except, perhaps, female prisoners.[25] The Zulu spared no effectives and no cattle. They terrorized the region in consequence, and were thus safe from attack themselves. They knew, as every general staff knows in spite of the doctrine of some statesmen, that the objective must not only be the extinction of an enemy army but his materials and morale and those of the civilian population as well.

The African states, whether old ones like those of the Baganda, Banyankole, Banyoro, Bushongo, or later ones such as the Zulu, Zande, and Masai, were very apt at exploiting a victory. Perhaps no one did it with more thoroughness than the Zulu. They were formerly a chivalrous group, fighting for the pure love of athletics. They waited for the other army to get ready, considering it below themselves to take any advantage. They thought it rather mean to take all the enemy's cattle, and they never harmed women and children. Chaka, however, modernized them. Generosity never occurred to him, for he preferred to take his foe at a disadvantage and slaughter every man, woman, and child if he so chose. Civilized deceit was his delight. Kidd reports that if he could save work for his own troops by promising quarter which he never intended to grant, he did so, only to slaughter the beleaguered afterwards.[26] This sounds like the cynical

[25] Junod, *op. cit.*, p. 449.

claim made by our fellow citizens at the outbreak of every modern war, "Our veneer of civilization is really very thin."

Kidd's horror need not impress us. Chaka made a real transition from the primitive to the civilized. His work sounds much like modern power politics which prefers to gain military ends by political techniques when it can. He ceased considering battle an athletic event and abolished the game laws protecting the fallen foe. In sport hunting these rules are all very well, but in food hunting or war, the quarry is just as dead if shot sitting as on the wing. Chaka pursued the defeated instead of holding a dance, and he did away with potential enemies when he caught them. Hence, in the end, such a reign of peace surrounded Zululand that he had to go far afield to find anyone to fight.

Although the surrounding tribes often borrowed Zulu ideas, many of them could not emerge from the primitive enough to exploit a victory because of the lack of discipline, or timidity, and the mutual distrust which Junod claims was the result of their frequent earlier defeats and the cause of their recent ones. The Maputju, he says, considered themselves the Zulu's equals, but were courageous only when out of danger.[27]

Both Polynesians and Melanesians generally but not always exploited a victory. It must be admitted that the best Melanesian fighters went about this in a thoroughgoing manner, which the Polynesians did not. The great value of heads to the Melanesians dictated the complete annihilation of the defeated without pity or hesitation. No one states this with more vigor than Mrs. Coombe, who in other places says that her informants knew not war.[28]

The Iron Age Celts were as thorough in their exploitation as Chaka's Zulu. Apparently they left nothing standing when they conquered a country. Avienus, speaking from tradition, says that the ravaging Gael always left desolation where prosperity once dwelt.[29]

Here, then, are some of the ways the sinews and muscles are flexed. But the brawn of war is futilely exercised unless it is directed by the eye and brain of Mars, which is the subject of the next two chapters.

---

[26] Kidd, *op. cit.*, p. 304.
[27] Junod, *op. cit.*, p. 450.
[28] Coombe, *op. cit.*, p. 220.
[29] Rufus Festus Avienus, *Ora Maritima*, p. 586.

Chapter 6

Intelligence, Surprise and Countersurprise

All eyes and ears is the second office of a general staff; it inspires the foe with terror and its friends with confidence. The general relies upon it to know what the enemy is about to do, and even to estimate what he is thinking. It is the intelligence function; its news is secret news. It is espionage and, just as important, it is counter-espionage. It seeks to enable its commander to surprise the foe, and by its assiduity to throw an aura of mystery around his plans. Regardless of the unwarranted romance with which the civilian invests it, it is most important, and no military body, group of armies or squad, can afford to do without its functions of intelligence, surprise, and security for one moment, and no victorious one ever has. The fog of war is never perfectly pierced, but the effort must be made.

That this includes primitive warriors is no accident. The primitive fighter does not fall behind the modern in this feature, and for reasons which it is hoped will be apparent. Indeed, its very alertness is primitive. Only its techniques have developed with need.

The chief-of-party must utilize every possible source of information regarding the enemy in order successfully to wage war. Military intelligence in the ordinary reconnaissance forms known as "scouting and patrolling" was so highly developed among the American Indians, for example, that it has not been surpassed if even equalled by the ground troops of any military power. Nonliterate man was not primitive in a derogatory sense, that is, undeveloped in the use of military intelligence. This point has theoretical significance; therefore, attention is called to it with considerable strength.

Certainly some of the books written by white travellers have grossly exaggerated the Indian's scouting powers. Many of them have ascribed some organic superiority to him, some mysterious hyperacute sensory system innately beyond the capacity of civilized man. Such theories are, of course, basically unsound. No man can develop his sensory acuteness in all ways. He will develop his perception along the lines of his occupation and interest. The American Indian was a marvellous scout because his life depended on it, both as a hunter and a warrior. Craft acuteness of this order is common enough in civilized life.

Most American groups departed for war with from adequate to more than adequate reconnaissance patrols to gather information and to offer the service of security. Often the scouts would locate the village of the enemy and spy it out for several days before telling the main body to come up to attack. The Teton scouts prepared stone shelters on high ground which would screen them from the enemy villagers.[1] The Comanche appointed the scouts for each expedition. After having discovered the enemy position, they returned and set up a pile of bison chips near their own main body. The scout leader went in front of the pile of chips and sang a war song. This pile constituted a rallying point during the engagement, while the song was an attestation that the intelligence offered was true.[2] Reconnaissance was provided for the Iowa by some three to four scouts who left the camp secretly in advance of the rest of the war party. When they were ready to inform the main party of what they saw, they sang their war bundle songs in such a way as to convey the correct information.[3] The Menomini and many others sent their scouts right up to the edge of the enemy village.

Often the scouts were disguised for purposes of concealment. Many Plains scouts daubed themselves with mud, often fashioning wolf ears of the same material on their heads both for disguise and for magical purposes. Leaves and branches were utilized for camouflage when available.

Various ways of conveying intelligence to the rear were used, some of which have been mentioned. Sometimes the scouts, often called "wolves," made specific wolf howls; or would run in zig-zag lines back to camp; or would run in the four directions to inform the main body that the enemy was in sight. In the South American jungle, as in Africa, the ceremonial drum was used to convey military intelligence over considerable distances, although the system was by

---

[1] Densmore, *Teton Sioux Music, passim.*

[2] Lowie, *op. cit.*, p. 811.

[3] Skinner, *Societies of the Iowa, Kansa, and Ponca Indians*, p. 687.

no means as well developed in South America as in Africa.[4] The well-known smoke signal technique and the famous Plains sign language also served the reconnaissance patrols well.

Some tribes merely chose their scouts from among the clever men, often changing them daily to prevent fatigue. There were a few, though not many, who had permanent professional scouts. The men were generally those who had Wolf or Coyote for their supernatural guardian. This was true, for example, of the Kutenai. Those who had Wolfe societies, or lodges in which certain members were Wolves, generally utilized them as scouts. For example, the officials known as Wolf Hide Bearers in the Oglala Wolf Cult performed this duty.[5]

It is interesting to note that Wolf in one form or another was the patron spirit of war all over the Plains.[6] He was primarily the genius of the intelligence service, the ruthless, crafty, cautious hunter. This may well be taken as symbolic of all Plains, or of all American Indian warfare. Its prototype was the shrewd stalker and, as Wolf's depredations depended upon intelligence, the Indians hunted men in the same manner. The service of intelligence was the one branch of their art of war which was perfectly developed.

One method of gathering military intelligence or effecting counter-reconnaissance practiced by many Indians was the use of magic. Among the Flathead there was an especial class of shamans who were believed to be able to project their vision wherever they wished.[7] When a Northern Saulteaux chief had chosen his war party, a shaman would smoke and send his pipe into the air in the direction of the enemy. The enemy shaman did the same thing, apparently in the spirit of sportsmanship. When the enemy pipe arrived, the chief of the party smoked it almost to the finish. The shaman then made a speech. After this a great noise was heard first in the east, then in the north, then in the south, and at last in the west. At this a bat appeared and told the council the position and strength of the enemy. These people also had shamans who could gaze into a smoked glass

---

[4] Karsten *op. cit.*, p. 5.

[5] Wissler, *op. cit.*, p. 91.

[6] Robert H. Lowie, *Plains Age-Societies: Historical and Comparative Summary*, Anthropological Papers, American Museum of Natural History (New York: 1916), XI, Part 8, *passim.*

[7] Harry H. Turney-High, *The Flathead Indians of Montana*, Memoir 48, American Anthropological Association (Menasha: 1937), p. 29.

and describe the enemy strength and position.[8] Perhaps shamanistic military leadership was most highly developed on the North Pacific Coast.

Counter-reconnaissance was secured in the Southwest by shamans causing dust storms to blow. The Teton liked to attack under the cover of rain, so the shamans sprinkled a wolf hide to make the rain come. Wissler relates that the Oglala Hide Bearers of the Wolf cult could make the weather cloudy to screen a raid. Those woodland people who had war bundles often sought military information from them by elaborate ceremonials.[9]

The gathering of information by actual spies or intelligence operatives within the enemy lines or villages was quite rare in America. It was common in Africa, as will be seen. This may or may not have been the result of the great linguistic variation of America. There is some reason to think that the Iroquois Confederacy used this device, and Flathead informants insist that they did. Their language contains words meaning to dress as a Crow or a Blackfoot with the intent of visiting the enemy camp for purposes of espionage. According to Karsten, espionage among the Jibaro covered every detail as well as any modern *Deuxieme Bureau* could desire.[10]

The African Kingdom of Dahomey maintained a well organized spy service in the villages its king intended to assail. No modern power could excel Dahomey in this. Their king went to war on a sure thing, thanks to his G2. A shrewd bit of intelligence work, not unknown to modern powers, was performed in Nigeria. Neutral towns were bribed to bring news of any movement on the part of a suspected enemy. Ambushes were prepared upon receipt of such intelligence with expectable results.[11] Neutrals have never been popular with belligerents, nor has harboring hostile spies increased good feeling towards them.

The Zulu were most adept at gathering military information, as the next chapter shows. But able as these warriors were, they were not above using shamanistic rites for intelligence purposes any more than

---

[8] Alanson B. Skinner, *Notes on the Eastern Cree and the Northern Saulteaux*, Anthropological Papers, American Museum of Natural History (New York: 1911), IX, pp. 165f.

[9] Skinner, *Social Life and Ceremonial Bundles of the Menomini Indians*, pp. 100ff.

[10] Karsten, *op. cit.*, p. 20.

[11] Talbot, *op. cit.*, p. 237.

were the Saulteaux. Their functionaries would observe two vessels in which magical mixtures had been brewed, one representing the Zulu and the other the enemy. The behavior of the froth in the vessels was thought to foretell victory. Perhaps the shaman set two sticks in the ground likewise representing each side. The side would lose whose stick would first be blown over by the wind.[12] The king would also send spies to acquire some property of the enemy chief over which he and his shamans could perform magic.[13] Such statements seem necessary to remind us that in spite of their fine war system, the Zulu were a nonliterate people. Yet while the army was on the march, magic was not of paramount importance, though there were "doctors" aplenty along in a staff capacity. Reliance was really put on scouts sent by twos and threes ahead of the advanced guard. When the enemy was located the main body was informed by runners.[14]

Military intelligence was highly developed in Oceania. The Melanesians were most expert in this work, for the same reason that the American Indian was. The Kiwai Papuans normally sent out scouts called "ghost people" to estimate resistance and to spy out the land. Their chief function was to aid in accomplishing the surround of the hostile village.[15]

In addition, both Melanesians and Polynesians tried to obtain intelligence from the behavior of animals and other magical means. Birds were thought to give notice of the enemy in New Britain. Omens were observed and their appearance would alter a war party's behavior. A snake on the road, for example, indicated that the enemy was in position on the boundary, and the war party disposed itself accordingly.[16] A bird flying across the path of a Samoan party was a bad omen, and if they saw a rainbow behind them instead of in front, they postponed the attack.[17]

Practically every type of military intelligence method was utilized by the Eurasiatic barbarians. The arctic tribes relied heavily on magical and ornithological methods. Bogoraz says the Chuckchee relied

[12] Kidd, *op. cit.*, pp. 308f.

[13] Krige, *op. cit.*, p. 268.

[14] *Ibid.*, p. 274.

[15] Landtman, *op. cit.*, p. 159.

[16] Brown, *op. cit.*, p. 154.

[17] *Ibid.*, p. 169.

heavily on incantation. The arctic tern was considered both their chief sentinel and *Deuxieme Bureau* against sudden attack.[18]

The Iron Age Europeans were somewhat more realistic. Julius Caesar said that it was the regular habit of the Gauls to compel travellers and merchants to halt and to tell all they knew of other peoples, even against their will.[19] He thought the motive in gathering such tactical and strategic information was creditable, but said the Gauls' lack of analysis and intelligence critique led them into fatal gullibility. Their visitors often told them some very tall tales.

One of the chief functions of military intelligence is to effect surprise on the enemy. The principle of surprise is one of the greatest in the art of war. He who has effected a surprise has gone far towards victory.

The American Indian, as well as most other nonliterates, was adept in the use of surprise. Especially is this true of the hunters. Such expertness has given rise to a plethora of remarks of the following type. This one is by DeVries on the Leni Lenape of Delaware:

> As soldiers they are far from being honorable, but perfidious, and accomplish all their designs by treachery; they also use many stratagems to deceive their enemies and execute by night almost all their plans that are in any way hazardous.[20]

This Dutch remark regarding the uses of the principle of surprise is pure nonsense. The principle always has been and always will be important. The only critical remark to be made on this score applies to almost all Indians, which is to call attention to their almost complete reliance on this principle to the exclusion of most of the others. As for the comment on the treacherous character of the Leni Lenape, DeVries would have done well to have omitted it. There is no more damning chronicle of white treachery than that contained in his Journal. Most of the Dutch victories over the Indians were accomplished through broken promises and the mass murder of undefended villagers.

The French explorer Romans made a similarly condescending remark regarding the Chickasaw to the southeast, but most of his sneers are applicable to almost any modern commander.

---

[18] Bogoraz, *op. cit.*, p. 646.

[19] Caesar, *op. cit.*, iv. 5.

[20] DeVries, in Clark Wissler, *The Indians of Greater New York and the Lower Hudson,* Anthropological Papers, American Museum of Natural History (New York: 1909), III, pp. 281f.

> They make war by stratagem, surprise, or ambush, despising us as fools for exposing ourselves to be shot at like marks. A man's valour with them consists in their cunning, and as he is deemed the greatest hero who employs most art in surprising his enemy; they never strike a blow unless they think themselves sure of a retreat, and the loss of many men is an infamous crime laid to the charge of the party.[21]

Apparently intelligence was condemned in the soldiers of Romans' day. Cannon-fodder attitudes are not well-considered today, however, and apparently the Chickasaw had truly modern views.

One would expect the simple hunters of Africa to be expert at surprise and to rely almost entirely upon it, but it is surprising to discover that such a well-organized, efficient kingdom as Dahomey did the same thing. In spite of the most civilized preparations made for war, the Dahomeans were really tactically simple. Reliance on surprise as "the essential tactic of Dahomean warfare" marked them as primitive warriors after all. In commendable contrast, however, they themselves were very hard to surprise. Their vast network of spies in enemy territories prevented this. They knew the enemy's situation even better than did the Zulu. They knew his terrain, his population, his resources, and generally his intentions.[22]

The Nigerian Oronn relied on surprise very much as did the Ojibway killing a hut-full of Sioux. This would be expected of hunters. The Oronn chose some compound apart from the others and took great pains to hew a secret path through the dense brush almost up to the house. There they lay in ambush until some inhabitant left his house to perform a chore. They would shoot him in cold blood and flee down their secret path. Often the dead man's kin, gathering in sorrow around his corpse, would senselessly provide another target.[23] Nigerians so valued the principle of surprise that no one of a war party was allowed to scratch the terrible insect bites of the region for fear the slight noise might alarm the enemy.[24] Note again another Ojibway-Jibaro surprise murder method from Nigeria. A small band would creep up to an enemy house at night. They would silently pour water on the mud wall so that they could cautiously dig away a hole with their fingers. They would peer through this to find the sleeping head of the house and shoot him with a

---

21 Romans, *Natural History of East and West Florida* (New York: 1775), p. 70.

22 Herskovits, *op. cit.*, I, pp. 15-17.

23 Talbot, *op. cit.*, p. 236.

24 *Ibid.*, p. 233.

musket. Talbot says that to this day fear of this fate impels the Oronn chiefs to build their sleeping rooms in the center of the compound and to erect thick, low mud walls around their couches.[25]

Even the southeast Bantu did not hesitate to use such primitive methods before Dingiswayo and Chaka civilized them. Kidd says that some tribes accustomed themselves to raw meat so that they could subsist in ambush for days without betraying their presence by fire. They would sneak up to a kraal at night and station killers at the door of each hut. Others would go to the rear and fire the houses in the Jibaro fashion. The witless inhabitants were killed as they crawled through the low doors on their hands and knees.[26]

The principle of surprise was highly developed in Melanesia, as with all simple folk. Polynesians used it less, in fact often threw away any advantage it might have given them in order to conform to their ceremonial pattern. The blacker people, though, relied on it almost entirely. Brown says that the men of New Britain "did not consider it to be any disgrace to use treachery, concealment, or ambush in war; in fact, these were to them the proper way of carrying on war."[27] Neither do civilized soldiers consider any of these things disgraceful, but we need not dwell on that.

After commenting on their dislike for close fighting and love of boasting, a missionary says of the Gaua warriors on Santa Maria, Banks Islands, that six men like to lie in wait for one victim. If the first shot fails, they take to their heels and wait for better luck next time. If they succeed, they may expect the dead man's kin to try the same thing on them.[28] The same author describes a descent from the sea in San Cristoval, Solomon Islands, Northern Melanesia. The landing was not made until darkness. Then the enemy was surrounded. Dawn was awaited so that no victim could escape in the dark. The war cry was given in the first light and the butchery began.[29]

It is useless to repeat that in an over-reliance on surprise the European barbarians revealed their savagery. The use of "treachery," which the moralistic writers are so fond of attributing to men without writing, is and must be essential to warfare, including anything

---

[25] *Ibid.*, p. 237.
[26] Kidd, *op. cit.*, p. 304.
[27] Brown, *op. cit.*, p. 154.
[28] Coombe, *op. cit.*, pp. 57f.
[29] *Ibid.*, pp. 219f.

we can foresee in the future. Indeed, the recent war indicated a marked return to the savage *reliance* on the principle since without surprise the attack airplane has little value against military personnel.

The surprise element was well undertaken by certain ancient Germans who were trying to cross the Rhine against the Celtic Menapii who were trying to prevent their passage. There was a good plan in this action as well. The Menapian service of security had been too good for the Germans to rely on brute surprise, so they had to think up a ruse. The Germans then pretended to retire to their own land and the Menapian scouts reported all clear. They went three days away to effect this stratagem, but in a single night the fine German cavalry wheeled and attacked, catching the Menapii complacent and unprepared. The Menapii could only die.[30]

Nonliterate tribes have not been described as submilitary because they used surprise but because they relied almost exclusively upon it. The ancient Germans used it as just described, but did not give up because their original surprise attack failed. Nevertheless, they were not above the common American or Melanesian night surprise and surround. The Roman Tacitus said that the Harii, a tribe of Lugii, were a strong, fierce, artful people. They liked to paint themselves and equipment black and attack on the darkest nights, striking "like an army of ghosts." They were universally successful, partly because of their phantasmal appearance, for "in every battle after all the eye is conquered first."[31]

The same author shows that the Scots could also make able use of this principle. His father-in-law Agricola once divided his forces in the face of the enemy, which should have brought him to Custer's fate. As it was, the Scots apparently were shrewd enough to appreciate the blunder and tried to take advantage of it. They attempted a night attack by combined forces on the weakest legion, chopping through the pickets and charging the sleepy Romans.[32] Tacitus made a poor amanuensis here for his parent-in-law. In this passage, however, it is implied that the Scots made an able combination of the principles of intelligence, surprise, cooperation, mass, and concerted effort. The battle finally went to the Romans due to their superior handling of the last three of these principles. Even then the defeated Scots

30 Caesar, *op. cit.*, iv. 4.
31 Tacitus, *op. cit.*, 43.
32 Cornelius Tacitus, *Agricola*, 25-26.

saved themselves from extinction at the hands of a determined and vengeful foe by proper use of the terrain.

The Viking raids were famous for the use of surprise. The Norse were quite capable of fighting pitched battles, but they were not above the use of the night surprise, stealthy house-burning, and murder which would do credit to Ecuador, Papua, Minnesota, or the Congo. It is said that this practice was not well thought-of, but it was used nevertheless. The Icelandic sagas speak of one Earl Rognvald who came with his men by stealth to the house of King Vemund while the latter was feasting. This they surrounded and fired by night, burning the king and his men, and appropriating their ships and property.[33]

The use of the principle of surprise among the Paleo-Siberian reindeer nomads is reminiscent of the folk east of Bering Strait. Chuckchee warfare was remarkably like that of the Eskimo, with whom they often fought, even crossing Bering Strait to do so. The Chuckchee are described as being frank with their enemies and often fighting stand-up battles of sorts. Most of their stories of past wars, however, are tales of "surprise, nightly attacks, and murder of the sleeping."[34]

Confronted with an aggressive enemy relying on the principle of surprise, any group which wishes to survive has but one answer, eternal vigilance. This means able observation of the principle of security. A United States Army publication says, "Security in a military sense means measures to prevent surprise. A commander may be excused for being defeated, but never for being surprised."[35]

Such security may be obtained by information regarding the enemy, which means continuous reconnaissance. In the field, there must be covering detachments flung to the fore, rear, and the flanks. Military intelligence work must be constant. Correct formations must be observed on the march, in camp, and in battle to prevent any initial surprise from being successful. Concealment and cover must be used intelligently. Fortifications must be built within reason, but not enough to permit defensive Maginot complacency. After all, aggression and initiative are the best protection against surprise. An enemy will hardly ever surprise you if you have him on the defensive or on the run.

---

[33] Snorri Sturluson, *The Heimskringla*, W. Morris and E. Magnusson, trans., 4 vols. (London: 1893), I, pp. 93f.

[34] Bogoraz, *op. cit., pp.* 645f.

[35] *Tactics and Technique of Cavalry,* p. 5.

The miserable observation of the principle of security by most American Indians is frankly incomprehensible. It would seem that the aggressor who so completely relied on surprise would take pains to see that he himself was not surprised, but this seldom occurred and the clever scouts of the Great Plains were the worst. While living in the Middle West the Sioux had no concept of the principle. They did not learn it when they moved onto the Plains, nor did any of the non-agricultural Plainsmen. The semi-agricultural people developed their system of sentinels and Cossack posts as well as did any small detachment of white troops. The bison hunters had their teachers but were unwilling to learn. The farmers were seldom surprised. The bison hunters normally were. The core pattern of Plains war was to sneak into a village, steal a few good horses and women, and to slaughter some of the sleepers before the hostile party was discovered. The hunting tribes rarely erected effective works or even fences around their villages, though they had the raw materials at hand. They never learned the value of posting sentinels, although both the defenders and attackers relied entirely upon surprise and shock. In light of the perfect state to which they developed intelligence, it is incomprehensible why they neglected the other side of the picture, the reply to enemy scouting and surprise, the service of security.

Certainly one thing is clear: Contiguity and need are no assurances of diffusion. For example, the Plateau Kutenai considered that every healthy young man's nightly job was to patrol the camp and its environs as mounted vedettes. The nearby Flathead, whom they often fought, never did so and were almost always soundly beaten by the Kutenai. The Kutenai chose their camp sites for defensive positions. The Flathead preferred to camp in hollows on open ground surrounded by trees, the most vulnerable positions possible. Yet the Flathead did fence their camps with stakes and ropes on which were hung rattles to give the alarm. The Kutenai never thought of doing such a thing.[36]

The Siouan neglect of security stood them in bad stead in their Minnesota war with the Ojibway. The latter were clever at surprise. They also obtained gunpowder sooner than the Sioux, which they used to good advantage. In those days the Sioux lived in permanent mud huts when they were not on the march. It was no trick for the Ojibway to make grenades, sneak up on the undefended villages,

[36] Harry H. Turney-High, *Ethnography of the Kutenai*, Memoir 56, American Anthropological Association (Menasha: 1941), pp. 162f.

toss a bomb into the smoke hole of each hut, and accomplish a telling victory in a few minutes.

It is easy to overestimate Ojibway superiority. Had the Sioux formed the Confederacy of Five Fires soon enough, they might have changed the story. In effect, the Ojibway planned to rout the Sioux from Minnesota because they themselves were being pressed by other Indians, who in turn were being squeezed westward by the white settlers.

The Plainsmen and Plateau people as a whole showed that they had some knowledge of the principle, for their march security was excellent, as shown by several passages of this work. But when camp was made, only the maize-growers of the Plains could guard themselves. Could it be that men with only their lives to save are unwary while those with full bins are cautious?

The expectable response to an enemy who deals in stealth is stealth.

That the Plains villages normally went to sleep at night with neither sentinel nor fortification is a fact. Sentry-go would have been a normal function of their military lodges had they but seen it that way. This did happen, but rarely. This duty was often the work of a whole sib in the Northeast Woodland.

Le Moyne wrote that the Creeks of Florida protected their villages from an enemy notorious for clever stealth by moat and palisade. Sentinels were posted whose scent was so keen that they could smell a foe from afar. Should a village be surprised through the neglect of the sentinels, the culprits were given a ceremonious execution in the chief's presence.[37] Le Moyne claimed to have been an eye-witness of such punishment; if so, he witnessed a degree of discipline very rare in nonliterate America.

Observe, too, the disciplined state of march security observed by the neighboring Timucua. Le Moyne says:

> When Saturiwa went to war his men preserved no order, but went along one after another, just as it happened. On the contrary, his enemy, Holata Outina, whose name, as now I remember, means 'king of many kings,' and who was much more powerful than he as regards both wealth and the number of subjects, used to march with regular ranks, like an organized army; himself marching along in the middle of the whole force, painted red. On the wings, or horns, of his order of march were his young men, the swiftest of whom, also painted red,

---

[37] Le Moyne, in John R. Swanton, *Early History of the Creek Indians and Their Neighbors,* Bulletin 73, Bureau of American Ethnology (Washington: 1922), pp. 379f.

> acted as advanced guards and scouts for reconnoitering the enemy. These are able to follow up the traces of the enemy by scent as dogs do wild beasts; and when they come upon such traces they immediately return to the army to report. And, as we make use of trumpets and drums to promulgate orders, so they have heralds, who by cries of certain sorts direct them to halt, or to advance, or to attack, or to perform any other military duty. After sunset they halt, and are never wont to give battle. For encamping they are arranged in squads of ten each, the bravest being put in squads by themselves. When the chief has chosen the place of encampment for the night, in open fields or woods, and after he has eaten, and is established by himself, the quartermaster places ten of these squads of the bravest in a circle around him. About ten paces outside of this circle is placed another line of twenty squads; at twenty yards farther, another of forty squads; and so on, increasing the number and distance of these lines, according to the size of the army.[38]

This statement is valuable not only for its description of march order, scouting, and patrolling but particularly for its revelation of the unusually effective service of security for the camp at night. This is remarkably modern, except that the camp was not ringed by outposts according to the principle of increasing resistance in numbers but by increasing resistance in the valor and efficiency of the posts.

The ferocity of the Apache corn-thieves forced a division of labor on the Pima which withdrew their male strength from productive work in the fields. Enemy parties were expected at from weekly to monthly intervals, so sentry-go around the camp by day and night was the chief duty of the men. The women were perforce the tillers. The Apache liked to attack under the cover of a storm, so stormy nights brought on particular vigilance. Dogs were trained to warn the village of the approach of strangers, and all the trails were guarded. The Pima liked to build little fires around the camp at night, hoping that the foe would come near them and thus reveal themselves.[39]

An exception to the poorly guarded Plains hunting villages is found among the Assiniboin. These people posted sentinels in a ring some two to three hundred yards away from the camp circle and at intervals of from fifty to sixty steps. It no doubt paid them.[40]

The people of the forested portions of South America tended to rely on the village chickens and dogs to give warning of an approach-

---

[38] *Ibid.*, pp. 6f.

[39] Frank Russell, "The Pima Indians," *Annual Report 26*, Bureau of American Ethnology (Washington: 1904-1905), pp. 200-205.

[40] Denig, *op. cit.*, pp. 548f.

ing enemy. The war drums were then sounded and friends gathered from afar. The assailants abandoned the attack in such an instance, having no stomach for an effort against an organized position.

This area was notable for the rudimentary use of chemical warfare in security, the closing of areas hard to defend by noxious gases. Chemical warfare based on capsicum was well known among the Arawak and Carib. Fires were lit and laden with capsicum so that the fumes would blow over ground which they wished to interdict to the enemy, thereby releasing fighters for other spaces. The attack also built rings of fire around the village and threw in capsicum to windward. This is nothing more nor less than the use of prohibitive gas areas. The advanced party of the attack consistently introduced peppers on coals into the cracks of unwatched houses to force out the inhabitants. The defense likewise threw capsicum grenades to irritate the attack.

A similar prohibitive use of noxious materials is reported for Nigeria. Before an engagement scouts were sent ahead secretly to lay magic leaves along the route the enemy must take. Talbot says that this was not superstition but a clever use of juices from virulent fruits which would make the hardiest warrior howl with pain if he should step on them. Men are said to have gone mad from such agony.[41] The Nigerians did not hesitate to use pure magic, however, as they decked the thoroughfares with the limbs of dead enemies to guard against surprise. Sometimes roads were interdicted to the foe by bringing thither magic stones taken from the temples. Goats were then sacrificed and, as their blood was spilled over the stones, the names of the deceased members of the chief secret societies were recited so that they would act as sentries. Farther south the Bechuana likewise relied on the sentry value of tortured and sacrificed beef blood rather than on their own eyes, ears, and wakefulness.[42]

In contrast with this savagery, the post-Dingiswayo Zulu used the principle of security much as a modern army would. In safe country the regiment marched in extended regimental formation, with scouts to the flanks and rear. Close order was maintained on entering the theater of operations to prevent stragglers from being sniped. About ten companies preceded the main body in the service of security, with the additional intent of persuading the enemy that they were the

---

[41] Talbot, *op. cit.*, p. 235.

[42] Kidd, *op. cit.*, pp. 310f.

main body. Passwords and countersigns were used to prevent surprise on the march and in camp.[43]

The principle of security was observed by a few Melanesians, but with reference to protecting themselves while on the march rather than by guarding or fortifying their villages. The practice of fortifying the villages was well developed in Polynesia. Polynesians on the march or about to engage in an action took great pains for their security. One missionary says that in Samoa a war party moved in a body with advance and rear guards, while two or three scouts were sent to locate the enemy.[44]

It was said at the outset of this work that the material culture of war would be dealt with very little. For the same reasons but little will be said regarding primitive military engineering. Certainly the archeologists have written enough on this subject to satisfy anyone. There are, however, a few remarks which could be made regarding the lack of understanding of the principle of security by that branch of anthropology. There is no doubt that the earlier investigators of the pueblos of Southwest United States erred in attributing too much military significance to the pueblo structures. A healthy reaction set in, but when an archeologist says that the pueblos were not fortresses at all, he has erred. The enemies of these people dealt in surprise. Furthermore, many of the pueblo structures were admirably adapted to defense. If they were not so used we can dismiss much of the sympathy most people have had for their builders. True, not all the buildings were adaptable for defense, but it is difficult for a trained soldier to believe that some of them were not. It would be extremely hard, for example, for the trained eye to view the *casa grande* as anything other than a fort, even if poorly sited with reference to the defensive terrain.

So let it be. Fortification of the camp according to the principle seems to have been best done by the best farmers. Is this not expectable? They had something to lose. Furthermore, their socio-economic systems provided food and training in ways whereby enough group labor could be summoned to erect the primordial forts. There is no use to go to Peru to see Ollantay Tambo. That work could not be taken today except with good artillery and air support. The Mandan-Arikara-Hidatsa group had quite enough. So did many others. The Canichanas of Southwest Amazonia entrenched their vil-

[43] Krige, *op. cit.*, pp. 273f.

[44] Brown, *op. cit.*, p. 166.

lages against surprise. They used these little citadels as points from which they could raid their enemies.[45] Most of the villages in Ecuador were protected by approaches full of traps and pitfalls meant to kill or maim. They had to be approached with great care. The walls of the houses were strongly built and loopholed for arrows. Similar deadly pits are common in Malaysia, as anyone who has served in the Philippine Scouts or the U. S. regulars can relate. Such things are only sensible. They do not lead to the introversion, in a particularly extrovert activity, that can only mean defeat in the long run.

---

[45] Church, *op. cit.*, p. 104.

CHAPTER 7

Battle Plans

IS IT NOT A TRUISM THAT EVERY HUMAN ACTIVITY OF ANY COMPLEXITY must be planned? Any business venture, scientific experiment, or athletic contest succeeds largely because it was soundly planned. Now war is an extremely complicated activity, requiring close teamwork according to the principle of cooperation. That such work requires planning seems too obvious to mention, despite the fact that many primitive actions are practically planless. One might say with some justification that it is planning which in part takes war out of the classification of murder.

The necessity for planning is too patent to be elevated into a military principle. The pertinent generalization is called the principle of simplicity of plans. Regardless of careful attempts to prevent surprise, to gather intelligence and to make meticulous plans, war contains too many unpredictable eventualities to permit any complexity of planning. The "fog of war" is dense at best without the commander needlessly increasing it. "Simplicity should be the keynote of tactical procedure in plans, orders and execution. Only the simplest plan has any success in war. Never attempt anything complicated. A simple plan, whose success does not hinge upon a number of contingencies, is always possible."[1] It is not planning which is military and non-civilian. Any man or woman in active life knows that. The essential non-civilian element is simplicity. Study the work of the world's great captains and be convinced. Anthropologists of recent years have commented on the tendency of human culture to expand and grow complicated beyond any requirements of practical utility, apparently just for expansion's own sake. Is this not also true of planning? Every sociologist knows that unnecessary complexity, complexity beyond the requirements of the situation, is one great cause of social problems. Most of us in our really honest moments will

[1] *Tactics and Technique of Cavalry,* p. 327.

admit that our lives, our work, recreation, and certainly college courses of instruction are planned to death. It is careful planning that the work of the world demands, not that complex planning which is the refuge of the unimaginative and fearful mind. This sort of thing may be tolerated in civilian life, but it will not do in war.

There is no need so to sermonize the modern soldier, for he appreciates the principle of simplicity of plans. There is no need so to preach to the sub-civilized warrior, either, for it is difficult to get him to follow any plan at all. Where plans are used they are always simple. The small forces involved and lack of troop specialization alone would guarantee that.

Let us first consider the Eskimo, for he was so pacific that elaborate battle practice was too much for him. However, contacts with un-Eskimo ideas did contaminate the west Eskimo to the extent of having some kind of method. Nelson says that the old way of making war among the Bering Eskimo was to lie in wait around a village until night, then to steal to every house and barricade the doors from the outside. The men of the village being thus confined, the attackers could leisurely shoot them with arrows through the smoke holes.[2] This reveals a rather simple method. The principle of offensive was observed, as throughout America. The chief element, however, was the reliance on surprise. This was not as easy to accomplish as it might seem, since the Bering Eskimo made a half-hearted effort to guard their villages.

A complete lack of planning is exhibited in Apache tales. The Apache under Geronimo were the last Indians to give the United States Army any field work, but when they were fighting the old aboriginal wars with the Pima, they must have relied on ferocity alone. Jicarilla war folklore shows complete lack of methodical planning.[3] It relates that very soon after men came upon earth from the underworld, a chief led a war party against some other men. The commander allowed the enemy completely to surround his force of five hundred during a parley. When the parley failed, it was no trick for the foe to kill every one of the five hundred.

So it was, too, in California, where simple murder and feud were more popular than war. The Kato hardly tried more than to lure some witless individual into close quarters in order to destroy him.

2 Nelson, *op. cit.*, p. 327.

3 Pliny E. Goddard, *Jicarilla Apache Texts*, Anthropological Papers, American Museum of Natural History (New York: 1911), VIII, p. 196.

Stand-up fighting was not in favor except in pitched battles, and these were long-range affairs with arrows and infinite dodging.[4]

Skinner lamented that the Menomini of Green Bay, Wisconsin, never fought in the open with large bodies of troops, and lacked method in warfare. Their faith was pinned on ambuscade and raids by small parties.[5] Quite aside from the competence of the Menomini, such criticism has little meaning. Skinner had the grand strategy of the War between the States as an ideal, which would have been fatal in the woods of northern Wisconsin. It is true, though, that most of the Algonkian peoples, particularly those of the east, never rose above the technique of the raid, which made them easy prey for white men and Iroquois alike. Some of them could plan a surround, as soon will be shown, but many of them could plan no more than a bloody game of tag.

Strangely enough, it was not in the east of the Algonkian range that one found the best fighting men. The good warriors were not near the Iroquois and other astute tribes, but in the west, confronted by the incompetents of the Great Plain. For information on the Central Algonkians, reliance is put on the works of Frances Densmore. One cannot forbear to remark that there is more insight into military ethnology in this musicologist's reports than in the combined works of many other experts.

The Ojibway were good examples of Central Algonkian superiority. It is apparent that their greater success in part relied on a social organization which could bring large numbers into the field. Though this book has shown them capable of fatal and primitive incompetence, yet they were one of the few American tribes outside the central civilizations who had any *strategic* sense. Miss Densmore clearly indicates that the Ojibway were capable of planning to occupy an entire region, and of accomplishing that objective by war.[6] I say by war, for it will be recalled that the wilder tribes of the Southwest United States were partly responsible for shrinking the pueblo area not by war but by a simple nuisance technique, making it unprofitable for the peaceful corn-growers to hold on. But it is an historically authenticated fact that the Ojibway did plan to drive the Sioux out of Minnesota onto the Plain, and that they accomplished that mission, despite the fact that their material equipment was very little better

---

[4] Kroeber, *op. cit.*, p. 152.

[5] Skinner, *Social Life and Ceremonial Bundles of the Menomini Indians*, p. 97.

[6] Densmore, *Papago Music, passim.*

than that of the Sioux. The Siouan tribes could not comprehend strategy or campaigning. None of their leaders or councils had the ability or authority to plan and carry out such an objective. This one fact was enough to throw the balance on the side of the Ojibway. Like the Iroquois and the Germanic Chatti, they could go to war as well as to battle.

Le Moyne wrote of the simple southeastern Timuca, saying that they and their chief Holata Outina never indulged in anything recognizable to his Seventeenth Century training as a battle. He said that they were content to call it a day if any one man, no matter how insignificant, was killed. This gave adequate excuse for a rather elaborate style of head-hunting.

Yet one cannot be so sure that Le Moyne gave a good analysis. He was an artist accompanying the military expedition of Laudonniere, and his accuracy of reporting is questionable. He describes as a typical Indian skirmish one which used support and reserves, a rarity in the field reports. The Timuca seem to have scouted the principle of objective and mission, or rather their missions were different from ours. In another section of this book commander Holata Outina is said to have been able to organize his people into admirable formations, which is not consistent with planless savagery.

It might be that Le Moyne, Romans, and many other early observers could not recognize a battle when they saw one, hence they reported that the tribes had no battle method. This has become almost an *idee fixe* in the civilian anthropologist and civilized military mind, and one might ask why. The reason is not hard to find.

Skirmishing as light troops was not the European style at the time of the early reporters. From the centuries following Gustavus Adolphus and culminating in Frederick the Great, the musket had developed enough efficiency to make it the chief weapon of war. This reinstituted the infantry as the Queen of Battles, leading to its present, or at least recent status as the chief arm of any battle. It might be that since the Battle for France and the Ardennes counteroffensive the textbook tenet, "The infantry mission is *the* mission," has suddenly become obsolete, but it worked for over three centuries. The primary infantry weapon, the musket, was still an inefficient fire device. It was slow to load and of short effective range. This, at least so it was thought, necessitated the musketeers firing shoulder to shoulder in serried ranks by platoons in order to get any effective mass fire. The movement part of the action had to be supplied by pikemen. This massing of infantry destroyed its maneuverability and made the mobility of its heavy lines as nothing. This was a transitional period of infantry tactics and was evidently a mistake. This can be said definitely since two British generals could not rid themselves of the pretty Frederician tactics in America. Braddock was defeated by the sound tactics of fire, movement, and utilization of the terrain. His failure necessitated another campaign for the west. General Pakenham conducted a Frederician parade before New Orleans and suffered complete defeat at the hands of Jackson's Indian fighters. Therefore, because the American Indian failed to array a dress parade, he is accused of having no battle method.

Africa was capable of many carefully planned actions, but all the Negroes were not so competent. The Ibo and several other simpler Sudanese never rose to such levels. "Warfare among the Ibo was more a matter of affrays and raids than of organized campaigns."[7] The Ibibio had adequate man power and a good command principle, but they made no formal arrangements. They set out at dawn in an unorganized mass, murdering such enemies as they found on the way. They could conduct an engagement of several days' duration, were organized and commanded as age-groups, but the fighting took place apparently without plan as the occasion seemed to demand. The planning principle could be expected only among the better organized African states. Yet this certainly did not take place automatically. The efficiently organized kingdom of Dahomey, with all its force and authority, could think of nothing but the grossest animal surround, which was indeed a plan, but a simple and inflexible one.

One remark frequently made about Melanesian war is that it lacked method, while another, constantly repeated, is that the Melanesians did not know war in any recognizable sense. Such statements are hardly borne out by the facts. For example, Armstrong says that there was "no real war on Rossel" because the islanders do not fight in the open but "murder secretly in safety." He laments the lack of a stand-up fight between ranks or spearmen.[8] This is just a repetition of the desire on the part of some reporters for the natives to fight in close order in the old Frederician manner. Why, indeed, in a forested country should they abandon the use of cover and "fight in the open"?

[7] Meek, *op. cit.*, p. 242.

[8] Wallace E. Armstrong, *Rossel Island* (Cambridge: Cambridge University Press, 1928), p. 106.

Perhaps the typical Melanesian killing was the man-hunt, which required little plan or method, but Melanesians did know something else. In the Solomons, for example, individual man-stalking was done to earn blood money, but the islanders also made planned punitive raids on whole villages and apparently had plenty of inter-group actions.

The consistent battle plan of primitive war was overwhelmingly the surround and dawn attack. The time chosen was when the enemy would be sleepiest and most unwary. The surround itself was an old method carried over from the surrounding of herd animals in hunting. It relies almost entirely on surprise. It has something of a formation, insofar as the surround is really a line bent into a circle. Recall that the principle of correct formation does not demand that the battle line be straight.

When the Kutenai scouts reported contact with an enemy camp, the chief ordered his men forward cautiously. As the simple approach column arrived at the proper spot, one man turned to the right, the next to the left, the next to the right, and so on until the sleeping camp was surrounded. When the first two men met they knew the circle had been formed. These two men then touched the men next to them in the direction from which they had come. When this touch signal reached the chief, he blew on his whistle and the Kutenai fell on the hapless sleepers.[9] This was almost the identical battle plan used by such Central Algonkians as could make any.

The Ecuadorian Jibaro likewise made the attack by night or just before dawn. A house was cautiously surrounded. When a person opened the door to come out he was shot and the attackers rushed in to massacre the inhabitants. If they were not able to penetrate the house by violence or chicanery they set fire to the thatch, forcing the inhabitants to come out and be killed or remain within and be smothered. The attack intended to slaughter every defender, an observance of objective unlike the common North American practice. The inhabitants could expect no help from the other villagers for they, at the first sound of tumult, bolted their own doors and waited for the enemy to set fire to their own houses in turn. The only hope of escape was to break through the besieging ring as individuals, and that was a slight one.[10] The dawn attack, then, was typical of South America outside Peru or Colombia. The Chiriguano of the Gran Chaco, for

[9] Turney-High, *Ethnography of the Kutenai*, pp. 167f.
[10] Karsten, *op. cit.*, p. 26.

example, assailed an enemy town at dawn with much noise. The first attack was so furious that it could not be sustained for long. It had to win at once or lose.[11] This remark is applicable to most users of the dawn attack and surround.

The bulk of Melanesian war had only the same story to tell: the preference for the dawn attack, an exaggeration of the old animal hunting surround, linked with an over-reliance on the principle of surprise noted so often among the simpler subjects of this study. A counter use of the service of security, the posting of sentinels and watch, seemed no more to have occurred to most Melanesians than it did to the Plains Indians. This carelessness is very difficult to understand, since the enemy habitually relied on such surprise methods. That a culture will produce a response to human needs, material or nonmaterial, is not automatically certain.[12] The dawn attack preceded by sea voyages and a descent upon the coast are also common in Melanesia. A good example is given in Abel, *Savage Life in New Guinea.*[13]

The dawn attack using infiltration as well as the surround was popular in New Guinea. Just before sunrise the Kiwai attempted to enter each bushman's house quietly and tapped the individual inhabitant silently but adequately on the head, which was removed on the spot. Since this was done with the greatest caution and organization, and since the enemy posted no sentinels, no villager was left alive. Should some wretch awake and give cry, he would benefit himself and his fellows but little. The Kiwai were awake, organized, and in command of all principal positions, which the villagers were not. The Kiwai found it paid to be able to distinguish friend and foe by painting themselves with white pipe clay, even though some enemy might use the white stripes as an arrow target.[14]

The Kiwai plan was, in other words, reliance on the dawn attack, surprise, and exploitation by wiping out every enemy life. A rudimentary command function shows through and the element of simplicity in the plan is apparent. A single file approach order was maintained, preceded by able scouts observing the principles of intelligence and security. The principle of objective is very plain. The

[11] Church, *op. cit.*, p. 234.

[12] Coombe, *op. cit.*, pp. 219f.

[13] Charles W. Abel, *Savage Life in New Guinea* (London: London Missionary Society, 1902), pp. 138f.

[14] Riley, *op. cit.*, pp. 263f.

stupidity of the bushman enemy and his unwillingness to learn from experience is also apparent.

> The principle of utilization of the terrain is most important in battle practice anywhere.
>
> Terrain exercises a controlling influence on all military operations. Properly utilized it is frequently the decisive factor. The elements of the terrain are the concealment, cover, facilities for movement and opportunities for observation and fire which it affords, and the obstacles it interposes to fire and movement. Every individual and every unit in every situation, whether moving or stationary, should seek the natural advantages of the terrain, and avoid its disadvantages.[15]

Terrain often defeats civilized troops, too, when confronted by savages who know how to use it. Braddock found this out. The Inca likewise made little or no progress in subduing the eastern face of the Andes though, according to Garcilasso de la Vega, the Inca Rocca sent his own able son Yahuar-Huaccac against the tribes with as many as fifteen thousand men.[16]

Some American Indian tribes disregarded every other principle of war but this one. Typical of such actions were those of the Canadian interior. These people could only effect adequate fire, without movement, and use the terrain skilfully. Their actions were completely ineffectual, since their overreliance on terrain was an indication of their cowardice rather than an opportunity to launch a telling offensive.[17]

Proper use of terrain was almost always observed in Africa. Even the simple Kerri-Kerri of the Sudan used natural hill tops for village sites. The bases of their precipitous cliffs were artificially fortified by ditches hidden by verdure.[18] The Americans and Africans as a whole used the terrain skilfully in the offensive, but the latter surpassed the Indians in a defensive use of nature.

The principle of utilization of the terrain was well observed in both Melanesia and Polynesia. Brown says the Samoans "took every advantage of ground or position which would afford shelter," which they would not forsake until the enemy was in retreat. In typical fashion he scorns their use of shelter as "treachery and ambush."[19]

---

[15] Tactics and Technique of Cavalry, p. 6.

[16] Church, *op. cit.*, p. 195.

[17] Skinner, *Notes on the Eastern Cree and the Northern Saulteaux*, p. 165.

[18] Olive Macleod, *Chiefs and Cities of Central Africa* (Edinburgh and London: W. Blackwood, 1912), p. 287.

[19] Brown, *op. cit.*, p. 169.

Approaching the military threshold, the Polynesians could be expected to utilize the terrain in both defense and offense. Buck cites an example showing fine tactical sense in forming the battle line. The attacking side used two taro swamps to protect the flanks, and chose a site for a prepared position which would afford good retreat in event of defeat. They then offered battle, but in spite of their pains, were defeated.[20]

Some Melanesians prepared a position in the old days. By this one means that they accentuated the natural advantages of the position by art. If time permitted they often cleared away the bush in order to have a clear field of fire. This fell into disfavor in the New Hebrides when fire arms brought about a preference for sniping instead of mass fighting and mass arrow fire.[21] This is an interesting example of a quick response of tactics, a part of the nonmaterial culture, to a change in material culture.

There was a fair indication that the principle was well observed in Eurasia. When the Chinese first descended from the plateau and started forming their nation, they were opposed by certain Turkic tribes who resented the intrusion into their land. Chinese tradition says that the Turki often fought them and, if possible, attacked with a swamp at their back. If the Turki were successful the swamp was not needed, but if they failed they retreated through the swamp where the Chinese could not follow. This was possible because the Turkic tribes were horsemen and negotiated the swamp which was impassable to the Chinese infantry.

Caesar relates a clever and painstaking method of the Gaulish Bellovaci which is reminiscent of the Manuan Polynesians just mentioned. This enemy had prepared for him a set of ambushes surrounding an open plain of about one square mile. They tried to make Caesar give battle on this field. The open country itself was "fenced every way by woods or by a troublesome river."[22]

Appian tells of an instance wherein a group of savages mistook Augustus for a general with Braddock's intelligence. They used much more energy than the Indians in preparing the terrain, but this time without success. The transalpine Iapydes, "a strong and savage tribe," had trounced the Romans twice in twenty years, had raided both Italy and the Roman colonies, so Augustus set out to make them

[20] Buck, *op. cit.*, p. 43.
[21] Humphreys, *op. cit.*, p. 57.
[22] Caesar, *op. cit.*, v. 56.

cooperate. He had to traverse a steep, rugged road to get into their territory which they had made more unpleasant by felling large trees across it. They made constant assaults on his flanks, but Augustus was not Braddock. He had flank guards marching on the ridges paralleling the main advance, and so avoided disaster. The Iapydes fled to defensible thickets when finally defeated, but eventually came out on the promise of amnesty.[23]

In the far east the Aryans found a rather able tribe of Dravidians called Puri blocking their passage through the Himalayas by erecting blockhouses at strategic points. The Vedas tell how the Aryans of Tritsu overcame them, however, but only by the intervention of their god who destroyed the Puri forts for his devotees.[24] The incident is quoted from a Vedic hymn to Agni, the fire god, in whom we see the Latin counterpart Ignis, the fire. The clear implication is that the Aryans managed to make a Jibaro-Kiwai sneak-up on the wooden Puri forts and drove the inhabitants out by putting fire to them. While the Puri did take advantage of the Himalayan terrain, even accentuating it with blockhouses, they seemed to neglect the service of security. The prime function of fortification is, of course, the accentuation of terrain difficulties for the enemy. It was mentioned elsewhere that fortification was an outgrowth of the principle of the defensive, but proper utilization of the terrain is also offensive as well. Like most features of simple and civilized material culture, field and permanent fortification begins with natural advantages and improves on them.

The only modern elements in actions described so far are simplicity in plans, the dawn attacks and surround, and a rather good utilization of terrain. Yet there were nonliterate peoples who approached efficient battle planning. The tribes of the American North Pacific Coast were reportedly among these.

Almost all of their travels, including military approaches, were by sea. Thus, a war canoe or group of them would attempt to round the point of a bay without being discovered. The attackers would paddle as close to the shore line as they could, taking every opportunity for concealment offered by rocks and trees. Upon being observed, or upon approaching the shore line of the village, those detailed to paddle would exert every possible force while the bowmen would deliver as much fire as possible. When the shallow water was reached the archers would jump from the canoes, rush to the shore

[23] Appianus of Alexandria, *Roman History,* x. 18.

[24] *Rig Veda,* vii. 3, 6.

line, and continue to deliver such withering fire that the enemy could not effectively organize. The other half of the party would beach the canoes, then form a line of shock troops for the assault. Since they were armed with particularly terrible clubs and encased in slat armor, this assault was very effective, and if the enemy's service of security had in any way been lax, it was almost certain to succeed.

This was almost as effective and tactically sound as the procedure of a landing party of modern marines. It was aggressive, so obeyed the principle of the offensive. Unusual among Indian fighters, these tribes had specialized troops and used them according to the principle of concerted effort. They followed the principle of concentration of effort, but that was almost inevitable in Indian warfare. They obeyed the principle of economy of force, and afforded a perfect example of the use of combined fire and movement. The plan was simple and practical, and the surprise element was used to the fullest degree. The Northcoast people utilized the terrain as much as possible, and no modern officer could deny that they used the correct formation to accomplish the objective. They, like other Indians, were not lax in gathering intelligence and, as with others, their mobility was almost perfect. They could also exploit a victory inasmuch as they got what they wanted in the way of goods and slaves, destruction of property, and so on, although from our standpoint they might have done this more efficiently. However, if all the American Indians had been as able tacticians as they, this might have remained a red man's continent much longer than it did.

If Adair was an accurate reporter, the southeastern Indians were fairly successful battle planners. He said that the typical war party contained from twenty to forty men if a long distance was to be covered in order to avoid providing information to the enemy by numerous tracks. Invasion of contiguous territory where this secrecy was not needed frankly employed the principle of mass to overwhelm the foe by numbers. Surprise, again, was the chief element, and the loss of many men even in victory was not highly considered. The extremes to which they went to guarantee surprise were astounding. Very clever approach formations were used, and the command element was strictly in control. They liked to be pursued by the enemy so that they could lure him into the hollow of a crescent formation in South African fashion. The surround in any form was their chief motive for movement, in contrast with the more static operations observed elsewhere in America. Tactical employment was well observed on both sides. Intelligence work was really intelligent, bolstered by clever signal communications. The fire-fight from cover was begun on signal and not before, and was usually adequate. If the action was long enough and the occasion demanded it, the formation was changed according to an altered situation.[25]

The mock retreat with intent to lure the enemy into a trap was also known to the ordinarily inept Plains fighters. The Assiniboin were probably the most methodical fighters on the Plains when they set their minds to it, which they often failed to do. They obtained intelligence and security by clever scouting, of course, and the approach was made by night. All the advantageous ground was occupied before dawn. Surprise was often accomplished by the use of decoys, just a few men who were sent to make a feint at the enemy camp. Upon apparent defeat, these men fled, drawing the unwary enemy into an ambush. The Assiniboin also liked to make the foe leave his camp in disorder by firing the prairie grass to windward of the camp.

However, such astute though simple plans were the exception rather than the rule with the Assiniboin, who usually proceeded as follows. After dawn had broken, a group of horsemen chosen out of the distinguished warrior class would charge the enemy camp, firing and howling as they went. These people did as much damage as possible, but were ordinarily content to pass on through, driving as many horses before them as they could. They were followed by an echelon of footmen who advanced without order, file, or line. This group, acting on the good principle of fire and movement, would have destroyed the enemy if it had observed any cohesion at all. But each man fought individually and accomplished individual and poor results.

The actual battle was no more than a mildly dangerous game. The shrieks were horrible, especially if a warrior fell. His friends howled and tried to get his body, while the foe screamed in exultation. Actually very little damage was done if the parties were about equal. If the warriors remained bunched, the technique was to snipe the strays. Neither side wished to attack unless there were plain chances of an overwhelming smother. Otherwise the action degenerated into a boasting and feather-waving parade punctuated with mutual insult, no doubt a very fine thing to witness. The chiefs made some ef-

[25] James Adair, *The History of the American Indians* (London: E. and C. Dilly, 1775), pp. 382-388.

fort to plan battles according to the situation, and during the action shouted advice which everyone entirely disregarded.

The Seri of Sonora and the islands of the Gulf of Lower California were remarkably modern in their use of planned actions, although McGee, on whose reports we here rely, describes them as being "devoid of military tactics." This is the standard remark. The Seri were not only capable in comparison with their neighbors, but in comparison with the American Indian as a whole and with nonliterate warriors anywhere. McGee says that they acted on a preconceived plan, generally using a small group as a pivot of maneuver while the main body attempted ambush or a surround. A use of reserves, extremely rare in America, is mentioned. They sought every advantage of position and number, used cover intelligently, and planned their avenues of retreat in case of defeat. McGee scorns them for their lack of "open face-to-face fighting," and "that sense of fairness which finds expression in the duel." He might rather praise them for sensible use of preparatory fire followed by a shock attack which sought to brain the harrassed enemy.[26]

The Seri were characterized by an implacable animosity for other Indians and for the whites. Their highest virtue was to kill a foreigner and their greatest crime was to marry one. Their life was communal, self-centered, and ethnocentric. Despite the ethnologist's reiteration that the Seri were not tacticians, they managed to keep their own land against all comers — white, red, and mixed — until very recent times.

The later Zulu were quite capable of making plans, not only set ones for all occasions, as most of the foregoing were, but individual ones for specific situations. Their supreme commander, the king or some *induna* appointed by him on the eve of departure, gave much thought to planning the entire campaign. He left as little to chance as possible.

Later Zulu methods left little to be desired. It has often been alleged that the great militarizing kings borrowed their basic ideas from white sources. Competent Africanists, however, see in this an unwarranted effort to discredit Chaka's originality. True, he lived at the time Napoleon was conquering Europe. He had heard of Napoleon and tried to emulate him, but in all fairness his battle order

[26] W. J. McGee, *The Seri Indians,* Annual Report 17, Bureau of American Ethnology, (Washington: 1895-1896), pp. 254ff.

was not Napoleonic, nor European at all except in its success. It possessed all the characteristics of good tactics, and it had originality. Its fluid, mobile flanks were not only his own idea but are worthy of imitation. In all, it was a parallel invention of the great fools-mate which has been successful against incompetent commanders from the Bronze Age to the Battle of Tannenberg.

> Either before or just after this sprinkling, the men were drawn up in a semicircle and instructed by the officer in supreme command as to the routes to be taken, what regiments were to form the right horn, and what the left (of the crescent). Then the warriors, once more reminded of their challenge and exhorted through praise of departed kings, dashed forward to the attack. The Zulus attacked in the form of an *umkhumbi*, or semicircle, usually making a feint with one horn, while the other, concealed in the bush and grass, swept around to surround the enemy. The 'chest,' consisting of the greatest number of men, and also the most experienced [for the 'black' (young)] regiments always form the horns, now advance and tried to crush the enemy. Behind them was a large force which came to their aid when the army was in difficulty, or joined in the pursuit of the enemy, while the commanding officer and staff took up their positions on high ground to watch and issue directions, which were delivered by runners.[27]

This description of a Zulu action leaves one amazed at its modernity. It was realized that the main effort would be to the fore, and the strongest and oldest regiments were entrusted with the job of being "chest," or the widest and central part of the crescent's belly. The enveloping movement was extremely clever and very mobile. The young men were assigned to that job.

The Zulu formation was primarily an offensive device. The principles of cooperation, of the combined, planned employment of all forces obviously working in concerted effort were carefully observed. The commander was able to concentrate his forces at the critical point because he had planned this beforehand. The integrity of tactical units was well observed. The withholding of the reserve is an example of the economy of force. Fire and movement were used, but the aggressive movement was stressed and fire was only incidental. The plan, of course, had to be altered for every engagement, but it so followed a customary pattern that an able enemy commander could predict it. But how much more so is this true of all other nonliterate plans! They were so stereotyped that they should have deceived no one.

---

[27] Krige, *op. cit.*, p. 275.

The principle of surprise was observed by masking part of the enveloping force by utilization of the terrain. That the Zulu used correct formations for the job at hand is proven by their mastery of the region. It was a mobile formation, acting forcibly and with dispatch. Intelligence had been gathered ahead of time so that the commander knew what he was doing. As for exploitation, the Zulu did that in a most thoroughgoing manner, as noted elsewhere. Other African kingdoms achieved considerable tactical success, but the Zulu went as far as nonliterate man could.

Almost all Eurasiatic peoples used some kind of plans which could be recommended today. Even some of the simplest Siberian tribes could make rudimentary ones and carry them out. Bogaraz, for example, records an action between the Siberian Chuckchee and the Eskimo on the American side of the Bering Strait. A large party from Asia landed on St. Lawrence Island under the cover of fog. The largest portion moved around the Eskimo rear. A small pivot of maneuver moved cautiously forward to engage and immobilize the enemy. Fog lent almost complete surprise. The blow from the rear was a telling one and the islanders lost their lives and women.[28]

In general one might say that the plans of primitive war had to be simple since they had to be standardized. This standardization was too weak to tolerate any real thought. Each man was too much his own general, certainly in America. Any violation of the simple patterns of battle would have been resented as much by friend as by foe.

[28] Bogoraz, *op. cit.*, pp. 656f.

Part II

The Concepts of Primitive War

Chapter 8

The Socio-Psychological Motives

Why do men go to war? This plain question has no plain answer, for no single thread runs through all wars. Man's motivation for every simple act is complex, so how shall it be outlined for war, which is not a simple activity? Every war is fought for more than one motive, spurious or real, appreciated or unrealized. Every individual warrior joins the colors for more than one reason. It is characteristic of successful social institutions to have a bundle of functions, as every human activity has a bundle of utilities. War is an institutionalized behavior pattern even among nonliterate men, and the basic function of every social institution is the maintenance of the psycho-physical equilibrium of its clientele considered as individual persons, and the balance of those persons within the social system. In brief, the primary function of a social institution is the maintenance or restoration of a feeling of well-being in persons and their groups.

A very profound motive for going to war is to resolve life's tensions, to escape from unhappiness caused by frustration in other realms of existence. War is one of the most effective devices ever invented for this cathartic purpose. Life at best is full of frustration, thwarted ambitions, unfulfilled wishes—all of the sorrows and disappointments with which humanity is only too familiar. People become involved in personal dislikes which develop into hatreds, often irrational ones. Now in civilized groups, and even more so in nonliterate ones above the simplest individual food-gathering horizons, the release of these hatreds toward members of the we-group is intolerable. To be sure, personal feud has been very common among loosely knit nonliterate groups and, until recently, in isolated areas of civilization. Nevertheless, the maiming and destruction of personal foes within the group interferes with the efficient functioning of the group, weakens the front against the common enemy, and reduces the economic productiveness of the workers in a society perhaps already underpopulated.

The poor hygiene and obstetrics of nonliterate groups make the excess of male births over deaths too small to waste effective population by feud, even in those areas where the vendetta is tolerated. Thus, if this amassed hate can be transferred or sublimated from socially undesirable expenditure on the we-group and wreaked with little or no control upon the out-group enemy, then war, bloody or otherwise, has served a great socio-psychological utility, whether perceived or not.

Man's balked wishes and denied ambitions in time tie him into tight knots of frustration, crying for release. War is one such release. It allows desires disapproved within the group to find an approved outlet. The piping times of peace are often boresome except for the very fortunate. *Ennui* seems to be a price of domestication, and man, the self-domesticated primate, suffers from it more severely than any other creature. The orderly processes of group living, with their constant repetition of all-too-familiar activities, frustrate the universal wish for release from boredom in new experiences. By contrast, war is the most exciting exercise in the world. The real struggle of fighting is more thrilling than the mock opposition of games; the real man-hunt is incomparably more stimulating than the slaughter of animals. War is the great trigger-release of pent-up emotions, and it is apparent that more than one tribe has realized this. The Winnebago, for example, recognized that war affords an excellent release when the load of sorrow becomes too great to be borne.[1]

Many tribes, indeed, were more realistic in conceiving of war as a flight-from-grief device than we are. Fletcher and La Flesche mention the Omaha as having recognized it in general, and particularly for a father grief-stricken at the death of a child. In addition, the spirit of the man slain by the Omaha father would act as a guide for the child in the next world.[2] It is a well-recorded fact that in some Plains tribes a man through grief or disappointment would deliberately seek military death, would "give his body to the enemy." One could join the Crazy Dog Society, the members of which association often considered their bodies ceremonially votive to enemy weapons.

The forms which sexual jealousy and disappointment take vary tremendously in the cultures of the world; only their universality seems to be constant. War throughout the ages has been a method whereby the jilted, the snubbed, and the cuckolded could obtain release and restoration of self-respect. Miss Densmore says that a Teton Sioux,

[1] Fletcher and La Flesche, *op. cit.*, p. 594.

[2] *Ibid.*

upon being teased about his girl's infidelity, would go to war even though he knew the report to be false, and even though he was in no mood to fight. Before the fight he asked his comrades to tell the girl that he hoped he would be killed.[3]

A Flathead husband had definite rights to wound or kill both his adulterous wife and her lover if he caught them *in flagrante.* If he could not do this, but still had reasonably certain knowledge of his betrayal, he could go against the enemy and strive to count *coup.* Should he be successful, he would ride into camp singing his war song. He would shoot an arrow into the *tipi* of his persecutor, preferably at the place where the cord bound the poles together, thus making it fall down. He could shoot one of his rival's finest horses, and the seducer could do nothing about it. To be sure, the husband had to have grounds for his suspicion. If the suspected man were innocent, he would resent these acts as unwarranted aggression and take steps to obtain revenge. But if in the right, the husband could thus destroy property belonging to his wife's lover just as often as he could manage to count *coup.*[4]

Having conquered an enemy, there are no reasons why nonliterate tribes should have then indulged in gloating, orgiastic victory dances, except that tensions were thereby released. Such victory, scalp, and other dances afforded opportunity to tribes righteously to vent all possible spleen against a defeated foe, his scalp, one of his captive members, and his very name, regardless of the source of the ill-humor. Victory has ever been strong medicine. The victory dance restored the equilibrium of the ante-bellum frustrations and those caused by the war as well. They were also a necessary rite of passage indicating the return to normality of statuses which had been seriously disturbed by the war.

Perhaps the weakest expression of victory gloating was to be found among the simpler California tribes. For instance, the Yurok were absolutely subtactical and to all intents a warless people. Their scuffling amounted to no more than feuds wherein little blood was shed. They had practically no sense of victory. When a feud was closed, the warriors of *each* side danced in opposing lines, fully armed, while the compensation money was magically being purified of the ill-will between the rows. There was no true victory dance, for the dance

[3] Densmore, *Teton Sioux Music,* p. 357.

[4] Turney-High, *The Flathead Indians of Montana,* pp. 95f.

after victory was participated in by both combatant parties. Such practices were common to several California tribes.[5] The more military Maidu frankly tortured prisoners after victory in gloating vengeance, but lacked the refinement of the Northeast Woodland in such matters. The simple Pima farmers of the Southwest were openly orgiastic in their victory celebrations, reportedly much to the disgust of their chiefs. The leaders thought the death of an enemy a sufficient crime against humanity without the riotousness of a disorderly dance which was wasteful of goods and food. Their disapproval was contrary to accepted behavior patterns, however, and they could only express their opposition verbally.[6]

Such gloat-dances were not absent from the more advanced American Indians. An anonymous relation quoted by Swanton says that the Choctaw had orgiastic dances after victory wherein little sons and nephews were given portions of fresh scalps so that they, too, might gloat.[7] Such a practice must have been effective in conditioning the children to the war pattern. The neighboring Creek set legs, arms, and scalps taken from the enemy on poles with great ceremony, after which the shamans cursed the foe with a "thousand imprecations."[8]

Such tension-release dances have not been confined to native America. They have been a complicated and important feature in the life of almost every African tribe, and have actually formed one of the high arts of Polynesia.

The use of fighting and its accompaniments for tension-release has been barely mentioned by reporters on Greco-Roman civilization, but it took place nevertheless. Our barbarian ancestors, however, knew it well. They did not possess the artistic and recreational outlets that we have. Their lot was hard, and their material culture was inadequate for the fulfillment of man's basic needs. War offered them a means of sublimating their blocked wishes. They must have been bored much of the time when at peace.

Some of the passages in Caesar might be interpreted as illustrating the tension-release motivation in barbarian fighting. Certainly the Norse poems given the berserker a very prominent place. This man, as heedless of danger as a member of a Plains military no-retreat so-

[5] Kroeber, *op. cit.*, p. 50.

[6] Russell, *op. cit.*, p. 205.

[7] Swanton, *Source Material for the Social and Ceremonial Life of the Choctaw Indians*, p. 169.

[8] Swanton, *Early History of the Creek Indians and Their Neighbors*, p. 378.

ciety, or as a Malay who has run amok, had all but vowed his body to the enemy, for he sought danger at every turn.

Civilized warriors have also fought for glory. Psychologists and psychiatrists have no more than scratched the surface of man's search for prestige and ego-expansion. We know the wish for recognition is strong, and that its fulfillment will be sought in whatever field of endeavor society permits. Certainly war has been a convenient device for this type of wish fulfillment.

Denig reported that he was "acquainted with no (Assiniboin) Indian who has risen to distinction without success in war being the principal cause of his advancement."[9] Success in hunting, religion, generosity, and all else were honorable, but they were only garnishes to the fount of honor. The Assiniboin were simple Plains hunters, but such attitudes were just as common among the more cultivated southeasterners. Swanton says that a Creek might be famous for oratory, stoicism under trial, or wisdom in council, but if he had not been on a war party he bore no title and was classified as a boy.[10] Young men performed the menial labor, were submitted to many indignities, and were excluded from the councils of manhood until they had performed a warlike exploit.

Man's desire for emulation and invidious comparison has been noted by many writers. Most Indian cultures north of the Rio Grande contained economic and social organizations so weak that war was the chief means whereby an ambitious man could obtain the privilege of looking with contempt upon some and being looked up to by others. The chief type of social stratification in America, then, was a military aristocracy into which anyone could be inducted upon performing certain specific deeds. It could hardly have been otherwise. Fame and glory were motives for living greater than life itself. An Iowa father might say to a son, "Go out and die so that I may hear of you to the end of my days. Increase your name. If you are shot in the back and fall on your face I'll be ashamed, but if you are wounded in the front and fall on your back I'll be proud."[11]

Such honors were not all empty ones. A man on the Plains could not be deemed a chief until he had acquired a certain number of standardized war-honors. The term "chief" among the Plainsmen and

---

[9] Denig, *op. cit.*, p. 525.

[10] Swanton, "Creek Social Organization and Uses," p. 366.

[11] Skinner, *Societies of the Iowa, Kansa, and Ponca Indians*, p. 686.

many tribes of the Plateau simply indicated such war-honors, for their chieftains were ordinarily without authority.

Just after he had created the Legion of Honor, Napoleon was chided by one of his generals with the words, "How could you be interested in such a toy!" The rising dictator replied, "Men can be controlled with toys." The appeal of an especial honorific military costume is very strong. The privileges of costume and face painting have been so extensively dealt with in the literature that they will only be mentioned here. The Sauk and Fox allowed even the grave of the valiant dead to be decorated with poles signifying the number of the enemy he had killed and scalped.[12] The very brave Kansa, Osage, and neighbors were allowed to tattoo their breasts and be one of the two splendid bodyguards of the chief. Even the less brave but fairly successful warriors among them were exempt from all kinds of vengeance, could be present at all parties the chief gave, could whip ungrateful guests, and were the camp, hunting, and ceremonial police. *Coup*-counters among the Crow and neighbors could paint their tents with representations of their valor, could use an especial interior drape within, and wore distinguishing costumes, such as ermine tails on their shirts. While the love of personal display on the Plains could be satisfied only through war, military honors were sometimes more solid. Members of the war societies and those entitled to wear the war-bonnet among the Oglala Sioux could walk into any tent where food was being cooked, blow the whistle of the war society, and appropriate any or all of the meat.[13] There were many public offices to which a man could not aspire until he had counted one or more *coups*.

Notable among such political honors was membership in the Plains war fraternities. In the west, where the chieftainship was particularly weak, these associations were the only political devices other than the pressure of custom and the joking-relationship which kept the camp in order. They were the police, and their power over offenders was almost unlimited. On the eastern Plains the war societies were the administrators of the chiefly and tribal decisions, and were composed of men of great valor and honor. Among the Ojibway and others they were exempt from all labor. They were exempt from blood vengeance and could marry immediately after any successful

12 Bushnell, *op. cit.*, pp. 13ff.

13 Wissler, *Societies and Ceremonial Associations of the Oglala Division of the Teton-Dakota*, pp. 15f.

war party regardless of the number of wives already espoused.[14] To be sure, they had many dangerous duties. The *akicita* societies often could not retreat before an enemy, and it was not always safe to serve as tribal executioner.

The whole complex of Plains war honors, or *coup*, formed one of the most interesting social traits in all nonliterate life. Their complexity would make their discussion too lengthy for this work, and they have been excellently reported elsewhere. The point to be emphasized here is that these honors were for the most part individual, depending upon personal valor and accomplishment rather than on group military success. Certainly the brave individual is honored in modern armies, but the winning of the war is the primary object of civilized states. Among almost all American Indians, by contrast, war existed to bring glory to the individual, and since war was relatively safe, everyone was happy even though few tactical, strategic, and economic advantages for a whole people were obtained. One might observe that almost the same remarks could be made of the knightly *coup*-counters of our mediaeval period, and with the same impermanent results. The modern attitude of the Ojibway wherein "the leader of a war party gets all the credit if it is successful," was extremely rare in primitive war.[15]

The result of such a war motive, the preening of the adult male, was disastrous for the military efficiency of the American Indian, and caused a state of tactical confusion and military incompetence comparable to that of the European early mediaeval period. Aside from a few negritic tribes in Africa, the individualistic head-hunters of Indonesia, and the lowest of the Melanesian societies, the American Indian outside the areas of intense cultivation and state-building stood at the bottom. He would have been no match for most African tribes, while the Polynesians would have slaughtered him with as much efficiency and probably more dispatch than the whites did. His prime motive was individual glory, which made disciplined, planned teamwork impossible. It obviated protracted campaigning. The honor went to the individual, not the village, band, or nation. It tended to make fighting the work of assembled individual champions. While it is too much to say that war based on individual bids for role, status, and recognition was the only thing which prevented most American

[14] Skinner, *Political Organization, Cults, and Ceremonies of the Plains-Ojibway and Plains-Cree Indians*, pp. 490ff.

[15] *Ibid.*, p. 491.

Indians from becoming soldiers, certainly no truly military people ever rose who were burdened with such tactical and organizational ineptitude.

It is not implied that Africa was free from such practices. There was no real difference between the satisfaction of the basic wishes through military media in Africa and America. The human ego needs puffing up, and there is always enough atmosphere of this kind in war. It is granted that all men enjoy renown. The Indian was only more childish than most in his admission of that fact. It would take a large volume, however, to describe in detail the victory dancing, group and individual gloating of the militarily efficient Zulu.[16] Most of it was no more than the familiar *coup*-counting in Bantu. Power and wealth can always belong to those who can capitalize on human vanity, a fact which the Zulu princes understood well. The real difference between the American and the African was the former's fatal emphasis on the individual.

War contributed to the determination of role and status also in Oceania. The method of becoming a *tsunaum* (chief) in the Solomons by raiding for war-honors was reminiscent of the *coup*-counting of the American Great Plains. Since the Polynesian social system had developed a nobility based on divine descent, individual war-boasting could not take paramount place, although it was very important. Individual honor was the basis of Polynesian beheading. Brown said that he had seen successful warriors dance in the public square before the chief, each bringing his captive head to throw before the prince with appropriate remarks of self-praise. The warrior would juggle his war-club ceremoniously and receive the chief's thanks and the crowd's acclamation. Heads were not ordinarily kept as permanent trophies, as in Melanesia. Sometimes the relatives of the slain were allowed to take them away after they had served as *coup*-counters. The chief cause of war in Samoa lay in some disparaging language or behavior towards a chief, or some rival claim to his honor, so it behooved him to praise his protectors. The African king of Dahomey held a similar levee wherein he publicly praised and rewarded victorious officers.[17] So did the kings of mediaeval France.

The honor motive and ideal in Samoa was strikingly similar to that of the mediaeval military gentleman. Buck reports that jealousy for

---

[16] Krige, *op. cit.*, pp. 275ff.

[17] Herskovits, *op. cit.*, II, pp. 89ff.

honor also was a powerful cause of war among the Mangaian Polynesians.

This personal bumptiousness characterized many of our barbarian ancestors—the same prestige-seeking through war so often observed elsewhere. The satisfaction of wishes for prestige, the road to glory lay in war, but there was also the desire for gain which impelled Germanic youth to enroll in someone else's war as proto-mercenaries. Caesar's Gallic war is, for the first part at least, all but monopolized with a discussion of economic war waged by land-hungry tribes rather than a search for prestige. This contrast will be discussed in the next chapter.

The honor motive is not as apparent in the literature on Eurasia as it is elsewhere, but it does appear. Scythian behavior, for example, resembled a Crow *coup*-counting council. The governor of each district held an annual wine feast at which all Scythian men who had slain a foe during the year dipped into the chief's bowl. Those who had killed several could bring two cups and drink from both. Those who had killed no one had to sit aloof in disgrace.[18]

Tacitus reported *coup*-counting among the able Chatti, who were so military that they went forth to war and not to battle. Their youths did not shave or cut their hair until they had killed an enemy, so cowards and weaklings remained unkempt always. At a Chattian's first killing he stood above his spoil and shaved, advertising that he was now worthy of his kin and country and had paid for his birth-pangs. The elite warriors wore iron rings on their fingers, which were otherwise badges of shame, symbolizing slavery's chains. This was, of course, a boast of pride that they could afford to wear a servile badge without disgrace. This elite band owned no property and did no work, always knowing that they would be welcome to anybody's food, which they wasted without regard for their host's welfare.[19] Such behavior was a clear parallel to that of a Plains military association.

Revenge is so consistently reported as one of the principal causes of war that it requires detailed analysis. Why should the human personality yearn to compensate for its humiliation in the blood of enemies? The tension-release motive plays a part here: Revenge loosens the taut feeling caused by the slaying or despoiling of one's self, clan, tribe, nation. Even the hope for revenge helps the humiliated human

[18] Herodotus, *op. cit.*, iv.
[19] Tacitus, *Germania*, 30.

to bear up, enables him to continue to function in a socially unfavorable environment. Fray Camposano wrote of the Mojos of southwestern Amazonia to Philip II of Spain that, "The most valiant were the most respected and their patience under injuries was only dissimulation for subsequent vengeance."[20] Revenge, or the hope of revenge, restores the deflated ego, and is a conflict motive with which mankind must reckon with universally.

The revenge motive has been strong in African war, and has always been more marked among the simpler people socially organized on a sib basis than in areas with strong over-all tribes. The chief among such folk has never been able to assert the national or political interest over that of the clan, hence the vendetta has been the cause of much bloodshed in such simple societies.[21] The loose organization of the Nigerian tribes, for example, probably made revenge their paramount military motive, although they recognized enough social authority to put this on a somewhat broader tribal basis than would the Bushman or Hottentot. Yet the Ibo did not fight for economic reasons but for noneconomic reprisal, so war with them was more a penal than a military measure. In the absence of strong central authority, every individual and kin group had to be its own court and executioner in order to survive.[22]

This universal method of wiping stains from the individual or collective mirrored self has been apparent in both Melanesia and Polynesia. It was not as strong in the well-knit Polynesian societies as elsewhere, for vengefulness has always been more productive of feud and vendetta among peoples with strong sibs and loose over-all societies. But nations can suffer mass humiliation and have sensitive honors as well as families. The primacy of the revenge motive, however, seems to retard the development of real war and eventually becomes a nuisance to its practitioners. It is reported that the Maori welcomed the white prohibition of revenge warfare.

The vengeance motive appears to have been more often mixed with others in Melanesia than in Africa and America. The Kiwai of Papua fought to take heads in vengeance for enemy depredation, to deter him from further hostility, and to acquire skulls to enhance the prestige of individuals.[23] The Solomon Islanders made war because

---

[20] Church, *op. cit.*, p. 104.
[21] Meek, *op. cit.*, pp. 240ff.
[22] *Ibid.*, p. 7.
[23] Landtman, pp. 240ff.

an outsider spoke disparagingly of, or cursed, their chief or his chiefly symbols; because a foreign chief injured them; because of theft of pigs, canoes, or women; because someone had illicit intercourse with a chief's wife or daughter, or rejoiced in an unseemly manner over their misfortunes.[24] But battle has also been sought in honor of a new house for the chief or the assembly, the launching of a large canoe, the death of a chiefly personage, or the birth of a son.[25]

The vengeance motive was important in Eurasia, but it does not seem to have as much relation to the rest of the culture as noticed in the Americas, Africa, and Oceania. After having observed the pattern elsewhere, one would expect the revenge motive to be strong in Siberia where the social system did not develop strong groups beyond clans. The lack of vital tribal spirit made interclan fights for revenge more penal in quality than military. The Chuckchee held the whole clan of a murderer responsible for the blood of a fellow, and demanded compensation. If this was refused, a hereditary blood feud might spring up between clans.[26] The Gilyak, too, held an offender's clan responsible. This was very serious, since an unavenged soul could not enter a desirable afterlife. For similar reasons, the clan's vengeance was visited upon animals. The life of a clansman at the claws of a bear had to be expiated with the death of a bear, any bear. The obligation of vendetta existed for three generations, during which time each clan submitted to a type of martial law until the affair was settled. This might be quickly done if the clans were neighbors. If they lived at a distance "a military expedition on a small scale is arranged."[27]

In Britain vengeance was even more keen if on a more tribal scale. Widsith often sang of the gold-adorned chiefs seeking "vengeance for their warriors and their wives."[28] In old Ireland the king of Ulster fought to punish the Connaught clansmen "who dared to take spoil from the north."

It has often been said that men fight for booty and beauty. The economic motive will be analyzed in the next chapter, while the net which has long enmeshed Mars and Venus will be discussed at this point.

---

[24] Brown, *op. cit.*, pp. 150f.
[25] *Ibid.*, p. 156.
[26] Bogoraz, *op. cit.*, pp. 659-661.
[27] Czaplicka, *op. cit.*, pp. 61-70.
[28] Widsith, in Cook and Tinker, *op. cit.*, lines 35-45.

If it is conceded that the reflection of the self in the mirror of the general community is important enough to impel a man to risk his life, the prestige mirror of Aphrodite has even more emotional import. Sex is an important consideration in work, play, eloquence, or war. Whatever the ethos of the group, prestige-conferring activity is sought avidly by the male that his glory may shine in the eyes of his own and other men's women. Much has been written about the role of women in war, and most of it is too fantastic for review. But war is an important complex in the cultures of most societies, and women form too large a proportion of any populations to be left out of the discussion.

Without commenting upon the importance of women in the war complexes of civilized societies, it is most obvious that they have always had a role, although a subordinate one, in the fighting of nonliterate groups. They were conditioned to their roles in the tribal war just as they were conditioned to the rest of the culture.

Feminine social pressure often influenced the nonliterate warrior to take up arms in a quarrel which might or might not be his own. In the light of such facts, the opinion that women inherently hate war is not borne out by the facts. Why should they?

In an unsuccessful war of defense women may suffer as much as combatants, but women have been, are, and so far as anyone can see, will be essentially civilians. But women are just as enthusiastic for aggressive war as their men, leaving civilized people out of the discussion; this is testified in hundreds of pages of field reports. If riches infallibly get social adulation, men try for that with the urging of their women. So with piety, and all the other socially desirable traits. If the patterns of culture emphasize military preeminence, the women are not far behind urging the male to fight.

Let us view the opening of hostilities in America. When the recruiting season opened, women who had lost sons, husbands, or other relatives were very apt to visit the lodge of any distinguished warrior and urge him to wipe away their tears with enemy blood. Teit remarked that when a Flathead war party was announced by proper authority, the band sang and beat on buffalo hides before the lodges of warriors, urging them to enlist after the common western method. Those who joined up rode around the camp circle all night singing, as more and more recruits joined the procession from time to time. The women followed the horsed procession, singing and urging the men to volunteer.[29] It has been observed elsewhere that membership in the Plains military societies carried with it many dangerous obligations as well as privileges. To hold the office of Lance Bearer in the Kit-Fox Society of the Oglala Sioux meant almost certain death. When a candidate for this office had been chosen the women stood outside the lodge and cheered while the members sang the ritual within.[30]

The Arikara were a rather peaceful group of farmers on the margins of the Plains whose women, could be expected to love peace, if any could. Instead, they played an important part during the two-day war preparatory ceremonial. The musicians in this hate-raising dance for recruits were men, but the dancers were appropriately feminine.[31] They dressed in their husbands' clothes and danced round and round in a circle. From time to time an Arikara woman would step into the circle and harangue the five to six hundred persons in the great lodge about her husband's valor in order to increase that of the recruits. During the preparatory dance of the simpler Comanche, the instrumental music was supplied by beating a bison hide. Men held up its one side while women held up the other.[32] Women have usually played a part in the recruiting and preparational activities of nonliterate societies, and their influence upon the prospective combatants has undoubtedly been great. Women shone in the reflected glory of their men, often being allowed, as among the Teton, to wear or carry distinguishing ornaments indicative of their husband's success.[33]

It was very common in America for women to accompany a departing war party for some distance to encourage the men. The wives and mothers of Ojibway men slain by the Sioux got the captured scalps, and the party of departing warriors was led from the camp by women either afoot or in canoes.[34]

---

[29] Teit, James A., "Salishan Tribes of the Western Plateau," edited by Franz Boas, *Annual Report 45*, Bureau of American Ethnology, Washington: 1927-1928, *passim*.

[30] Wissler, *Societies and Ceremonial Associations of the Oglala Division of the Teton-Dakota*, pp. 15f.

[31] Lowie, *Societies of the Arikara Indians, passim.*

[32] Lowie, *Dances and Societies of the Plains Shoshone, passim.*

[33] Wissler, *Societies and Ceremonial Associations of the Oglala Division of the Teton-Dakota*, p. 17.

[34] Skinner, *Political Organization, Cults, and Ceremonies of the Plains-Ojibway and Plains-Cree Indians*, pp. 490f.

Although not typical of America, among some tribes a number of women actually accompanied a war party, usually performing some supply function. The Shasta women, who also danced on the flanks during the war dance, went with the warriors to cook and carry supplies.[35] A woman who had lost a relative to the enemy went with an Hidatsa party to provide cooking, mending, and encouragement. She received a scalp if they took one, which she carried in the subsequent victory dance.[36] The peaceful Pima always took one or two women along in their revenge expeditions against the predatory Apache, always females who had lost relatives to the ferocious foe.[37] Bossu said that Choctaw women might venture to help their husbands even in the field if they were fond of them. So, too, in Guiana the women kept by their husbands' sides and collected the spent arrows for them, although taking no part in the actual fighting.[38]

Women who actually fought have been authentically reported, but they were as rare in fact as the legend of them is extensive. Female marching clubs with war insignia were well-known, but such battalions were not tactically operational. The Great Plains had many harmless women's associations patterned after the male war fraternities. To be sure, in times of grave danger and defeat, women in all places have been known to defend themselves and their own as best they could, but every warrior, primitive or civilized, has known that women are essentially unfitted for the hardships of service. The Britons under Boadicea were conquered, and that may be accepted as the symbol for the whole idea.

On the other hand, it should be noted that a woman could take the field, count the same standardized *coups,* and thereby be admitted into the police-soldier *okitcita* lodge of the Plains Ojibway.[39] Even then she did not wear the *okitcita* feather, which a relative wore for her, although she had all the other privileges. And it should be recalled that the Amazon river was named for the fierce South American women. The Carib considered fighting the characteristic of manhood, but their enemies and victims, the Tapuya, allowed women to fight alongside their men. One supposes that the observation that the

[35] Kroeber, *op. cit.,* p. 298.

[36] Densmore, *Mandan and Hidatsa Music,* p. 145.

[37] Russell, *op. cit.,* p. 201.

[38] Roth, *op. cit.,* ch. 28, *passim,* especially p. 764.

[39] Skinner, *Political Organization, Cults, and Ceremonies of the Plains-Ojibway and Plains-Cree Indians,* pp. 490f.

Carib normally defeated the Tapyua has no bearing on the discussion.[40] Abbe Durand says the women of the South American "Juruas" fought savagely side by side with their men. Nevertheless, only in Africa were there real female fighters in the male sense.[41]

The Kiowa regarded their women highly, and a warrior sought praise and honor from the females. One of the two important women's associations was the Old Woman Society, composed of old or middle-aged women. A man starting forth to war would always pray to the Old Women, promising them a feast upon his victorious return. If success followed him, he would accost them in session upon his return, light a pipe, and present it to each member in turn that she might smoke it. The warriors then brought water for the sisterhood who drank and prayed again for their welfare. At length the leader of the war party arose and told of his deeds. Then one of the society's officers cut a piece of meat and buried it while praying. And so she did with a morsel of each type of food served.[42].

When the Tlingit warriors of the North Pacific Coast departed for battle in their canoes, their wives gave them little wooden images. Once in their canoes, the men threw these back to their wives. If a wife failed to catch the image, her husband would presumably die in battle. The wife of the leader had to have stones tied about her blanket, just like her husband had while on the expedition. She dressed her wooden image like her spouse. She also provided herself with a long board which she called her "canoe," causing the wives of the other warriors to sit with her thereon from time to time and pretend they were on the expedition. They took great care that the board did not tip over lest the real war canoe meet the same disaster. They ate from the same dishes which were customarily used by the warriors.[43] Jibaro women met every night during the absence of a party to dance and chant incantations to the time of rattles and snail shells. Thus their men were enabled to shed the enemy's weapons, to prevent surprise by him, and to avoid his vengeance for the defeat inflicted upon him.[44] Likewise the Chirguano women of the Grand

[40] Church, *op. cit.*, pp. 102f.

[41] Smith, Edwin, W., *The Golden Stool* (London: Holborn House, 1926), *passim.*

[42] Lowie, *Societies of the Kiowa, passim.*

[43] Swanton, "Social Conditions, Beliefs, and Linguistic Relationships of the Tlingit Indians," pp. 407f.

[44] Karsten, *op. cit.*, p. 24.

Chaco often marched in procession with bodies bent and singing mournful songs during the absence of the war party.[45]

It will be seen later that the wives and daughters of the Jibaro, having ceremonially participated in the war, fell under the same blood uncleanness as their victorious men, and had to undergo the same tabus and lustration. Therefore it is not surprising in the light of this feminine magical power that tribes whose patterns were sufficiently complex to contain true divinities often had female war goddesses and valkyrs. When the Hopi of Powamu worshiped the war gods, a *katcina* appeared in the guise of a warrior maid.[46] If this sort of morale-stimulating behavior had military value, and it has, it might be said that women often did perform a tactical function.

Women were the leaders at the victory rituals. If they went forth ahead of the departing warriors for a space, they also went forth to meet them when they returned victorious, for their real job began then. When the Plains-Ojibway warriors returned with honor, they blackened their faces and made signals. Women came out to meet them, gave them presents, and in return got the precious scalps with which they would soon dance.[47] Almost the same trait has been observed among the distant Papago of the Southwest.[48]

The victory dance, called by many names in various tribes and containing many and diverse features and complexities, always contained this one feature throughout America wherever it was held. Women took at least equal part with the men, and generally they were the primary actresses within it. Examples could be cited at great length, but the following will suffice.

The ritual among the Assiniboin was characterized by a chorus of women who sang in praise of war and warriors, although they did not especially eulogize the present victors.[49] The first ceremony of the Omaha was principally a scalp dance by the women. They did all the dancing, the men merely providing the music. The men had their own dance later.[50] The role of American women in victory was exemplified by the simple Wind River Shoshone. Three dances were

[45] Church, *op. cit.*, pp. 110f.
[46] Fewkes, *op. cit.*, p. 74.
[47] Skinner, *Political Organization, Cults, and Ceremonies of the Plains-Ojibway and Plains-Cree Indians*, pp. 490f.
[48] Densmore, *Papago Music*, p. 187.
[49] Lowie, *The Assiniboine*, pp. 90f.
[50] Dorsey, "Omaha Sociology," p. 330.

held when one of the enemy had been killed. The first was one in which the women danced with the scalps on poles. In the second dance the men took their best horses, tied up their tails and, taking the women on behind them, rode about the camp singing war songs, this time the men holding the scalp poles. This ceremony was succeeded by a dance on foot. Each man stood between two women whom he embraced in the circle which was formed. The dance was clockwise to slow drumming and song. This was followed by another dance in which young people alone participated. The men stood in a row, each facing a woman in an opposing line. The women now walked backward, followed by the men. A man would then choose a woman and bring her over to his side, as also women would choose men and bring them to their row. The women would then walk backward pursued by the men, and so on until the figure was stopped by the chief.[51]

The early settlers were often impressed with the ferocity of Indian women, as European colonials have been both in Africa and Asia. Women had an important emotional role to play in war. Because of the very high place of women in the social organizations of many American peoples, this ferocity, while not universal by any means, is not surprising. Among the well-organized peoples of the North and Southeast Woodlands the power of the women over captives was quite marked. Mooney says that by tradition the Cherokee had a body of female dignitaries called the War Women or Pretty Women who had the power to decide the fate of captives, and who might have had the power of declaring war and peace, as among the Iroquois. This power of the Iroquois matrons is well attested. A captive under this system was an enemy until he had been adopted, which meant that some clan or family was willing to receive him. Since kinship among these people was counted on the female side, such questions of mercy and adoption naturally fell to the women.[52]

Mooney surmised that such customs would mitigate the severity of war, but this should mislead no one. The institution he describes resembled little the evils of war softened by the feminine touch. This touch was too often applied with a hot coal. Our forefathers on the continent were not all liars, granted a certain amount of exaggeration and romance. It is admitted such women had the power to spare or condemn the captive, and condemned they often were, for there is no evidence of an innate desire of American Indian women to dull the

[51] Lowie, *Dances and Societies of the Plains Shoshone,* pp. 650f.
[52] Mooney, *Myths of the Cherokee,* p. 489.

bite of war. The Omaha women mutilated the bodies of the fallen,[53] while some of the Upper Dakota allowed their women to torture prisoners to death. Such examples could be cited at length. Women reserved their role as the conservers of life to the we-group. They had been conditioned as children to war psychology just as had the men. They were also denied the excitement of actual fighting. They were the ones who lost their inestimable economic male providers to the enemy; it was they who had been deprived of their affectional partners through his deeds. If they were thoroughly angry about it, one need not be surprised.

Sexual intercourse in connection with war was apparently not as common in America as in Africa. An example of the essential fear of sex at such a crisis is found among the Iowa. In contrast with the preparation ceremonies of some tribes, an Iowa woman was not allowed to attend the sacred ceremonies to the war bundles before the departure. Neither could a warrior have intercourse during the four days needed to purify himself in the preparatory sweat bath.[54] The Kutenai also had this fear of sex during war.[55] Like the Kutenai, the Mojos of southwest Amazonia fasted and were sexually temperate for a long time before war in order to attain invincibility. Compare this with the Hindu attitude which will be described later.[56]

Yet war was oftener a signal in America for more license than abstention. The girls of an Assiniboin camp fell easy prey to the seductions of the young victors.[57] It was very easy for a young Crow who had just counted *coup* not only to have an affair with one of the young girls but with almost any married woman. It was rather expected that under certain conditions a successful warrior could do so even with the husband's disgruntled knowledge. It was the common Crow custom for warriors gathered around the campfire of a war party to boast of their adulteries. Should the cuckolded husband later hear of the boast, or even be present to hear it first hand, there was nothing he could do but divorce his wife, which was allowed him even though she had been faithful. It is well reported that a young man could often dispense with any go-between, his or the girl's parents' objection, and marry at once after counting *coup*. Among the Flathead it was

[53] Dorsey, "Omaha Sociology," pp. 312f.
[54] Skinner, *Societies of the Iowa, Kansa, and Ponca Indians*, p. 686.
[55] Turney-High, *Ethnography of the Kutenai*, p. 127.
[56] Church, *op. cit.*, p. 103.
[57] Denig, *op. cit.*, p. 558 and *passim*.

seldom that a youth who had counted *coup* would be refused by any girl's parents, even though they might have objected before. Their reasoning in this matter was sound. A man who had counted *coup* used the same skill, daring, and vigor needed to be a great hunter and therefore a good provider. According to their thinking, a man who was intelligent, brave, and skilful, was a good warrior; he was therefore a good hunter and provider, and was a desirable son-in-law in a perfectly logical sequence.[58]

America and Africa observed the sex motive quite differently. African men did not enlist because the women performed some dance or other, or expected them to go out and get killed. The expectation was the chief's. Women did not commonly wear some special costume simply because their husbands were man-killers. War success was not the ordinary prerequisite to marriage. True, Chaka always promised his soldiers vast sexual joys as soon as they should conquer the whole world, but he was loath to release an able warrior from his celibate garrisons. The fact is that women in Africa generally occupied an humbler social position than they did in America as a whole. Instead of finding themselves important in the military complex, they were something in the way and to be feared. This is not saying, however, that women had no part in the causation of African war.

Women were not needed to bolster up Zulu courage, but they took their toll of cowards. Girls sometimes disrobed in the presence of a cowardly fiance to shame him, afterwards breaking the engagement.[59] The female war dance before the dispatch of the war party was rare in Africa. However, one has been reported in Ashanti where only women with participating husbands danced.

One rare female element existed in Africa—the real Amazon soldier. It is reported that the female guard of the King of Dahomey constituted a genuine group of fighters, not a parade organization. It is said that they made stronger soldiers than the men because of their hard lives. If this is true, it is at variance with the generally recognized female inferiority of physique. This, too, might be the result of cultural rather than genetic influences. These female fighters had changed their sex in their own estimation. They had their own units, specialized tactically and in armament.[60] They endured hard discipline, and were actual shock troops in the attack. They were sup-

[58] Turney-High, *The Flathead Indians of Montana*, pp. 86, 133.
[59] Krige, *op. cit.*, p. 279.
[60] Herskovits, *op. cit.*, II, pp. 89f.

posedly all virgins and were theoretically "the king's wives."[61] Without casting any doubt on the competence or ferocity of these women, let the reader recall the type of action fought by the Dahomeans and he will suspect that women could do as well in them as men.

Privileges of sexual license to successful warriors were rare in Africa, but they were granted. Apparently Africa was not a suppressed continent. The soldiers of the Masai garrison-kraals were bachelors, yet the prepubertal girls lived in the kraals with them as servants and concubines. These girls married retired soldiers upon arriving at puberty.[62] Even Chaka had to make some concession to humanity, so permitted his celibate soldiers to philander with unmarried girls providing they were not his personal feminine reserve in the military kraal's *isogodlo.* The king handled the sex affairs of his soldiers with the same authoritativeness he used in their tactical discipline. He forbade their marrying until they were mature men. Sometimes in his gentler moments he might command all the girls of a group to marry a whole regiment without asking the consent of either.[63]

The magical influence of the stay-at-home women on the men in the field was a factor in Africa as elsewhere, being especially marked in the kingdoms of the Kitwara Empire. A wife's observance of tabu in her husband's behalf was both exacting and onerous. The absent warrior husband's behavior could in turn harm his family at home.[64] The tabus laid on the Zulu home people were quite thoroughgoing, and they applied to the whole clan. For example, the village had to keep strict silence during the absence of a war party. Great "bitterness" would overtake an absent warrior husband should his wife close her door. The family fire had to be lit every night so that the absentee would have light. Very little farm-work was done, and then only in the cool of the morning. If work were done in the heat of the day, any thorn in the absent soldier's foot would burn, any stump he might knock against would hurt him. It was tabu to mourn the dead until the army's return, even if a messenger should bring bad news, and illicit mourners were fined. Any sex activity would hurt the warriors and cause their defeat. The Zulu women could not quarrel while the army was away. They might wear no ornaments and

61 Forbes, I, p. 23f, in Herskovits, *op. cit.*, II, p. 85.
62 Hollis, *op. cit., passim.*
63 Junod, *op. cit.*, p. 470.
64 Johnston, *op. cit., passim.*

their skirts were worn inside out. They painted their faces with ashes, earth, and other dirt. They beat large stones together and rattled small ones to keep death from their husbands. The men's huts had to be swept and fire made in them to encourage their return. These are but examples from a lengthy list of observances.[65]

On the other hand, femininity constituted a greater threat than a help to the African warrior, not even excluding the civilized Mediterranean litoral. Elements of this were noticed in America, but the fear of women in the western world did not compare with the dread they inspired in Africa. In America the warriors were like strutting cockerels before the women. African warriors had to avoid the softening effects of femininity during war for their own and their comrades' sakes. A wounded Ibibio could not let a woman see his blood flow, for it was his masculine strength. It was nothing if a man saw a woman's blood flow, for she was inferior anyhow and any feebleness which might come to her was of no account.[66] Neither would these people permit the dangerous female to witness the peace-making rites. Zulu women directed their unfavorable magic against the enemy by running naked before their own troops before they set forth.[67] Zulu warriors might not cohabit with their wives after the shamans had "doctored" the army lest they lose their keen vision and hence their lives. Women might not see the ox-throwing rites of mobilization, nor might they eat any of the meat of this ceremonial slaughter. They had to keep afar off unless they had passed the child-bearing age. Zulu commanders distrusted recently married men and sent them home until their first child had been born. Junod reports that after the Mooudi battle a certain Zulu slayer took grave offense at a stay-at-home man who touched his food. This man had cohabited with his own wife, and the slayer thought his carelessness might cause his death or that of one of his kin.[68]

The sex motive was present and strong in Oceania. It was very apparent among the Fly River Kiwai. However, some observers may have exaggerated the importance the women themselves put on an enemy head. Yet an enemy head was a necessary requirement for marriage, for the males who had the women in gift placed high value upon this trophy. In any event, the man had to have a head in order to

[65] Krige, *op. cit.,* pp. 277f.

[66] Talbot, *Life in Southern Nigeria,* pp. 223, 243.

[67] Krige, *op. cit.,* p. 275.

[68] Junod, *op. cit.,* p. 483, footnote.

marry.[69] If a non-killer married, he lived in the men's club house and refrained from regular, child-begetting intercourse with his wife. When he fulfilled his murderous obligation he and his relatives wore red paint instead of the usual ceremonial black, and a son begotten at this time was supposed to become a great fighter. A first son who was not a "blood-son" was humiliated when he grew up.[70]

Nowhere did people more frankly connect sex and war than did these Kiwai. Like many people, they had a complicated war magic, much of which was connected with their own genitalia and that of the slain enemy. War magic and fear-suppressing rites among the Kiwai were also related to the secretions of their wives' and even mothers' genitals. In contrast, the sex relation was fraught with danger to the male, particularly the fighter, as was the case with many, many tribes.

The husband of a pregnant woman endangered himself and his comrade, so he stayed at home. Men contemplating an expedition had to live in the men's house to avoid any intercourse, matrimonial or otherwise. Neither could their food be cooked by women accustomed to intercourse.[71] War chastity was likewise demanded of the New Britain fighter.[72]

Kiwai matrons sometimes accompanied their husbands, who obligingly failed to kill an occasional enemy so that the women might dispatch him with digging-sticks or daggers. The Kiwai considered mangling the wounded particularly woman's work. Codrington reports Melanesian women cheering an attacking party with cries and beating upon trees.[73] They only acted as cooks in New Britain, but were stimuli to cruelty toward prisoners and the abuse of the dead.[74]

The Polynesians did not develop the military chastity required among many peoples in America, Melanesia, and Africa. The Polynesian men demanded chastity of their wives while they were at war but they did not impose it on themselves. Beauty and booty were joint motives with the men, and while war was a woman-gathering job in part, captive women were chivalrously treated, in contrast with their slaughter and cannibalization in Melanesia. They were consid-

69 Riley, *op. cit.*, p. 271.
70 Landtman, *op. cit.*, pp. 24f.
71 *Ibid.*, p. 149.
72 Brown, *op. cit.*, p. 154.
73 Codrington, *op. cit.*, pp. 306f.
74 Brown, *op. cit.*, p. 153.

ered the spoil of their Polynesian conquerors, but their status was that of wives, not concubine slaves. They were offered no degradation and their children succeeded to their fathers' names and property.[75]

War in Polynesia was primarily men's business. Women were allowed freely to pass through enemy lines without hurt or insult even if it were known that they were carrying food to their warrior husbands. This is in marked contrast with Melanesia, where such women would have been slaughtered as gleefully as if they had been men. In further contrast, note the paradox that, while Polynesian women were most considerately treated by the enemy, they often formed a fair fighting auxiliary, which they did not in Melanesia. They often assisted their husbands in the battle line by parrying spear thrusts with short clubs, or catching the enemy points with thicknesses of cloth.[76]

According to sources available, Eurasian women played a very great part in war. Caesar certainly reported no lack of spirit among the German women in the band of Ariovistus. The Germans arranged their wagons so as to make retreat impossible, setting their women on them so that they would beseech the advancing men with tears not to deliver them to Roman slavery.[77] Tacitus likewise said that the Germans placed their women and children where they could behold their valor. Wives and mothers supplied the men with food and exhortation, and delighted to view their wounds. He said the Germans wrested many a victory from apparent defeat because the women bared their breasts with pleas that they fall not into enemy thralldom.[78]

Women egging men on to war, sometimes to an unjust war, is a common situation in the Norse legends. In the Lay of Biarki (*Biarkmol Him Foinu*), Skuld, the wife of King Hiovarth of the Gauts (Goths), persuaded her husband to revolt against his hero-overlord Hrolf Kraki, which he successfully did. The poem brings out the sex motive on Hiovarth's part, and the economic one for his carls, who would receive the booty, as well as the political ambition of Skuld.[79]

---

[75] *Ibid.*, p. 172.
[76] Buck, *op. cit.*, p. 160.
[77] Caesar, i, 51.
[78] Tacitus, *Germania*, 7, 8.
[79] Hollander, *op. cit.*, pp. 6f.

Women have always had political ambitions as well as men, and who would not prefer to be a first-rate queen instead of the wife of a princeling? Gyda, the daughter of King Erid of Hordaland, spurned even the hand of the great Harald Fairhair until he made himself master of all Norway. Said she, "I will not waste my maidenhood for the taking to husband of a king who has no more than a few folk."[80]

If one sees the valkyr strain in the Nordic women, so likewise he observes that the men were not above woman-raiding. King Helgi harried Sweden in those days, "and got plenteous plunder, and laid hands on Yrsa the queen, and had her away with him."[81]

The Aryan of India was egged on to war by women as vigorously as in Germany. The *Ramayana* has several passages in which wives and mothers behaved very much like those reported by Caesar and Tacitus. But in contrast with many another tribe, the Aryas had achieved a great respect for sexual restraint by the date of the Vedic hymns. While they hymned the virtues of heavy drinking, they considered that their victories over the licentious Dasyus were due in part to their own continence. Specifically, the hymns ascribed the victory of the Aryas over the Asuras entirely to the former's *Brahmacharya tapas,* their semi-mystical stability of character which resulted from their sexual control. This is very reminiscent of Kutenai thinking.

The Aryan women, if we are to believe the hymns, were likewise valkyr fighters. How much of this is just another Amazon myth is hard to say, but the *Taittiriya Samhita* praises the women who were organized into troops for both offensive and defensive warfare. The *Rig Veda* definitely states that the weapons of the non-Aryan enemy were made by their women.[82] The hymns also relate that the non-Aryan girls formed troops against the invaders which were in no wise inferior to the male battalions.[83]

The political ambitions of the Nordic princesses call to mind the fact that the political motive for waging war is not a primitive one, nor has it often been found among primitive warriors. This trait has belonged principally to areas with fully developed or rudimentary states such as Middle America, the Iroquois League, Peru, and the best of Negro Africa.

---

80 *The Heimskringla,* I, ch. 3, p. 93.

81 *Ibid.*, ch. 33, pp. 49f.

82 *Rig Veda,* v. 9, 30.

83 *Ibid.*, v. 51, 80; vii. 78; viii. 19, 33, 91.

The better-organized Polynesians, though, were a political people and were capable of waging war for political supremacy. This is not found anywhere in Melanesia, nor among all Polynesians. Earlier writers not only erred in thinking the gap between Melanesian culture and that of Polynesia was greater than subsequent research has shown, but they also considered Polynesian culture much more of an unity than it ever was.

In Mangaia, Hawaii, and elsewhere, the power motive was a strong one. The great courtesy of the Polynesians has often been praised. Yet when motivated by real military ambitions, they were capable of casting aside their ceremonialism and seeking power, and were not above the basest treachery and breaches of hospitality in attaining it. The political rewards of victory were high in Mangaia. A successful leader could become lord of the whole island, so powerful that he could depose the otherwise omnipotent hereditary high priests and pay his leading warriors with liberal grants of land.[84]

Likewise it was to be expected that the political motive, the desire to spread the power of one kinship group over another, to increase dominion of princes and chiefs, should have bulked large in parts of Eurasia. The Metal Age folk who practiced the institution of the state knew it well. Widsith sang of the northern kings who "won more lordship with the sword, of King Offa who forced the Angles and the Swaefs to be one."[85]

The connection between military enterprise and religious cult is not new, nor is its history completed. Among the Teton-Dakota, the Omaha, and similar folk, those at home continually sang ritual songs for the absent war party.[86] The young Siouan warriors were consecrated to the divinities with abuse, fasting, and sweat-bathing.[87] It has not been long since we have had such orders of fighting monks as the Templars, Knights of Malta, and Teutonic Knights. The better-organized Siouan warriors had to fast four days before a war party, and their leader abstained from food and women even more completely than did his warriors.[88] The religious motive generally has pointed away from primitivity when conflict has been undertaken in

[84] Buck, *op. cit.*, p. 161.
[85] Widsith, in Cook and Tinker, *op. cit.*, lines 39-48.
[86] Dorsey, "A Study of Siouan Cults," p. 492.
[87] *Ibid.*, p. 444.
[88] *Ibid.*, p. 390.

the service of the gods. This is because the simpler societies have had no definite gods.

For example, the religious motive in the pure has not stood out very clearly in Melanesia and tropical South America, except with reference to the *mana*-acquiring element in head hunting. Polynesia, however, was an area of true gods, some of whom were definitely war gods. The religious motive was, in consequence, very powerful. The lords of Mangaia, for example, were fortunate in having a Valhalla motive to spur on their warriors. Men killed in battle went to a special warrior's paradise where they danced with their old friends and former enemies. All others had to face the "ovens of Miru in the lower Avaiki."[89]

The presence of war gods was attested among those Eurasiatics who had any gods at all. Some of them apparently went to war in honor of their gods, but this is by no means clear. In such excerpts as we have, most of the war-god idea seemed to be a wish-fulfillment cult directed toward inevitable victory. This apparently was true of India, at least. The Aryas had an unconquerable war god in Indra, who led them in their conquests like Yahveh led the Israelites as a pillar of fire, or as Huitzilopochli conducted the Nahua into the Vale of Mexico. Like many other war gods, he fought the other divinities in the pantheon, and when he won, so did his devotees. The early concept of Indra was not pacific, as it became later, for it was he whom "steed-possessing men," pressed into battle, invoked.[90] Many Africans likewise have thought that the real battle is that between the heavenly hosts, of which the one on earth is only a mirror.

Before taking up the great civilized motive, let us turn again for a moment to a type of tension-release warfare, the recreational. A fact which some people have failed to realize is that war is often fun. Frankly, men enjoy soldiering, the dangers of which have been exaggerated. Proportionately few people are injured or killed in war. No one has explained why this is so, why marksmanship is so fatal against animals while it is almost impossible to shoot a man. Let one contemplate the millions of dollars spent on equipment and organizational devices located far behind the lines in the theater of operations or the theater of war, the thousands of dollars worth of ammunition, the vast amount of energy expenditure needed in our day of mechanical efficiency to do what? Kill one man! Governments have com-

[89] Buck, *op. cit.*, p. 161.
[90] *Rig Veda*, iv. 42.

piled statistics on that. Now if we have so much trouble killing people with all of our devices for doing so, what about the nonliterate folk?

War stories are still the most entertaining stories, and in order to spin yarns there must be wars. Wissler's discussion of the Blackfoot makes this clear. With them the military yarn was the most important form of entertainment, and the Blackfoot insisted that it be a true one. Plains life was probably very monotonous, and therefore the successful warrior had not only provided pleasure for himself in manhunting but was a public benefactor in relieving the *ennui* of his fellow-tribesmen.[91]

Much primitive war was more of an athletic than a military exercise. Of course, one sought to kill a human and risked being killed himself, but dangerous games have always been the most fun, especially those which look more dangerous than they are. When a Plains warrior got more honorable *coups* for slapping a living enemy in the face, for being first to whip a corpse, for taking a bow or blanket from a living man than for slaughtering a hundred troublesome enemies in ordinary battle, he was indulging in an athletic event, not war.

California informants admitted as much to Kroeber. They knew that war looked more dangerous than it was. They remarked that an arrow flew straight to the mark in animal hunting while it seemed to fly right by a man; modern musketry and marksmanship experts can testify to the same phenomenon. They also knew that they were athletic humbugs rather than killers, although they would not have said so in so many words. These tribes knew how to make stone arrow points, for they used them in hunting. Yet with the full knowledge that stone-tipped arrows were the more dangerous, that they produced more nervous shock and bleeding than blunt shafts, they carried headless arrows to war. Warriors would return from an engagement bristling like pin-cushions. Their wives would pull out the simple wood arrows, and they would live to "fight" another day. Kroeber also found the Mohave willing to admit that the wish for new experience was their primary cause for going to war. They liked to see new lands and peoples.[92]

Landtman points out that the inter-clan and intra-village hostilities in Papua were exercised with much self-restraint. They were gen-

[91] Wissler, *Social Life of the Blackfoot Indians,* pp. 32-36.

[92] Kroeber, *op. cit.,* p. 727.

erally held at night by the light of torches held by women. The observer might think that the battle was frightful from the noise and expenditure of rage. The opposing sides went at each other with whatever was at hand, but deadly missiles were aimed at the legs, not chests, and deaths were rare.[93]

Here was a social pattern which tolerated internecine fighting, but one wherein the tribal concept had become important despite the emotional significance of the sib in everyday life. Unless viewed from the standpoint of a game, the whole thing seemed impossibly futile.

How far this motive has figured in the patterns of culture of the whole world is very difficult to understand from the field material. It may often be inferred, and the inference is strong. Since ordinary nonliterate life has never been very exciting save in its hunting and military aspects, these two were probably developed far beyond the rationale of economics and security.

---

[93] Landtman, *op. cit.*, p. 148.

Chapter 9

The Economic Motive

Nonliterate man's motivation for war contrasts markedly with that of civilized man. One generalization seems valid regardless of the identity or efficiency of the culture under consideration: Civilization wages war for more coldly calculated motives than does nonliterate society. Civilized war need not be primarily derived from hate. Merely want is required, and out of the frustration of a wish hate can be built up. In essence, the paramount motive in civilized war is overtly economic or covertly economic through politics. The economic motive was rarely strong in pre-metallurgical war, and was sometimes entirely absent.

Examine any war waged by city-building peoples and the economic motive is either openly supreme or so important beneath the surface that it ranks with the admitted motive. To be sure, the simpler societies have not been entirely unappreciative of the economics of war, nor have all tribes and cultures been equally blind to this civilized motive. Furthermore, the contact with civilization during the imperialist epoch led to a more economic approach to war than nonliterate conditions had previously appreciated. This has been historically recorded for North America. The westward pressure of white settlement, the appearance of the horse, and the introduction of the fur trade are cases in point. Neither was the economic motive completely absent from pre-Columbian America. It was merely undeveloped in the noncivilized areas, while such people as the Toltec knew it well. Its poor expression fitted the pattern of meager development in all economic techniques among most Indians. Starvation was never far distant on a continent which proved to be a land of plenty. The production of consumption goods and the storing of food never developed sufficiently to allow any large part of the male population to withdraw from work for long periods. Such conditions of culture could not and did not produce many or good soldiers, or states bent on improving the national wealth. The Indian was more concerned with keeping what he had than in improving his economic lot. Thus the motives, economic or otherwise, tended to fit into the patterns of the particular cultures.

Outside the high American civilizations the Indian's appreciation of the economic benefits of war tended to be individual rather than tribal. Such exploits, then, were thefts tolerated against unfriendly groups rather than war. There were some exceptions, to be sure. The Iroquois League recognized the importance of economic war from a tribal aspect. Furthermore, as stated, the recognition of the tribal importance of economic war seemed to have been growing toward the end. Typically, the Teton Dakota practiced two forms of war, tribal and individual. When the tribe as a whole needed horses, it was put on a war footing by tribal authority, and it fought for horses as a unit, as it did on the bison hunt. Individual "war" was indeed plain theft.[1]

Africa contrasts strikingly with America, for the economic element has been more important there, and nonliterate folk of that continent have possessed more effective economic techniques than those of nonliterate America, taken as a whole. Either the Negro developed an advanced technology for himself or he was not so cut off from the civilized world. After all, the Sahara, forbidding as it was, was not so great a barrier as the Atlantic and Pacific Oceans. For example, cattle-herding was diffused through the desert along the valleys of the Nile's headwaters. America's domestication of animals, except in Peru, was no more than rudimentary. The Negro also became a good metallurgist, in some regions surpassing in technique the best Peruvian work.

It is not surprising that the peoples of Eurasia should have attached more importance to the economic motive than anyone else. This is explainable by their greater economic success in non-military fields, being within the zone of diffusion from the Old World focal area. These remarks apply to the Metal Age peoples, however, for the old noneconomic motives were paramount among the others.

One marginal economic motive is seen in compensation for injury. No people seems to have been free from it, and it is for some reason frequently pled by civilized states to elevate their war to a higher moral level. Actually, it belongs as much to the realm of primitive penology as to primitive war and economics.

---

[1] Densmore, *Teton Sioux Music*, pp. 332f.

This concept, present in the internal penology of many American peoples, was often carried to considerable lengths in relations with outsiders, notably on the North Pacific Coast, in Southeast United States, and in California. In such instances the injured tribe would consent to remain on a peace footing if it or its members should be paid compensation in traditional amounts for the casualties claimed. Even the simple Yuki considered peace without payment impossible.[2] In such cases the economic ideas of the tribe had developed beyond the simplest primitivity. Usually such ideas have implied the concept of media of exchange. The tribes of the North Pacific Coast, for example, have rarely been surpassed in their reverence for wealth and the symbols of wealth.

Compensation for the death of a tribesman was not as important in Africa as in the American areas just mentioned. The custom did exist, however, for when a Nigerian war became tiresome, the elders of both sides and of some neutral town took a tally of the slain and audited the compensation. The victors, of all people, had to pay the most, since they had slain the most. Neither was the gross score all that counted. The social merit of the slain also required reckoning in the price-fixing, as in the Codes of Hammurabi and the Salic Franks. Thus a dead man with three wives cost more than a casualty with one; a rich, important man was worth more than a nobody. The balance had to be made up in cash and slaves.[3]

Another element lying on the margins of primitive military economics might be mentioned, although it will be given a more intensive discussion in the chapter on military values. This is the value of the magico-economic, of economic fetishes acquired by military means. There are several which, though differing from the capitalistic economy of modern civilization, were of economic-military significance to the practitioners. Head-hunting is in such a category. For example, the Jibaro warrior of Ecuador not only sought honor and fame when he took an enemy head but positive economic advantage. The captured head became an object of magico-economic advantage.[4] His behavior towards the *wakani,* the enslaved spirit of the man whose head he had taken, was definitely practical, for the slayer became invested with great insight into domestic affairs through its ownership. The women were the gardeners, but the owners of heads were their

[2] Kroeber, *op. cit.,* p. 178.
[3] Meek, *op. cit.,* p. 246.
[4] Karsten, *op. cit.,* p. 2.

advisers on all farming and herding affairs.[5] Such practices might not be deemed economic in a "principles" book, but Jibaro head-hunting obviously had a strong economic motivation. Nor were they the only people in the world who attached similar importance to head-hunting. The Dayak of Borneo put them far in the shade in this point.

The simplest economic military motive is thievery against the out-group. This is obviously so simple, or simply so obvious, that one is surprised to find that there were areas which had but slight concept of its value.

The technique of raiding the enemy to secure food and other goods was, for example, poorly developed in Indian America. True, the typical raid destroyed the enemy's property, but the idea of systematically appropriating it was not intelligently developed. The realistic Eskimo, of course, could be expected to conform to their intensely utilitarian pattern, and they frankly looted the villages and corpses of the defeated.[6] But let us consider the Great Plains. It would have been distinctly to the advantage of the hunters consistently to have raided the farmers for their superior food, but they normally burned the crops of the conquered tillers rather than appropriating them. One would expect the farmers and animal husbandmen of tropical South America to take the goods of the conquered, but several tribes did not. In their attempt to make a conquered village look as bloody as possible, they slaughtered all the domestic animals on the spot and left them.[7]

The exception to this situation north of the Rio Grande is found in Southwest United States culture. Both archeological evidence and ethnological tradition make the raids of the wild hunters upon the peaceful corn-growing pueblo-builders an outstanding fact in the area's prehistory. With the improvement of the material and non-material cultures of the settled peoples, it became more and more to the advantage of the wild men to scout the bordering hills, wait for the crop to ripen, choose a time when the villages or fields contained but few men, and to swarm like fury from the hills to capture the valuable maize. The pueblo area always centered on the San Juan Valley, and finally shrank to just about that region. The nuisance technique of the savages was an important cause of this restriction, along

[5] *Ibid.*, p. 47.

[6] Nelson, *op. cit.*, pp. 327-330.

[7] Karsten, *op. cit.*, p. 23.

with soil depletion and increasing aridity.[8] In the same area it was always profitable for the savage Apache to raid the sedentary and agricultural Pima. The Pima resented the Apache but could only exact profitless revenge from them. The Apache got the maize and live stock from the Pima, although at a price in their own blood probably exceeding the disutility of going to work.[9]

Yet on the whole, economic raiding was poorly developed in America and some other regions for reasons not too hard to find. There was too little technological or economic contrast between contiguous peoples. This is not saying that all Americans were on the same or similar technological and economic levels, but that the relatively poor and simple tribes were ordinarily close against other poor populations with simple technologies. Tribes which were savage, numerous, brave, and poor, were seldom contiguous to those which were rich, flabby, and easy prey to raiders. The rich were too apt to be the strong, while the poor had slight reason to raid their fellow poor. In addition to this it is by no means clear how much the fear of inimical magic attached to enemy property might have acted as a brake to military acquisition of goods.

The Plains tribes found a true economic *raison d'etre* for war after the introduction of the horse. The animal became the symbol of everything good and manly—valor, religious power, honor—but basically it was economic. A man rich in horses was rich in everything else, including wives. A horseless man was reduced to dependence on others, or to the standard of living of pre-horse days, which was certainly at the subsistence level for people not occupying good farm land. The horse became the chief Plains production capital in a very modern sense. As he was the end of war, he was also the means of waging it, playing a very important role in such military operations as the Plainsmen practiced. It might well have been that Plains war was kept typically to the level of raiding by small parties—hardly better than organized robbery — because the captured horse was ordinarily the property of the captor, not of the group. The economic importance of the animal made horse-stealing the Plains synonym for war.

---

[8] Alfred V. Kidder, *An Introduction to the Study of Southwestern Archaeology with a Preliminary Account of the Excavations at Pecos,* Papers of the Southwestern Expedition, Number 1, Department of Archaeology, Phillips Academy, Andover, Massachusetts (New Haven: Yale University Press, 1924), *passim.*

[9] Russell, *op. cit.,* p. 203.

Horse-stealing did not seek to inflict casualties on the persons of the foe. Indeed, it was hardly considered within the rules to kill or maim an enemy while sneaking his horses unless self-defense so demanded. The athletic war game idea, discussed elsewhere, was such that it was more honorable stealthily to cut the prized charger from the tether bound to the sleeping owner inside his *tipi* than to capture a hundred horses on the open plains. Among such people as the Blackfoot and Crow, horse-raiding was, indeed, more of a game than an economic enterprise. One Blackfoot hereditary foe, the Plateau Flathead, had a more realistic economic motive for horse-raiding, but the imprint of horse culture was strong enough to change the military terminology even with them. The term "horse-thief" became the honorific synonym for warrior, while the word in their Salishan dialect, "I went to steal horses from the Blackfoot," means "I went to war against the Blackfoot," whether horses were involved in the expedition or not.[10]

Piracy is a form of economic military endeavor with an ancient and somewhat honorable tradition. It is recorded that the Payaguas piratized on the Paraguay and Parana rivers for three hundred years.

This form of military theft has but recently been put down among our Eurasiatic selves. The Teutonic Vikings considered the economic motive almost the paramount reason for waging war, and piracy was their favorite technique. The resources of Scandinavia were too poor to maintain the somewhat brilliant Bronze and Iron Ages known to that area. Therefore the sea-kings clave the swanpath with their long ships for business reasons, linked with dominion. Military looting was an organized trade with them. More than once some chief possessing nothing but long ships gathered about him a mighty host of baresark men and proclaimed himself a king. King of what? Nothing but the wastes of the sea. There was naught to do but look about for some defenseless monarch, set upon him without the slightest provocation, kill him, his heirs and his men, and steal his land and throne. The Swedes had learned something the Jibaro and Kiwai had not discovered, but arable land was scarcer in Scandinavia.[11]

Organized war looting was not confined to the west of Eurasia. The Go-Harna episode of the Hindu *Maha-Bharata* epic poem shows that cattle rustling was a practice which the Arya king did not despise.

Victory looting is reported for all New Guinea and Melanesia in the monographs available to the writer. The theft of a New Hebri-

---

[10] Turney-High, *The Flathead Indians of Montana*, p. 62.
[11] Sturluson, *op. cit.*, ch. XXV, pp. 37f.

dean woman infuriated her group, not because of her sexual value but because of her economic worth as a gardener. Marital and extramarital sex partners were too easily obtained to have value in the New Hebrides, but the abduction of a producer was a blow to the village's self-sufficiency.[12]

Malinowski and Herskovits have shown us how different was the economic motivation of primitive societies from our own. This is also apparent in the prestige value inherent in war-loot among them. This factor might be considered chiefly in connection with the prestige motive, but since honors in this case were obtained through economic means, we will mention it here. Some students have been confused on this point, have been unaware that people might live in an economy other than an acquisitive one. The motive for wealth-getting, aside from immediate consumption, may be prestige as well as profit. To be sure, hoarded wealth confers prestige in civilization, as Veblen has pointed out, but among many nonliterates the prestige has lain not in hoarding but giving away. No one could think more of property than did the North Pacific Coast peoples, for example, although acquisition was more for prestige than consumption.

No one could have been more assiduous than a Kwakiutl chief in the shrewd and ruthless acquisition of food, canoes, slaves, Chilkat blankets, and copper pieces, and one of the best ways of acquiring surpluses in these was by war. But prestige did not follow mere acquisition, use, or hoarding. It consisted in the lavish way in which wealth was displayed, given away, or even publicly destroyed at festivals. Great men even fought by destroying property to see who was the richer and therefore more honorable. So, too, the marginal tribes still have gifting dances wherein the one who out-gives his rival, or her husband, is the man of the hour. To give away all the deceased's wealth at the Death Feast is honorable; for his kin to make contributions is magnificent. Now a successful warrior has a hard time to keep from acquiring wealth. Napoleon was no "Silverspoon" Butler, but he amassed a grand fortune. And it would be difficult for some nonliterate peoples to consider our leaders lords and chiefs if they knew that they behave in an unlordly and unchiefly manner by keeping the loot instead of giving it away.

Such motives underlay many of the horse-stealing wars of the Plains and Plateau. All but the finest captive horses were given away after

[12] Humphreys, *op. cit.*, p. 45.

a Kutenai raid, and if the circumstances were favorable, even the most prized were distributed to the unfortunate.[13] Assiniboin horse-stealing was frankly economic, but, as with other Plainsmen, honor went to him who captured horses only to give them away.[14] The victorious Choctaw chief in the south received honor not for his victory but for his generosity in distributing the booty. The beneficiaries were his warriors and the kin of those who had died in previous battles. Their grief was thus assuaged. The chief retained nothing but the "honor of being the restorer of the nation."[15]

Flathead women gave the victorious counter of *coup* a regular *charivari* until he made expensive gifts to all.[16] Assiniboin warriors went to a victorious chief's lodge after the victory dance and serenaded him with songs regarding his own valor. The chief was then supposed to come forth and make them a present of one of his horses. The serenaders then went to the lodge of each prominent man in turn where they expected similar treatment.[17] A young Teton, likewise, was very anxious to capture many horses. After a successful war-party, he would give away many animals at the next gathering, at which he discarded his childhood name for one of manhood suggesting his deeds of valor.[18] The giving of lavish feasts by a victor was common even if no loot had been taken. A victorious Jibaro slayer gave banquets to the community, although he and his wife and daughter could not eat any but the commonest foods since they were under blood tabus until purged.[19]

This gift-bestowal was not confined to successful, rich tribes. When a man of the Wind River Shoshone had slain an enemy he could expect the old men and women of the village to visit him during the night, singing and beating on sticks until he came out and gave fine robes to the men and meat to the women. The elders then went to the lodge of the other members of the party until they had collected from each.[20] Such pressure on victorious warriors was very common in America.

---

[13] Turney-High, *Ethnography of the Kutenai,* p. 165.
[14] Lowie, *The Assiniboine, passim.*
[15] Bossu, *op. cit.,* p. 103.
[16] Turney-High, *The Flathead Indians of Montana,* p. 63.
[17] Lowie, *The Assiniboine,* p. 30.
[18] Densmore, *Teton Sioux Music,* p. 357.
[19] Karsten, *op. cit.,* p. 38.
[20] Lowie, *Dances and Societies of the Plains Shoshone,* p. 821.

Charivari parties to victorious chiefs were lacking in Africa. True, the African kings and chiefs did make presents of loot, very lavish ones indeed, but no one dared exert cat-calling pressure to increase their generosity. Gift-giving by victorious chiefs was also common in Europe, although likewise without the element of ridicule. Tacitus commented on the Germanic youths' dislike of peace, how they would seek service under foreign chiefs if their own tribe were cursed by long years of quiet. The chiefs likewise preferred war, for from war came loot, and by loot one could maintain a large retinue, could make gifts of fine horses and weapons, could give banquets, and earn a name for generosity.[21]

War for the purpose of laying other peoples under tribute is hardly primitive. It belongs to such tribute empires as those of Rome, Peru, and Mesopotamia. It is the mark of civilized military robbery, too gradual and drawn out, too refined, and too productive for primitive society to appreciate.

Failure to collect tribute in goods was a defect in the economic-military patterns of American peoples outside the areas of intensive agriculture, where it was practiced with great efficiency, as attested by the thorough-going Aztec tribute rolls. A savage exception existed among the Sumu, a simple tribe of farmers in Central America. They, indeed, laid others under tribute of commodities and found it a marvelous substitute for work. Under their "kings" they began a rudimentary conquest empire in the Seventeenth Century, but it is not clear where they got such ideas. They lay too near the great Middle American civilizations to have been culturally independent of them, and they may have acquired such modern military and economic notions from the buccaneers who used them as mercenary sodiers.[22]

Tribute collecting, then, has been characteristic of rudimentary states. The getting of *scat* is one of the favorite themes of the Norse Edda. The Irish *Leabhar Gabhala,* The Book of Invasions, relates that the second invasion of the island by the Celts from Spain failed because of a pestilence. This gave the indigenous Formorians, who have come down in legend as sea-demons, a fine opportunity for setting upon the survivors. This they did, and they levied tribute upon

21 Tacitus, *Germania,* 14.

22 Eduard Conzemius, *Ethnographical Survey of the Miskito and Sumu Indians of Honduras and Nicaragua,* Bulletin 106, Bureau of American Ethnology (Washington: 1932), p. 82.

them of two thirds of the children, grain, and milk.[23] Herodotus said that the nomadic Scyths invaded and successfully held Asia Minor under tribute for long periods.[24]

Military slaving as an economic enterprise also belongs on levels above the lowest primitivity. It is certainly more productive to enslave a war captive than to kill him or to eat him. The brilliant rudimentary civilizations of Mexico and the Mediterranean basin might not have been built without the institution, so the world may have profited thereby. Such an opinion receives a blow when one understands that the Inca built his Peruvian greatness without it, but the Peruvians were able and willing to effect an efficient social organization.

Slaving was an economic military motive of only moderate importance in native America, for certain economic thresholds must be attained before the slave becomes valuable. The Plains hunters found the male captive a burden. He could not be sent for horses; he could not be trusted with weapons with which to hunt for his master; he was more of a nuisance than an economic asset, so was promptly killed, adopted, or sent home. The female slave, quite aside from her value as a concubine, was economically useful to the man and his wife. More than one woman was required to process the bison one man could kill. A woman's duties could be performed at or near home where she could be kept under surveillance.

The slave has therefore been valuable where the economic level, either through technological superiority or the presence of an easily exploitable natural resource, permitted work near home. An example is found in the legendary enslavement of the early Iroquois by the Algonkin. The latter soon appreciated the utility of agriculture and the disutility of the labor involved. So when the early Iroquois came north, the Algonkin enslaved these expert tillers, put the men in women's clothes, and set them to farming. As time rolled by, the Iroquois perfected their social and military organization to such an extent that only white intervention prevented the probable extermination of the eastern Algonkin by their erstwhile servants.

The Oregon Klamath and Modoc, each culturally simple people, went one step farther. While their economy had slight need for slaves, they went into the business commercially, venturing into Cali-

[23] *The Leabhar Gabhala*, in Henri Hubert, *The Rise of the Celts*, M. W. Dobie, trans., (New York: A. Knopf, 1934), p. 192.

[24] Herodotus, i. 106.

fornia in their *razzias* to enslave the Achomavi whom they carried to the international slave market at The Dalles, Oregon.

Skinner reports that the Menomini were consistent slavers. They took captives of both sexes and were none too kind to them. The Menomini did not try to capture or purchase many slaves, as they were never large-scale farmers, but slaves had some value to them. One Augustin Grignon said that he knew of two female slaves which sold among the Menomini for as high as two hundred dollars. These people preferred to raid as far as the distant Pawnee who, being taken so far from home, would have slight motive or opportunity to escape. The tribes of the North Pacific Coast made slavery almost as much a center of their economy as it was with the Arabs. Consequently, they were as fierce and as able warriors as this continent knew. In contrast, the Flathead frequently took male slaves in order to enhance the prestige of the captor, but finding them a burden, killed them off.[25]

A median attitude existed among the Plains Ojibway. These people, probably retaining a memory of past corn-growing practices, took captives of both sexes whom they did not torture but kept subjugated by fear of death. The women were taken as wives while the men were forced into a mild type of semi-slavery.

An extreme slaving attitude was found among the Sauk and Fox. The spirits of the foes a man had slain in his lifetime were perpetually enslaved to his service in the afterlife. Indeed, upon a warrior's death some dear friend would go to the edge of the grave during the funerary ceremonial and, by waving his war club toward the corpse of his comrade, bequeath to his spirit the ghostly servitors whom the donor's war exploits had amassed.[26]

No generalization can be made concerning slaving in South America. Some very ferocious people who also had lands to till never practiced it, while such gentle people as the Chiquitos of southwest Amazonia consistently enslaved their neighbors.

It has been noted that Africans as a whole fought better than Americans as a whole. They likewise had stronger economic motivation. Farming was most important in at least two great African areas, and was known to all save one. Serious farming, a fortunate geography, and a teeming population produced slavery, and slavery meant war.

---

[25] Turney-High, *The Flathead Indians of Montana*, p. 130.

[26] David I. Bushnell, *Burials of the Algonquin, Siouan, and Caddoan Tribes West of the Mississippi*, Bulletin 83, Bureau of American Ethnology (Washington: 1927), p. 14.

Many kingdoms of West Africa were founded for defense. Once they were established, the temptation to loot the scattered and less organized towns of their ivory, gold, and slaves became too strong. These kingdoms already possessed organized slave markets when the whites discovered them. They eventually became enormous slave factories. Actually what the Dahomeans called wars were no more than large scale slaving enterprises.[27] They were means of affording the king magnificent revenues, for he bought slaves at about five francs per head from his soldiers and sold them at much higher rates.[28]

Slaving, however, was not universally valued in Africa. The humbler tribes had no more use for the institution than did the bulk of the Americans. Even the great Zulu kingdom valued it no more than did the Sioux. Slaves were of no great value to herdsmen such as they, although at one time they were more concerned with slaves than in the great period. In the latter and magnificent day their slaving became most primitive, and they reverted to a preoccupation with the slaughter of survivors. Only attractive young women in later times were spared for sale into matrimony, and since this was true matrimony instead of sexual bondage, they were so well treated that they could hardly be called slaves.[29]

Slavery among the cruder south Sudan people could not have been of much importance, judged by the slight social distinction between master and slave. War captives could become their masters' heirs among the Makaraka, and could even marry free women. Lugbari slave women could marry free-born Kakwa,[30] all of which is in great contrast with Dahomean practice.

African slavery never reached the personal harshness recorded in the history of our civilization. Even in the well-organized and successful Congo Kingdoms slaves were given almost every right of freemen. If he could hoard enough, the slave could buy a slave to do his work. The interference of the white man changed this halcyon condition in many areas.

It is strange that the socially, agriculturally, and martially able Polynesians did not grasp the point of converting conquered folk into economically valuable objects more than they did. The Samoans, for

---

[27] Herskovits, *op. cit.*, II, pp. 70f.

[28] *Ibid.*, pp. 95f.

[29] Junod, *op. cit.*, p. 471.

[30] Leonard F. Nalder, ed., *A Tribal Survey of Mongalla Province* (London: Oxford University Press, 1937), p. 27.

example, made no attempt to enslave the conquered or to convert them into servile castes. All prisoners and wounded men were killed. If their territory was occupied, the surviving vanquished would seek refuge in a neutral town and eventually ask their hosts to intercede for them or help them expel their foe by force.[31] The conquerors were content with destroying the gardens and houses and with temporarily driving off their victims. The intercession of neutral hosts almost always got their homes back for the original owners.[32]

One cannot say that war-slavery was a particularly important trait among the agricultural peoples of barbarian Europe. Viewing the parallel development of the institution with the rise of civilization and the civilizing traits elsewhere, a somewhat greater development might have been expected.

The pastoral nomads perhaps practiced slavery most consistently. It would appear that the slave would have been more in the way among such wanderers than his slight economic worth would counterbalance. The captive's opportunities to run away must have been great, but the Scyths, for one, solved that problem. They used captives to milk their mares for them, and finding them valuable, blinded them to make them docile and immobile. The chronicler ascribes such blinding to "their not being tillers of the ground but a pastoral race."[33] The Scyths were able, shrewd, and hard enough to make slavery conform to the rest of their culture.

More surprising than the Scythian practice was the presence of slaves among the Siberian reindeer nomads and their neighbors, frequently mentioned in the works of Jochelson, Bogoraz, and Czaplicka. An adult captive was beaten to soften his spirit, which in the end only made him so treacherous that his master had to kill him. Actually, the Siberians preferred to kill all the vanquished adults and to take the more tractable youths and children. Siberian slavery was part of the reindeer complex. The victors therefore preferred to take a number of the enemy with the herds, for they were acquainted with the animals. The slave might earn virtual emancipation and a portion of his master's herd if he behaved. Women were sold as chattels, were worked hard, and were their masters' sexual subordinates, but in these things their lot was but slightly different from that of free women. Adult female captives were until recently priced at a

[31] Brown, *op. cit.*, p. 172.
[32] *Ibid.*, pp. 175f.
[33] Herodotus, iv. 2.

large bag of tobacco, from seventy-two to one hundred eighty pounds. Young girls were less dear.[34] Bogaraz and the other Siberianists state that in addition to this beating to tame the spirit, the arctic tribes tried to make their captives something less than fighting men by dressing them in female costume and making them otherwise behave as women, like the alleged Algonkin practice.

But it is the land which civilizes humanity in war as in all things. Economic land, the resources of nature in the service of humanity, is what makes man a food producer instead of a food gatherer, something new and uncommon in the world, instead of a parasite, which is something older and commoner than mankind. Archeology, history, and ethnology all speak of the mad scramble for arable land, and much farm land has been fertilized with human blood.

Despite the fact that many American Indian tribes were agriculturalists, the economic motive of acquiring more or better farm lands by force was poorly developed, save in the areas of intensive cultivation. The concept was well developed in such regions even if the technique lagged behind the conquest empires of the Old World. The patterns of culture for these people contained such ideas as a highly trained militia levy (Aztec), a well organized reserve corps and training *cadre* for conscript troops in time of emergency (Maya), and a highly trained, professionalized, disciplined standing army of regulars (Peru). Farm lands and other natural resources were systematically conquered, or brought under tribute control. Such features, together with a degree of urbanism, take the area of intense cultivation outside the discussion of "primitive" warfare and hence outside the scope of this study. Nevertheless, such societies strengthen the theory that cultural traits, including military ones, function as wholes within patterns and configurations. For this reason it is well to mention Peru, which from an economic-sociologic-military viewpoint was as modern in its pattern as the external British conquest empire or the internal one of the United States. In brief, the Peruvian monarchy systematically acquired territory by conquest with a trained regular army. Where such land in the hands of primitive farmers was unproductive, the empire brought the force of its civil service personnel and public works program—perhaps the most effective ever designed by any state in history or prehistory—to bear upon such land and its inhabitants. That such conquest was essentially benevolent though despotic is demonstrated by the consensus that such conquered tribes

[34] Bogoraz, *op. cit.*, pp. 659-661.

were thereby raised from a marginal economy to one of surplus. Peruvian conquest meant not only a regular tribute payment to go to the government and religion at Cuzco but a real rise in the standard of living of the defeated.[35]

The concept of territorial and political society, in contrast with kin-based society, was highly developed only in those portions of the Americas mentioned above. It was as much their failure to appreciate a land-space society as any other which made the American Indians the brave but wretchedly ineffective soldiers they were. It was tribalism which defeated them and made this a white man's continent far more than fire arms, a fact which those who overemphasize materials have not been able to comprehend.

It can hardly be said that the agricultural Indians succeeded much better than the hunters and food gatherers in their territorial military ideas. This has been stated before in the tactical discussion. The Plains hunters did protect their bison range, tended to think of certain hunting ranges and herds as theirs, and strove to drive off intruders. Their agricultural neighbors on the margins of the Plains erected rudimentary fortifications to protect the corn fields. Verendrye said the Mandan built minor strong points apart from the fortified villages to protect the fields and kept them well stocked with food even when not garrisoned.[36] This was unusual.

Of all the American tribes encountered in this study, only the Mohave looked clearly upon land as economic property and something to fight for as such. Kroeber reports that they could own, buy, and sell tracts as individuals. Indeed, one of the reasons for going to war was to acquire booty and slaves herewith to purchase tracts of land.[37] It is hard to understand how this simple California group acquired such a civilized concept on a continent where hunting or farming land was thought of in terms of kin ownership. This is especially mystifying since agriculture provided them with no more than half their subsistence.[38] For most Indians land was too involved with kin ownership or was not sufficiently scarce to matter economically or martially. The Jibaro might be taken as an extreme example. Their wars were spite wars which never aimed at conquest. They really feared

[35] George P. Murdock, "The Organization of Inca Society," *Scientific Monthly*, March, 1934, *passim*.

[36] Verendrye, *op. cit.*, p. 23.

[37] Kroeber, *op. cit.*, p. 744.

[38] *Ibid.*, p. 735.

and detested the farms and country of their foes, and vacated the same promptly as soon as victory was complete, for they considered the danger of occupying enemy land too great. Furthermore, there was an inexhaustible supply of free land available by simply clearing the jungle, so there was no need to conquer any.[39]

An exception to this disregard for natural resources from a tribal and military viewpoint is again cited by Kroeber. The Pomo, says he, were about the most peaceful of the California tribes. An extensive salt field lay within their range, and while they made no effort to prevent others from coming and gathering this most valuable commodity, they expected them to pay a royalty or tribute in the form of presents. Those who failed to pay were considered enemies.[40]

The failure to conceptualize economic land as nature functioning in the service of man generally held back the military development of nonliterate peoples unless their patterns included the intensive cultivation of some crop. Some Indians were effective farmers, of course, and yet did not become good soldiers, as the pueblo-builders attest. One might say, though, that a truly military people would attempt to capture the natural resources of an enemy, and we have observed that that American Indian seldom did this. Neither did they lay them under tribute, except in Middle America, Colombia, and Peru, or destroy them. Some effort was made against natural resources as such, to be sure. The Plains people consistently attempted to drive the bison off their foe's range and even fired the grass. Swanton quotes Simpson Tubby as saying that the Choctaw and their neighbors used to poison springs in enemy territory so consistently that the Indians preferred to drink from running water.[41]

The Jibaro example should not be taken as typical of disregard for territory in South America. It has been mentioned that the Caraio (Carib) and Tapuya fought for possession of the Brazilian littoral.[42] The Caraio ultimately spread over two thirds of South America, a very important fact of South American ethnology.[43]

Enough has already been said to show that war for new land was very important in much of Africa. Likewise, we have already seen

---

[39] Karsten, *op. cit.*, p. 16.

[40] Kroeber, *op. cit.*, p. 236.

[41] Swanton, *Source Material for the Social and Ceremonial Life of the Choctaw Indians*, p. 169.

[42] Church, *op. cit.*, p. 27.

[43] *Ibid.*, p. 28.

that it was not as important in Polynesia as one would expect. But the acquisition of new land was almost the paramount motive for major war in barbarian Europe.

War against the enemy's resources is an effective procedure, and is thought to be recent enough for modern moralists to inveigh against as something new. There are several passages in Caesar which show that both the Gauls and Germans realized that their forces and those of their foes were too large to live off the country, so they consistently attacked their enemy's grain fields as well as the supply elements in his army with the design of hamstringing his operations through hunger.

Several American tribes could be cited to show the slight concept of defensive war to protect their own land and wealth. This would have been surprising except for the lack of economic motivation, a condition brought about by defective agriculture and poverty of material culture. That such quiescence was lacking in Europe is clearly indicated by authorities which have come down to us. The Chauci, for example, were a superior and numerous people occupying a vast tract in west Germany. They made war on no one, undertook no raids, and depended on social justice instead of force to maintain internal peace. Yet any raider or land-hungry foreign chief would find them "with armies, horses, and men in abundance," and with plenty of intelligent ferocity should an attempt be made on their land and property.[44] To the east along the Vistula, likewise, the Hraeds resisted the Huns, fighting unceasing war "for home against the folk of Attila."[45] It is probable that our noncivilized ancestors fought better than many other peoples not only because they had learned better principles of war from the more civilized east but also because they had more to fight for, their fields.

The Samoans were good farmers and fair fighters, but they failed to hold the land captured. The fury with which the Jibaro destroyed all the food and food potentialities of their conquered foe is in point. Similar garden and animal destruction took place in both Melanesia and Polynesia, which also failed either to appropriate the soil or to make the conquered till their own gardens for the benefit of the conquerors. It no more occurred to the New Hebrideans to hold

[44] Tacitus, *Germania*, 35.

[45] Widsith, in Albert S. Cook and Chauncey B. Tinker, *Selected Translations from Old English Poetry* (Boston: Ginn, 1902), lines 119-122.

enemy land for more than a few days than it did to sell any of the tribal land. Actually, the victors were far more interested in the great victory feast they were to hold than in the economic advantages granted by victory.

Not all Polynesia was so stupid about economic expansion and the creation of rudimentary conquest empires. Buck shows that in Mangaia and elsewhere the Polynesians were capable of armed invasion by many canoes seeking homes and new farms. Sometimes the first comers were conquered and absorbed; sometimes they formed depressed castes. The raiding of garden lands with failure to occupy, as noted in Oceania and America, may be inherent in gardening, which is intensive agriculture, in contrast with true farming for grain, which is extensive. This is far from apparent.

As has been observed before, primitive war, in spite of the dancing about, honors-counting, scalping, and head-hunting, was remarkably tame. Perhaps this is because it so rarely was thoroughly economic. One might even be justified in observing that feelings were more often hurt than bodies, that primitive war was more psychological than lethal. In all but a few areas the bloodiness of primitive war has been greatly exaggerated. But one must recall that just a few casualties in a primitive economy at or not far above subsistence levels may be very important. The loss of the life of one producer in an Indian village might be economically more disastrous than the loss of a hundred in a community of comparatively similar importance among ourselves. Recall that in primitive economics the concepts of Land and Capital were slight; that of Labor was everything. So it was with our ancestors until the Renaissance. Therefore the loss of a small number of lives should not be dismissed as of no ecomonic importance.

A people whose keen economic sense stood in their way, a folk who overdid a good thing, were the Hausa in the African Sudan. The Hausa nations should have become great through their devotion to economic motives, but they overplayed the role. Even under their Islamic emirs they could effect no more than weak confederations with all but complete village and town autonomy. It is alleged that they failed politically because they counted wealth a greater prestige bearer than valor or gentle birth. It took a religious zealot to bring them together in the early Nineteenth Century.

CHAPTER 10

Military Values

DEFINITION OF THE CONCEPTS "VALUE" AND "ATTITUDE" HAS BEEN so difficult that there is a considerable variation in the use of the terms. It is, therefore, necessary for a work not technically in the field of social psychology to use the simplest definitions possible. A value, therefore, is defined as an object with meaning. But what, then, is the meaning of "meaning?" The word in this sense indicates that a trait, material or otherwise, possesses utility, while utility is the power of any object or trait to satisfy a human want. This leads directly to the anatomy and physiology of the human organism. The organism, being as it is, has certain needs, basic or acquired. The objects which satisfy these needs are useful and, being useful, are valuable. They have meaning. A cultural value, then, is an object or practice with meaning.

An attitude is the way people tend to behave toward a value. In the simplest words, an attitude is a tendency to act. Such an attitude need not call forth continuous action. An attitude is merely a habit, a learned response in the acquired nervous organization of the person, a tendency to respond in certain ways in the presence of specific stimuli. Such concepts are introduced into an ethnological discussion because the inspection of the attitudes and values of a people is only another way of studying its culture. Indeed, it might be the ultimately valid way. The former preoccupation of ethnologists with the overt was a matter of necessity, but it has become more and more apparent that the true nature of culture is covert. Overt behavior, all the tools and artifactual materials, are symbolic of the covert conditioned response. They are, perhaps, the values which satisfy the needs of man, but those needs are in the man. Tendencies to act toward such materials are also in the man whether he is in the presence of the tools or not. A man carries the skills needed to use his tools wherever he goes, whether or not he carries his tool kit with him.

Attitude and value—conditioned response and the symbol which evokes it—are opposite sides of the same coin. The functioning whole of an individual's habits or life pattern, together with his potential behavior, is that person's culture, for the carrier and transmitter of culture is the specific person. Persons do not have identical tendencies to act towards any particular value. Differences in heredity, anatomy, physiology, and experience will care for that. But the culture into which one is born finds him plastic material, so while the person is the transmitter and carrier of culture, cultural data are mass phenomena. Our habits are formed in sufficiently similar ways so that any culture as a going concern can function. Any society, as Malinowski has shown us, tolerates a certain divergence in individual attitudes and values. It is untrue that "savage" man demands absolute uniformity in obedience to custom, while the mark of civilization is "individualism." The tolerated divergences vary from culture to culture, to be sure, but if the individual is sufficiently indoctrinated and conditioned to the accepted mores to get along and keep out of his neighbors' way, nothing serious happens to him. If his attitudes and values are too much out of line with those accepted in his time and locale, he is maladjusted or disorganized. A culture which tolerates so much divergence in attitude and value that it cannot function as a working whole is in a state of rapid change or redefinition of values, or is in a state of disintegration, acculturation, and perhaps on the way out.

Military attitudes and values of nonliterate societies have always been extremely diverse. They have not had in common an instinct of war or pugnacity as has been supposed. There has been no uniformity, for instance, regarding hatred of the enemy, or a tendency to act in a uniform way toward some part of his body. In some places a scalp has been honored, in others heaped with abuse. The attitudes and values regarding military phenomena have varied according to the pattern of the entire culture, and this variation seems to have had all but infinite possibilties.

Since civilized, modern man has so sharpened his acquisitive tendencies, the problem of the loot and spoils might be the most obvious and therefore the easiest way in which to introduce this subject. This is, of course, part of the wider discussion of "things acquired from the enemy." The question of loot has been discussed under the economics of war, so we will turn immediately to the enemy himself considered as a value, either as a captive whole or in piece-meal. The living captive as a slave has had economic value, as noted in Chapter 9.

We are here discussing him as a prisoner rather than as a work animal or economic capital.

One of the greatest values the captive could serve has been as human sacrifice to a god who demanded such immolation. This permitted the substitution of a member of the out-group for the more valuable member of the in-group. Enough has been written on the gorier aspects of the religions of Mexico and Middle America for us to pass them by here. Suffice it to say that the pyramids of Mexico ran with the blood of thousands of victims annually. The sacrifice of a captive was often necessary for the appeasement of many Polynesian gods. Some Africans regarded prisoner immolation highly, nowhere more than in the west where thousands of victims were annually immolated in the Yam Festival. Indeed, it is to be suspected that human sacrifice has played a part in the religious history of every single group which has achieved civilization. Certainly not all of the victims have been war captives, but the bulk of them have been.

The significant point in the sacrifice of captives is that a rather high culture, indeed a civilization of sorts, has usually been attained before such practice has had any place in the complex. There had to be definite deities to whom sacrifice was directed, and specific, personalized gods were not characteristic of the simpler cultures. Such gods demanded organized, trained priesthoods with complicated rituals. In contrast with this, sacrifice of war captives has been a great rarity when the highest religious ministrant has been a shaman or "medicine man" seized with vague spirits, not gods. They possessed no rituals elaborate enough to demand such service. Human sacrifice to definite gods also has accompanied rather authoritative social organization with developed economic techniques.

Let us consider the marginal Plains Skidi Pawnee with their culture, authoritative social organization, and priesthood. Beyond them lay the socially anarchical Plains, without agriculture and without priests.

The Skidi Pawnee strove to capture a beautiful enemy maiden on each of their raids. This girl was then adopted into some very honorable Pawnee family where, to her surprise, she was treated with more consideration than the real daughters of the lodge. She became the pampered darling. Yet late one night she was rudely seized, stripped of her clothing, and her body half painted down its length from head, through groin, to foot with charcoal. She thus symbolized the junction of night and day. She was then strung up between two upright poles with cross pieces. Her adopted father was compelled to shoot an arrow through her heart just as the sacred Morning Star was rising. The arrows of the priests soon followed, and her body was horribly mangled before it had served its purpose. This rite of appeasement to the Morning Star was considered essential to Pawnee welfare, to success in all things and agriculture in particular.

The economic chapter described the Dahomeans as seeking prisoners assiduously. Suitable physical specimens were kept as slaves while the old and decrepit were decapitated at once for their heads. The enemy chiefs, however, were reserved for human sacrifice to the Dahomean pantheon.

Prisoners were sacrificed in Eurasia wherever the culture had developed gods demanding it. The Celtic devotion to the rite is well-attested. It existed in India, too, even before the Aryan invasion. The more primitive Tamil, for example, considered sacrifice-getting, sometimes no more than plain kidnapping, one of their prime motives for war. These people had a female fertility deity who had to be propitiated to fructify the fields, and captive boys and girls were often forced to breed victims for the sacrifice. The victim himself, aside from the cruel manner in which he was put to death, was not badly treated. A Tamil woman considered it an honor to have a child by a prospective victim. If we are to believe Herodotus, the Scyths sacrificed a vast number of prisoners to their war god.[1]

It appears, then, that captive sacrifice was not characteristic of the simpler cultures. The reverse is correct.

This does not mean that captives were not tortured or slain by simpler peoples. Kroeber reports torture by several simple Californian tribes, such as the Maidu and Gabrieleno, as a preliminary to execution. This was only spleen-venting, the release of tensions and emotions caused by the death of relatives and the other nuisance activities of the enemy. It had no theological value. Teit reported that the Coeur d'Alene of the northern Plateau mildly abused prisoners at the scalp dance.[2] This was the neighboring Flathead's only real reason for taking male prisoners. There is an old tradition on the Northern Plateau of tree crucifixion of war prisoners to some divinity, but this is highly doubtful. Spleen-venting seems to have been satisfac-

[1] Herodotus, iv. 62.

[2] James A. Teit, "The Salishan Tribes of the Western Plateau," Franz Boas, ed., *Annual Report 45*, Bureau of American Ethonology (Washington: 1927-1928), p. 190.

tory to such cultures. American field reports are filled with this tension release value of prisoner torture.

The Iroquois, as a sociological refinement, tied prisoners to stakes and wreaked almost unbelievable tortures upon them before they died. But if the man bore his torment with fortitude or even contempt, he was honored though not necessarily released. The children were brought to witness his brave death and taught to emulate his courage. In this way the dying captive served the purpose of indoctrinating youth to the war pattern. The Iroquois were a state-building people, and certainly not among the simplest people.

The royal Zulu by no means maintained Iroquois dignity in prisoner-abuse. If a defeated chief were brought home bound, he was reserved for the king's wrath. But the Zulu king required much shamanizing to enable him to meet the victim face to face, for the captive was magically potent even though bound. When the defeated chief came within striking distance, the Zulu monarch lept into the air and stabbed him repeatedly to demonstrate his own bravery. If the man had been brave, portions of his body were cut out for medicine to give the Zulu lord kingly qualities. The chief then chewed certain parts of the body and ate them, stopping now and then to spit out portions in the direction of the enemy. The slain chief's head was then made into a vessel to hold medicines, for they increased in virtue when stored in this manner.[3] This spitting portions of masticated enemy in the direction of the enemy had parallels in other parts of the world.

The greatest of all values to be obtained from the enemy in Melanesia was one of the enemy himself. This was not for human sacrifice, as among the refined, godly, and priestly Polynesians. The Melanesians did not understand slavery, neither did they need prisoners for refined ceremonial torture; but they could not be surpassed in childish cruelty. The spleen-venting catharsis of the Melanesian victory celebration has already been mentioned, but it was not considered complete unless witnessed by a slowly dying enemy. Abel quotes the following account of one of his informants which should be read in full.

> The war party had captured a man and a woman alive. As the canoes neared their home bay the warriors paused to put on their finery. The village was informed of the victory and the presence of spoils by conch shell signals. Joyful pandemonium set in ashore, and the homeguard began preparing for the feast. Their frenzied joy knew no bounds when

[3] Kidd, *op. cit.*, p. 309.

> they learned that the human spoil was alive. As the canoes neared the beach, twenty or thirty men came dashing into the shallow waters to lift the bound captives ashore on their spear points, taking care not to touch them with their hands, as this privilege belonged to the relatives of recent battle casualties. The captives were flung ashore and dragged to the center of the village where they were tied to two trees. The inhabitants and visitors from friendly villages were by then enjoying the most abandoned dance, which the captives were forced to watch. Women who had lost husbands to the enemy in former battles vied in cursing and torturing them. Tiring of this, the victims were trussed over a fire of coconut leaves and roasted alive. The drumming and dancing went on for days after the victims had been eaten.[4]

The person of an enemy was not always in danger in primitive societies. This was especially true of those who had strong ideas of hospitality. Persons coming to enemy villages voluntarily on the North American Plateau were almost invariably well treated. Among the Osage an enemy could run into camp where a certain official was bound to protect him, feed him, and care for his wants. The man was immune as long as he remained with the Osage, but his immunity came to an end if he returned to his own people.[5]

The attitude even toward prisoners was by no means universally hostile. Indeed, their presence might be desired for roles other than those of slaves. The Iroquois Confederacy suffered terrific casualties in its efforts to conquer a continent. A valiant young man was a most welcome captive if he would consent to drop his own tribal and kin affiliations, becoming an Iroquois and ceremonially taking the place of some Iroquois fallen in battle. This included taking over the dead man's name, property, and even his wife and children. Yet the captive sometimes was feared because of evil magic, the hostile gods, and other inimical influences which might have adhered to his person. He therefore had to be purged of being an enemy. Kroeber reports that the Mohave, after several days of song and dance, took new captives to the river and plunged in with them. The captives emerged as Mohave, and thus the tribe was magically innoculated against any sickness inherent in their enmity.[6]

Melanesia has just been mentioned as a torture area without peer, but this applied on some islands only to adult prisoners. The Solomon Islanders also recruited their depleted ranks from enemy children. The adults were cruelly slain and eaten, but enemy children were

---

[4] Abel, *op. cit.*, pp. 143f.

[5] Dorsey, *Siouan Sociology*, p. 237.

[6] Kroeber, *op. cit.*, p. 746.

taken into the clans of the wives of their captors. Upon adulthood they could not speak their native language and would not hesitate to fight their real kin.[7]

The body of an enemy, though dead, has often had value. The first few Plains warriors to strike the dead body of an enemy were given war honors. This often misled the pioneering whites into thinking that all Plainsmen mutilated the bodies of the slain, although mutilation of the dead was common enough in primitive war. Such mutilation in itself had social value. If the tensions and petty hates which everyone felt in connection with members of his own group could be transferred to the feelingless body of a dead enemy, the in-group was strengthened thereby. The Coeur d'Alene liked to bring home the body of a famous enemy warrior, if he were killed close to camp, so that it might be dressed up and set on a pole for exhibition.[8] The dead body of an enemy had *coup*-counting value to the Zulu, too, but not as much as on the American Plains.

The value of an enemy body for cannibalism has been a most important phenomenon. Many peoples ate the bodies of slain enemies for a great variety of reasons, ranging from attitudes of religion to just plain commestible ones. No generalization may be made regarding the state of culture of habitual cannibals for the world as a whole, for they have varied from the simplest to the most complex.

It is not surprising that the savage men of South America were cannibals. The Caytes of the Brazilian coast ate every wrecked vessel's crew. At one meal they ate the first Bishop of Bahia, two canons, the Procurator of the Royal Portuguese Treasury, two pregnant white women, and several children, shipwrecked in a French brig on the reefs of the Rio Sao Francisco in 1556. The particular Tapuya whom the Portuguese called Botocudo were as merciless and persistent cannibals as have ever been known.[9] According to one Gandavo, they were "so prompt and expeditious in their vengeance" that they often cut a piece from a man while he still lived, and cooked and ate it before his eyes.[10] The constant wars of the Cashibos of Amazonia were for the purpose of obtaining human flesh.[11] (One must recall that tropical jungles are ordinarily poor in meat game.) The Chiriguanos

---

[7] Blackwood, *op. cit.*, p. 43.

[8] Teit, *op. cit.*, p. 190.

[9] Church, *op. cit.*, p. 69.

[10] *Ibid.*, p. 71.

[11] *Ibid.*, p. 183, footnote.

of the Gran Chaco enslaved prisoners whom they kept at domestic service until delectably fat. They would then be killed without warning, and any man who refused to eat a piece of heart was called a woman, a terrible word in a warrior's mouth.[12]

Such practices were not surprising among South American savages, but what of the civilized Aztec? It is merely euphemistic to point out that the cultivated Nahua restrained themselves to religious cannibalization of human sacrifices, and that they did not eat much human flesh. This was a difference in degree, not of kind, and the religious rationalization amounted to little. It is doubtful if any cannibal could be forced to eat human food for whatever reason if he did not have a liking for it.

As Africa considered the person of an enemy of great value for human sacrifice, so did it think well of him as a food. African slavery was indeed mild, as noticed, but the captive could never tell when he and a number of his friends would be victims at some magnificent festival. West Africa surpassed America in sheer slaughter, fell behind it in refined torture, and far surpassed it in cannibalism. Ceremonial or hate-venting cannibalism has been reported for Africa, and a Plains or Winnebago note was struck by Meek when he observed an Ibo chief eating the raw heart of the King of Calabar with the boast, "This is the way I serve my enemies."[13]

Oceania was the cannibal area *par excellence*. The most valuable outgroup value in Melanesia was undoubtedly an edible enemy. The desire to obtain a cannibal meal ranked with vengeance as the primary incentive to war in Papua. Dead or alive, a slain or captive foe was taken home, although pains needed to do this were considerable. Most Melanesians claimed that their real motive was to insult their foes in this way and that they did not cannibalize for food *per se*. Almost all admitted, though, that roast enemy was savory and that they enjoyed it. Miss Powdermaker's Lesu people said that war captives were just another meat dish, wrapped in leaves and baked in the ovens, and savored as food without any idea of acquiring spiritual power.[14]

Cannibalism was practiced intensively on some Polynesian islands, while other groups had strong negative attitudes regarding it. Miss Mead says that cannibalism was never strong in Manua and probably

---

[12] *Ibid.*, p. 235.
[13] Meek, *op. cit.*, p. 71.
[14] Powdermaker, *op. cit.*, pp. 185f.

was never institutionalized. On the other hand, the whole war pattern was weak in Manua. For Polynesia, at least, one may say that cannibalism was apparently correlated with weak social organization. According to Professor Linton, regions of weak social control cherished the trait enthusiastically, while in those with strong central governments it was from weak to absent and was usually considered abominable.

For theoretical purposes it would be gratifying to conclude that such a correlation has been universal. But recall that in America it was the civilized Aztec who practiced cannibalism in contrast with the lowly tribes to the north who detested it. The advanced societies of the North Pacific Coast indulged in ceremonial prisoner cannibalism while the simpler tribes of the interior looked upon the habit with European horror. Actually, we know too little about the phenomenon to theorize about it.

The cannibalization of prisoners had dropped out of importance in Eurasia by the time any record became available to us, but this had not always been so. The builders of the pile villages of the Swiss Neolithic and inhabitants of certain areas in the Balkans and the Danube valley split human bones for the marrow, a rather certain sign of cannibalism.

But quite aside from their food value, scraps of the enemy body have been held in high esteem as trophies in many places. Again, such mutilation was not always indicative of the "lowest" or "most savage" cultures. The highly civilized Maya wore enemy jaw-bones as bracelets.[15] There is no reason to look down upon the Maya for such practices, as it is doubtful if any civilized people has been free from them throughout its history. But certainly the trait is not confined to rudimentary civilizations. In contrast with the Maya, the Gran Chaco Chiriguano brought home all kinds of scraps to expose to the mockery of the women and children.

Tokens of enemy bodies were insignia of military honor in South Africa. The simple Bechuana took off the navel and some of the surrounding skin as a passport into the cattle kraal of the victorious village where honors were to be bestowed. Here the shaman gashed each slayer on the thigh, a gash for each victim, as a sort of *coup*-count. The slayers then ate their scraps of skin.[16] The economic note

---

[15] Sylvanus G. Morley, *An Introduction to the Study of Maya Hieroglyphs*, Bulletin 57, Bureau of American Ethnology (Washington: 1915), p. 11.

[16] Kidd, *op. cit.*, p. 310.

was introduced by the BaThonga, who thought that a powerful ointment could be made of enemy flesh and blood which, smeared on the seed, would produce a good harvest. The mealies were again treated with the drug when they were two feet high. The blacksmiths bought it to mix with their ore, for otherwise they would get nothing but slag. Hunters treated themselves and their weapons with a similar ointment to improve their aim. Powder made from enemy tendons was spread along the paths so that foes stepping on it unwittingly would become unable to walk, and hence easy to kill.[17]

Bits of enemy flesh were used magically in Melanesia as in South Africa. For example, Miss Blackwood reported that in the Solomons a warrior would take a bit of the ear of any enemy chief he had killed, mix this with lime, bits of his eye-lash and pubic hair, and roll the whole into a bundle with a leaf. Before setting out on a party a qualified man would untie this bundle and blow a pinch of the mixture in the direction of the enemy, uttering the proper formula, which was supposed to make the enemy so blind and ill that he would become an easy prey.[18] While the most prized values obtained from the outgroup in Oceania were enemy scraps, nonhuman values were also sought. In addition to corpses, the Loyalty Islanders sought and prized the conquered chief's banner or mace of rare jade stone mounted on a handle and ornamented with Loyalty Island valuables. These royal standards were symbols of great honor.[19]

Simple scraps of enemy bodies apparently played a minor role in Eurasia, although archeology shows occasional bits of bone, mandibles, and cranial amulets prepared ceremonially.

The importance of non-capital scraps pales before the value of a whole head. The attitude that something of power is inherent in the human head seems persistent. Perhaps the greatest expression of head-taking has existed in the islands of the Pacific. The taking of enemy heads was not only the chief but only Indonesian athletic event. Stress was laid on the fact that among such people the head had to be an enemy head, not simply that of some disliked fellow-tribesman. The Jibaro of Ecuador had several attitudes in common with the distant Indonesian Dayak. The intra-tribal feud was popular with the

[17] Junod, *op. cit.*, p. 476.

[18] Blackwood, *op. cit.*, pp. 469f.

[19] Emma Hadfield, *Among Natives of the Loyalty Group* (London: Macmillan, 1920), pp. 117f.

Jibaro, but the heads so taken did not count. Only foreign heads had value.[20]

The Jibaro and Indians of similar culture, such as the Munducurus, were extremely clever in removing the bones from a head and drying it slowly so that it shrank to about the size of a human fist.[21] This work was done so well that the resultant miniature retained the features it bore in life. Even female heads were sometimes taken, but it was the stronger and more valiant male who provided honor for the slayer. But the Jibaro shrunken heads, or *tsantas,* were more than trophies. Their value was practical, not merely honorific. The Jibaros believed that the enemy's spirit was located in the head and that, though this spirit was thirsting for revenge, its malevolence could be turned into practical benevolence through the elaborite rites of the victory feast. The feast was not, therefore, merely the common gloat-celebration but a rite of deep spiritual import.[22]

The well-considered attitudes of the Jibaro regarding these heads as values has by no means been universal. It is doubtful if the Cocamas of the Upper Amazon could have attached such spiritual value to them because they took them in such enormous quantities.[23] The Jibaro, Dayak, Philippine hill tribes, and certain African people definitely sought to acquire the magical power residing in the enemy head in order to put it to work. Often, however, it seems as if head-hunting were mere trophy gathering. There was nothing in Eskimo religion which could possibly utilize an enemy head as a working fetish, but some Eskimo have been reported as head-takers. Nelson reports that the Bristol Bay Eskimo were content merely to set up enemy heads on stakes with arrows thrust cross-wise through the noses.[24] This sort of thing probably represented a simple gloat, and was very common.

So strong was the head-value idea in Oceania that on many islands head-taking was the primary motive for war, and anthropophagy was merely incidental. This strong attitude probably represented a diffusion from somewhere in the west, perhaps Indonesia. One tends to suspect a central focus of diffusion for all the head-taking complex outside America and Africa, or can we except these continents?

---

[20] Karsten, *op. cit.,* p. 13.
[21] Church, *op. cit.,* p. 78.
[22] Karsten, *op. cit.,* pp. 87ff.
[23] Church, *op. cit.,* p. 176.
[24] Nelson, *op. cit.,* p. 329.

Many Melanesians were zealous head-takers and skillful taxidermists. Recalling the theory of Polynesian origins, one would hardly expect them to fall behind the Melanesians in head-taking, for all their superiority in other realms. Indeed, Polynesian religion compelled some of them to take vast quantities of heads for temple furniture. They equaled some of the West African temple builders in this. Buck relates that one great lord of Mangaia took so many heads so that he could make an entire flooring for a new temple out of them. Raiding parties were sent out to attack isolated families, without declaration or intent of tribal war, simply to get foundation material for a new temple floor.[25] Since no first-rank warrior or member of his family was killed in the raids, the enemy tribes made very little of such occasions.

The Maori of New Zealand took enemy heads in order to pour insult on the foe, which was their prime defense of cannibalism. Skulls were placed on the corner pallisades of the stockaded villages, facing their erstwhile friends, in order to make the insult biting. An elaborate ceremony of "causing-to-look-backward" was held in which the heads were repeatedly pointed toward their former homes and urged in song and dance to bid farewell.[26] Enemy fragments were also made into jewelry and even fish hooks. This represented no attempt to get the man's spirit to work for one but was rather an expression of a first-rate hate. Captured heads were valuable in Maori diplomacy. The tattooed heads of chiefs and nobles were affixed to poles and spears and turned so that their friends could see them enduring insult and jest, but at the end of the war they were exchanged as part of the peace ceremonial. For a group to refuse to accept its own heads was to refuse peace.

While perhaps not exercising the skill and patience noticed in Amazonia or Malaysia, the Maori took some pains to cure heads. The commonest practice was to remove the brains and suspend the head over a pile of heated stones. A mat funnel was arranged to concentrate the heat on the suspended head. The trophy was occasionally removed from the funnel to allow the humidity to dry off, basted with fat, and put back in the funnel. The head was thus slowly dried and smoked.

The attitudes directed towards heads, the motivation behind such decollation, and the esteem in which they were held varied in Oceania

---

[25] Buck, *op. cit.*, p. 45.

[26] Frances Del Mar, *op. cit.*, pp. 57ff.

from trivial to the important political concept noticed in San Cristoval, Solomon Islands. There the chief's *mana,* and therefore his importance, was estimated by the number of skulls decorating his door. A petty leader might have as many as thirty, while a really important personage would have around a thousand. This was an attempt to answer objectively the question which all societies would like to know: Is the chief chiefly, the king really royal? An enemy skull was an objective test which even the great emperors of Mesopotamia did not despise.

Nowhere in Eurasia did head-hunting play the part it did in Oceania, Amazonia, and Africa, although the practice was by no means unknown. The use of amulets carved from human skulls in the European Neolithic sites hints of its very early importance on that continent. So likewise might the decorated and elaborately buried skulls characteristic of the Mesolithic of Offnet. European archeologists deduce that the care in burial and expensive decoration of such Mesolithic skulls indicate that they were honorific burials of prestigeful members of the we-group, and not enemies. From the many instances of honorable or even worshipful treatment of skulls taken from the enemy among living peoples, it is seen that such an interpretation is by no means forced on the student. In fact, quite the reverse is probable.

Asia knew a high head-taking complex even among civilized peoples. The Mon and Khmer, for example, although nominal Buddhists, have a survival of ceremonial head-taking wherein the spirit of the victim becomes a protective genius. These mainland people of Southeast Asia, however, are included in the vast head-taking area which covers Malaysia and spreads to Melanesia and beyond.

For nearer Asia, Herodotus reported the practice among the Scyths, whom he admired and therefore was not slandering. The prestige and recognition elements stood out in his report. The Scythian warrior not only drank the blood of the first man he slew in battle but decapitated every one he could. These heads were tokens of his right to share in the booty when the king distributed it. The Scyth then removed the scalps and prepared them carefully. The crania of enemies particularly detested were made into drinking cups. The poor man covered his captured skulls with leather, the rich man with gold. They did this with the crania of kinsmen if they slew them in judicial duels before the king. Such cups were the cause of much boasting.[27]

Legend has preserved the tradition of such behavior among our immediate ancestors in Northwest Europe, both Celtic and Teutonic. Furthermore, Poseidonius of Apamea and Strabo both distinctly said that mutilation of the dead was general in that area. Diodorus Siculus claimed that the Gauls were head-takers. The Assyrians, of course, carried this primitivity into civilization, and few if any peoples ever surpassed them in head-taking. And, speaking of the Semites, one might observe that David's decollation of Goliath did not shock the Jews. Herodotus furthermore says the plundering inhabitants of of Taurus beheaded war prisoners and set their heads as high as possible over the decapitator's house in order to bring its inhabitants under the heads' protection.[28] One cannot find a clearer statement of magical head-taking in the literature for Amazonia or Melanesia.

The Nordic Eddas rarely speak of head-taking, but they do mention the trait. The *Heimskringla* tells how the viking Earl Sigurd harried the Scots in company with other Norse rovers. He slew the Scots Earl Tusk-Melbridga and took his head, but as Sigurd rode along with the head bound to his crupper, he struck himself with one of the Scot's prominent teeth which infected his leg, causing his own death.[29]

The head is cumbersome to carry about, so it was to be expected that some tribes would be content with only the scalp. It is thought by some students that scalping was often a substitution, that some people who became expert scalpers were formerly head-hunters. It is believed by some, for example, that the Indians of Southeast United States were generally decapitators, often with a human sacrifice motive connected with a solar cult. It is contended that the Iroquois, having come from this area, turned into scalpers in their new northeastern home. It is also thought that the practice in America was formerly not as widespread as when the white man noted it in early historic times. It seems to have been rapidly diffusing from the south and east of the United States just at the close of Pre-Columbian times. Indeed, there are Indians who blame the white man for much of the speed of the diffusion, and we know that many of the pioneer governments were hair buyers.

---

[27] Herodotus, iv. 64-66.
[28] *Ibid.*, iv., 104.
[29] Sturluson, *op. cit.*, I, ch. III, pp. 93ff.

Scalping was particularly common in America and rare elsewhere, although there was no unanimity in the method of taking or preparing scalps in the New World. For example, the California Kato went so far as to take whole heads to dance over while many other California tribes, such as the Yurok, did not even take scalps.[30] The southern tribes, such as the Creek, were zealous prisoner-torturers and trophy-gatherers. Le Moyne said that special warriors were detailed to seize and drag away every slain or wounded enemy to a safe place and literally to skin the head, taking much more than the scalp, with reed slips "sharper than any steel blade." Enemy scraps, legs, arms, head skins were brought home and affixed on a circle of tall poles with great solemnity. The "sorcerer" then cursed the enemy with "a thousand imprecations."[31]

Here again was something more than simple victory gloating. The Creek, having acquired scraps of the enemy, could work evil against the surviving members of the tribe, a rather common attitude. On the other hand, some tribes had simpler ideas. The Flathead held no victory dance unless the war party had brought home something to dance over, to be thankful about, but their dances were mere hate-expenditure and tension release devices. The nearby Kutenai did not hold a dance if their side had suffered a fatal casualty.

The scalps might in some instances be relics of cannibalistic rites. Among the Menomini the scalps were the property of the women, but while they were still fresh the warriors licked the blood from them to symbolize the devouring by the sun of men slain in battle, that is, decomposition. Indeed, the Menomini warriors actually ate strips of roast enemy out of bravado and jeered at those who would not.[32]

The revenge gloat seems to have been the attitude impelling the Northcoast people to take scalps. The Tlingit took whole heads and, when leisure and safety permitted, scalped them so as to take the ears. These trophies were dried to permanence by the fire.[33]

---

[30] Kroeber, *op. cit.*, p. 157.

[31] Le Moyne, in Swanton, *Early History of the Creek Indians and Their Neighbors*, p. 7.

[32] Skinner, *Social Life and Ceremonial Bundles of the Menomini Indians*, pp. 116-123.

[33] Swanton, "Social Conditions, Beliefs, and Linguistic Relationships of the Tlingit Indians," p. 449.

The religious motive was revealed in North America most strongly in the Southwest, and among the simpler societies more pertinently than among the more cultivated pueblo-building peoples. Nevertheless, even among such peoples as the Zuni the religio-economic importance of the scalp was considerable. The Zuni felt that they had to induct each scalp-taker into the Bow priesthood for his own protection against the malevolent powers of the scalp. Such men became rainmakers for the benefit of the tribe and commanders in war. Nevertheless, they suffered a tabu against sexual intercourse for a year and had to be purified by very elaborate ceremonies, thereby conforming to the exacting ritual pattern of the pueblos.[34]

The fear of the scalp, the penalties a scalper must undergo, and the potential good a scalp might be made to serve have been clearly seen among the simpler Southwest people. Miss Underhill has reported this well for the Papago.[35]. Similarly, the Yuma had the entire skin of the head removed with great formality by a shaman and four assistants. Not everyone could do this or the skin would not keep its shape. At that, no small amount of skill and experience in dissection was required. This was a matter requiring several days. At home, the warrior who had slain the enemy lived with the skin for several days, affectionately talking to it to calm its spirit. As soon as the spirit was convinced of the love with which it was now surrounded, an elaborate victory feast was held. No one but the scalp's owner dared carry it to the feast. Indeed, it is alleged that it was physically impossible for anyone else to do so. At this time the Yuma and some of their neighbors kept the slayers under a number of tabus because of their blood-guilt. The owner held subsequent feasts in honor of the skin, and at his death it was thrown into the river and "drowned."[36]

Popular opinion which holds that scalping found its highest and most important expression on the Great Plains is at variance with the facts. The typical Plains tribe by no means conceived the scalp to have the social, religious, and economic value assigned to scraps of enemy bodies by many peoples. It is true that scalps were universally taken in the area, that they were valued, and usually danced

[34] Ruth L. Bunzel, "Introduction to Zuni Ceremonialism," *Annual Report 47*, Bureau of American Ethnology (Washington: 1929-1930), p. 527.

[35] Ruth Underhill, *The Autobiography of a Papago Woman*, Memoir 46, American Anthropological Association (Menasha: 1936), *passim*.

[36] Densmore, *Mandan and Hidatsa Music*, pp. 10-13.

over, shrieked at, and given some emotional importance. Yet the graded system of war honors, or *coup,* pressed the scalp far into the background of emotional importance.[37] A scalp was not regarded as a fetish fraught with benefit and potential danger on the Plains. It could grow no crops; it could win no subsequent battles; and a scalp as such had little value. It could even be divided and subdivided and put on poles to make it look like several with no apparent intent at fraud.[38] Any bit of human hair was primarily a trophy, a tangible bit of evidence of victory and valor. Often war shirts and horse ornaments were decorated with strands of enemy hair. The popular importance ascribed to Plains scalping is probably due to the fact that these people were the last fierce warriors encountered by the white man in the westward expansion.

While North America was the chief scalping continent, the practice was known in artic Asia, which, because of its proximity to North America, is an item of considerable interest. Miss Czaplicka says that the Ostyak, Vogul, and Samoyed were acquainted with scalping. Some Ostyak songs tell of eating enemy hearts, another trait observable on North America's Great Plains.[39]

Herodotus reported scalping among the more distant Scyths. After the victorious warrior had taken an enemy head he removed the scalp and carefully prepared it. He proudly used the scalp as a napkin, often sewing many of them together to form a cloak. Sometimes a Scyth would completely flay an enemy for the purpose, and quivers made of flayed enemy arms were highly esteemed.[40]

One must also consider the important category of military values acquired, in contrast, from within the friendly group, such as the vast host of amulets, charms, or fetishes which made "our" side victorious. The Ark of the Covenant fought for David, spreading emerods among the uncircumcized Philistines, and the Palladium fought for Troy. The legionary Eagles had military might in themselves which enabled Roman law to spread. Christians in the past have been known to parade the bones of the saints before the seried host, and the Winnebago had war bundles.

[37] Wissler, *Material Culture of the Blackfoot Indians,* p. 154.
[38] Lowie, *Societies of the Arikara Indians, passim.*
[39] Marie A. Czaplicka, *op. cit.,* 69.
[40] Herodotus, iv. 64-66.

The writings of Radin and Skinner on Winnebago and Menomini war bundles have been mentioned with regard to tactical magic. The Northeast Woodland of America had developed the war fetish about as highly as any area, although the Plateau Kutenai and Salish understood their fabrication. The Southeast Woodland was hardly less adept. Bossu said that the Choctaw always consulted their "Manitou" before going to war. The chief carried it, guarded by the warriors. On the march it was exhibited in the direction of the enemy, apparently to their discomfiture.[41]

Many such fetishes were personal rather than tribal. The Plains warriors acquired theirs through individual dreams and visions. Warriors would consult their "medicine" before going into battle and would often wear such animal scraps into the fray. Some people, such as the Assiniboin, acquired their war charms through the dreams of professional shamans who would collect handsome fees.[42]

The we-group granted many objects of military value to the African warrior, such as special decorations for killers and valiant men. Officers' insignia were highly prized in the eastern and southern African kingdoms.

European literature is likewise full of references to charms, amulets, palladia, and insignia. Weapons themselves were honor-fetishes as well as instruments of death. Everyone is familiar with that attitude in the Old World. "To have abandoned one's shield is the height of disgrace," says Tacitus of the Germans; "the man so disgraced cannot be present at religious rites, nor attend a council: many survivors of war have ended their infamy with a noose."[43]

One's name was often a military object of great value. Omaha warriors took entirely new names after they had been on a war party four days[44], while a Kwakiutl brave could assume a new name if he was able to eat a whole captive. The granting of permission to acquire a new and more honorable name upon the completion of some valiant exploit has been very common in the world.

---

[41] Bossu, *op. cit.*, II, pp. 89-94.
[42] Lowie, *The Assiniboine*, p. 33.
[43] Tacitus, *Germania*, 6.
[44] Dorsey, "Omaha Sociology," p. 324.

CHAPTER 11

Certain Military Attitudes

A SUMMARY OF THE ATTITUDE PATTERN OF ANY POPULATION WOULD describe the symbolic fabric of its culture as a whole, but the very complexity of such a work prevents its being undertaken for the world. The subject has been successfully studied for individual persons in case histories, and perhaps for very small, homogeneous groups. Such work has been intensive, and one cannot as yet work intensively with the world. Ethnographers have not employed such methods until very recently, and few subjective considerations are apparent in existing field literature.

For these reasons we are confined even in military affairs to attitudes towards war itself, towards the enemy, towards one's own life considered as a value, and closely allied considerations. That these attitudes are apparent despite the objectivity of field reports indicates that they must be endowed with great emotional importance. They are therefore discussed here as the greatest of military attitudes.

No generalization on basic attitudes towards even war and peace is possible for nonliterate peoples as a whole. There have been those whose attitudes were almost completely pacific while peoples like the Blackfoot considered fighting their chief delight. By contrast, war has sometimes been conceived of as a sorrow inherent in the universe which must be accepted.

The semi-agricultural Omaha, through Plainsmen, had essentially pacific attitudes. They considered aggressive war a disintegrating force. The mysterious *wakanda,* the great cosmic force, had decreed the existence of war, hate, and vengeance, and man must submit. Rites were said to control war and the turbulent, ambitious men who liked it, but the control was feeble.[1] War to such people was a necessary evil which they practiced efficiently, but the Omaha did not

[1] Fletcher and La Flesche, *op. cit.*, p. 402.

revere it as an end in itself, as their purely bison-hunting neighbors tended to do. The old men strove to spread the paramount doctrine of peace and order within the tribe. War was secondary, and its real function was protective. Aggression was considered more troublesome than beneficial.[2] Since war is life-wasting and marriage life-creating, it was inconsistent with "natural law" for a man on or about to go on the warpath to marry.[3]

The great variance in attitudes between such American Plains peoples as the Blackfoot and the Omaha is striking, making any genetic "human nature" theory for or against war seem naive. The only possible conclusion is that human nature, if such a thing exists, is anything but set and unchangeable but something modelled by the patterns of culture into which the particular human is born. While among the Blackfoot, horse thievery and *coup*-counting were the only real means of advancement, the Omaha had other means of acquiring prestige. The latter were a peaceful agricultural people surrounded by predatory and and parasitic hunters. They found that communal war distinctly interfered with more important activities. They were pacific by preference, but realistically conceived of war as something placed in this world by Thunder, which therefore had to be suffered.

Other American Indians found intense war a nuisance. The Iroquois League was founded as an experiment in practical pacifism, an institution to put down war. The Iroquois horror of needless bloodshed was probably real, for they believed in the brotherhood of man and the fatherhood of the Manitou, which they sought to impress on all peoples. Those who rejected this noble principle were thought unworthy of life, and fit only for extermination. There were peaceful people in ordinarily warlike South America. The Goaynazes of Brazil, nonagricultural hunters and gatherers, fought ably to protect their own persons and territory. Wanting peace bad enough to fight for it is not as paradoxical as it sounds.

Africa had some simpler cultures, even perhaps basically humbler people, than were found in the Americas. To the simplest, such as the pygmies and Bushmen, out-group killing was not a matter of glory but a matter of self-protection against stronger men. The Bushman killed Hottentots to get Hottentot cattle, since this was the easiest way to get the best food. Some pygmies and Negroes lived

[2] *Ibid.*, p. 211.
[3] *Ibid.*, p. 325.

in a state of economic symbiosis. The Negroes gave the Pygmies garden bananas and the pygmies hunted for the Negroes. If a Pygmy shot a Negro with a poisoned arrow for breach of contract it was because there were no courts to which the Pygmy could take his case, nor would he have understood them if they existed.[4] The glorification of man-killing has always required a higher culture than his. Only among the high cultures, such as the Dahomean, has the army been the symbol of the national vitality.

Cold-blooded slaughter has really never been approved by the bulk of mankind. All have understood the amenities of peace to a greater or less degree. Civilized and savage men understand that war requires regulation and that human death is full of *mana,* which is a fearsome thing.

Some African tribes had oracles who tried to settle disputes between villages in preference to fighting it out. There was killing enough, but peace was valued for its own sake. Indians of Southeast United States likewise had peace towns wherein no human life could be taken, not even an enemy's. The Nigerians had supernaturals who were the personification of pity and peace, and Ihi the peace spirit would take vengeance on anyone violating a formally proclaimed peace between two towns. Furthermore, they had rules limiting cruelty in warfare which had the force of international law.[5]

The BaThonga were not particularly warlike until the Zulu diffused their bellicose attitudes to them. The regimental organization of the later Thonga looks like a new addition to an old device, the adding of a new function to the old puberty rite. Junod thinks that the Thonga considered peace the normal situation. The adoption of war — a dangerous and abnormal status — was considered a *rite de passage.* This was especially true for the warriors, but the status of war placed the whole clan also into a condition of marginality. For example, the queen would enter the regimental circle quite naked during the rites, an otherwise unthinkable act. Other sexual tabus were relaxed, while ordinary sexual behavior came under stricture. The wild shouts at leave-taking, the swallowing of meat without touching it, the taking of emetics, the jumping over *ntjhopfa* branches, the medicine of oblivion, the triumphant return, the eating of captured oxen, were rites of separation from normal peace and re-entry

[4] Paul Schebesta, *Among Congo Pygmies* (London: Hutchinson, 1933), *passim.*
[5] Meek, *op. cit.,* p. 481.

into it, true rites of passage from the usual to the dangerously remarkable and back.[6]

Turning to Oceania, Miss Blackwood says that war so preoccupied the lives of the people on Bougainville that it monopolized their dreams. It is interesting to note that the colonial pacification of the coast has altered the dream content of the population, while the natives of the unpacified interior retain their dreams of killing.[7] Dreams are always a mirror of culture, so that if the native culture has been so altered by white administration that the dream content has changed, then acculturation has gone far. Aside from the advisability of stopping the interminable native wars, the white man has sometimes been unjust in accusing the male native everywhere of uselessness, laziness, and decadence. The men often considered war their *raison d'être,* and when this was abruptly terminated, no adequate reason for existence was substituted.

No brief for the old wars need be entertained. One simply observes that profound acculturation was to be expected by their prohibition. Neither do all natives feel that the old killing days should be brought back. There are many old Indians who appreciate the piping days of peace under the Washington-Ottawa administration. Miss Powdermaker says that some Melanesians think they have benefited, too, appreciating their present ability to move about among other people in safety.[8] Such appreciative natives do realize, however, that they have lost something by the disruption of the old military attitudes.

A prime consideration of the natives' attitude toward war is reflected in the constant repetition of observers that war as such did not exist in Melanesia. Attention has been called to this before. Almost every competent book states that battles were few, casualties negligible, but boastings many. From the standpoint of a truly competent and tactical tribe, the Melanesians were indeed military humbugs. The psychologist and sociologist see the importance of the war gloat, however, which the statisticians might miss.

The truth of this hinges on what one calls war. Such warless people have by no means been friendly and pacific. They have not been ignorant of how to shed human blood, nor have they abhorred

[6] Junod, *op. cit.,* p. 481.
[7] Blackwood, *op. cit.,* p. 566.
[8] Powdermaker, *op. cit.,* p. 215, footnote.

it. Neither have they been without social institutions which formalized man-killing. The lack of organized war may demonstrate certain points, but it should not be overstressed, as it sometimes is. Field ethnology no more demonstrates that a warless people are *per se* a kindly one than it shows that a monogamous tribe is sexually chaste. Armstrong, for example, relates that war was very unusual on Rossel Island, but that the natives were murderously inhospitable to visitors and strangers who chanced upon their coast.[9]

It is impossible to speak of Polynesia as one culture province regarding the importance of war attitudes. We know that the men of New Zealand, Hawaii, Managaia, and elsewhere considered war the most important part of their being. In contrast, Miss Mead says that it was of slight importance on Manua. One can judge from both ethnological and missionary sources that it was not considered very important in other parts of Samoa. Mead believes that the relative unimportance of war and war gods in Manua was due to "local differentiation upon a common base under conditions of isolation and differentiation in the size of the population."[10] Manua, then, never felt the influences which made war so important in Western Samoa.

In Mangaia of the Cook Group there existed the same pragmatic test of political superiority through war that has been cited for San Cristoval in the Solomons. The Mangaians glorified war, therefore the lordship went to the strong. Could it be that because the lordship was wrested by the strong the Mangaians glorified that which their masters cherished? Formerly in fact and today by tradition, he who is strong enough to take and hold the important English castle of Arundel is by that fact Earl of Arundel; this is a clear parallel to Mangaian line of thought.

Eurasian attitudes were almost universally bellicose and peace was esteemed only by a few. In very old times, according to the archeologist Childe, some folk were indicated as peaceful by the lack of weapons in their sites. Childe also says in many places that it is obvious that the pacific went down before the warlike, were exterminated, or became socially and economically subordinated to the war

[9] Wallace Armstrong, *Rossel Island* (Cambridge: Cambridge University Press, 1928), p. 108.

[10] Mead, *op. cit.*, p. 9.

chiefs.[11] While they were considered barbarians, the Celts were thought the most superior of that category by the Greek and Roman writers because of their warlike spirit.

Life is the dearest of all treasures in our civilization. It is the supreme value, as witness the horror with which western civilization regards suicide. The attitude that life as life holds the highest possible evaluation has great local variation, however.

Perhaps the greatest proof that civilized cultures are "better" than primitive ones is seen in this fact: Civilized man, no matter how humbly placed, probably has more to live for than savage man. Life rewards civilized man more richly. If this is true, the rise of western civilization has been in part the rise in the valuation of the individual life. Yet we know that the classical civilizations of the Mediterranean basin valued life rather cheaply, providing the life was not that of the individual concerned. One valued his own life and that of his immediate associates, but was rather extravagant in the expenditure of the lives of others. Even civilization has not always produced elsewhere in the world the high regard for one's own life that is found in the occident. Field reports show us that under strong religious motivation it has not been as difficult to persuade victims to undergo human sacrifice as one might think.

This is the very point. There can be little doubt but that there is some instinctive basis to the will to live, yet whatever this may be, it is capable of great modification by the conditioning culture. While there may be an instinctive basis to living, love of life scarcely seems to be as high among people who have not felt the civilization-plus-Christianity glorification. Nor is this entirely a matter of military bravery. It is impossible to generalize on the proposition that the non-literate man is or is not braver than the civilized man. Too many exceptions can be found on both sides. The conclusion is simply that the valuation of human life, including one's own, can be powerfully affected by culture — that cultural valuation is of tremendously greater importance than instinctive foundation.

The Jicarilla Apache of southwestern United States were a fierce, untamed people with a very humble culture. The myth of their first war tells how a chief led the party of five hundred men against the enemy. These men were surrounded, even deliberately allowed

[11] Vere Gordon Childe, *The Dawn of European Civilization*, 2nd ed., (London: Kegan Paul, 1939), *passim.*

themselves to be, and stood there to be chopped to pieces to the last man. There is no hint in the text that these were unusually brave men, that they were particularly meritorious, or, on the other hand, particularly blame-worthy. The myth simply reflects the fact that the Jicarilla, like many other people, had not been conditioned to look on life as we do.[12] Perhaps escape was out of the question for these Apache. Man, like any other respectable animal, is capable of great feats of valor when trapped beyond hope.

DeVries, an eye witness of the Indian wars on Staten Island, spoke very disparagingly of Leni Lenape bravery, but ascribed great feats of heroism to them when death was inevitable, including magnificent fortitude under torture.[13] But this valiant acceptance of the inevitable is not the point in question. We mean that under the drive of a culturally conditioned spirit of self-sacrifice or patriotism, religious expectation of reward in an afterlife and other such attitudes, men can be made to be contemptuous of death. Even among people with hazy ideas of life after death and with no concept of patriotism as we know it, warriors have been led to take an oath of no-retreat, tantamount to a suicide vow, merely for the honor involved.

Nowhere in the world has this been more apparent than on the American Great Plains. The Plainsman was undoubtedly a very poor soldier. He loved a sure thing and often ran from a real battle. He was often a poltroon, a man whose valor could only be trusted when put against inevitable death. But an outstanding characteristic of Plains sociology was the prevalence of military lodges whose membership as a whole, or certain officers thereof, could be induced to take a vow to retreat under no circumstances.

Among the Arapaho the leader and his four associates in the Dog Dance made such a pledge. They went into battle with scarfs trailing on the ground which at the beginning of the action they staked to the ground so that they could not flee.[14] The Arapaho Warrior Society had eight degrees. The third degree consisted of the Club Men, individuals in the prime of life, who in a bad fight planted sticks in the ground which they would not desert unless the head chief gave the signal for a general retreat. Some of the higher orders had

---

[12] Goddard, *op. cit.*, p. 196.

[13] DeVries, in Wissler, *The Indians of Greater New York and the Lower Hudson*, pp. 281f.

[14] Lowie, *The Assiniboine*, p. 91.

even more stringent no-retreat obligations.[15] Such a vow was taken by the Dog Society among the Gros Ventres, by the Mandan old men who had been admitted into the lowest (Foolish Dog) society, by the two leaders in the Mandan Buffalo Society, and others. The Blackfoot Brave Dogs could retreat from no danger.[16] The ten Kiowa Dog Warriors could not flee, and their leader staked himself to the ground.[17] The Inverted Warriors of the Cheyenne had to repel every hostile charge or die on the spot.[18] Some Dakota tribes had no-flight societies consisting of young men who had not yet distinguished themselves in war. The Oglala Dakota Brave Hearts had lance-bearers who could not flee. Even worse was the plight of their no-flight men who went into battle with such a vow but armed only with rattles or deer dew-claws tipped with iron. With these inadequate weapons they rushed the enemy and tried to stab them before they could draw the bow.

The Oglala had a society called the Kit-Fox. This was reorganized every spring and new officers elected. Among the important posts were the four lance-bearers who ranked just after the two leaders and the two pipe-bearers. To be elected a lance-bearer was tantamount to being elected to die, as these officials had to undergo every danger and be in the worst of the fight. Such men were elected to the society without their knowledge, and might even be chosen from outside the association's membership. The individual learned of his election from the society's Whip-Bearers who brought him to the society's lodge. Usually the man hesitated, although sometimes he was glad. Acceptance was almost certain, for no Plains Indian could hesitate for long while surrounded by the valiant circle of the association members with the herald of the society shouting his praises.[19]

The works of Lowie and Linderman on the Crow show that such no-flight men did not have to be organized into mutually stimulating

---

[15] James Mooney, "The Ghost-Dance Religion and the Sioux Outbreak of 1890," *Annual Report 14,* Bureau of American Ethnology, Part 2, (Washington: 1892-1893), pp. 987f.

[16] Clark Wissler, "The Blackfoot," *Annual Archaeological Report for 1905* (Toronto: 1906), p. 174.

[17] Mooney, *op. cit.,* p. 284.

[18] James O. Dorsey, "A Study of Siouan Cults," *Annual Report 11,* Bureau of American Ethnology (Washington: 1889-1890), pp. 21, 25.

[19] Wissler, *Societies and Ceremonial Associations of the Oglala Division of the Teton-Dakota,* p. 15.

associations. For any number of reasons, or for just plain *weltschmerz,* a young Crow might "vow his body to the enemy." His parents might grieve for him as one dead, but nothing would deflect him from his purpose of dying in an attack against hopeless odds at the first opportunity. One could not honorably and therefore tolerably escape the obligations once assumed. Neither could one thereafter flee from the enemy if the Crow dance-police should sit him on the lodgepoles during the Sun Dance ritual.

Some South Americans, like the Guarayos of the Southwest Amazonia, likewise have preferred death to surrender.[20] It is said that the Abiponian Mocobi-Toba of Patagonia have never been known to beg for life or mercy under torture.[21]

The Winnebago attitude toward the life of a member of the we-group had a strong economic tinge which is far from uncommon. The whole revenge complex which so saturates the field literature is an aggregate of attitudes toward the lives of fellow tribesmen as values. Often the valuation was bluntly economic, as among the acquisitive North Pacific Coast peoples. Revenge for a death which had not been paid for was a principal Tlingit reason for fighting.[22] This economic aspect of revenge often had magical connotations. The Jibaro boy was harangued by his father every morning that his gardens would be fruitful, his animals and fowls would prosper, and plenty of food would be his if he strove to avenge every wrong done by the enemy, even those committed long before.[23]

Almost every tribe has evaluated the lives of the members of the we-group so highly that effort has been made to keep peace within. The Jibaro, just mentioned, made very little attempt to keep peace within their own tribe because to them the effective we-group was the family, not the political tribe. Most people have gone far beyond that. Certainly the lives of fellow-tribesmen have been values of such importance that an unavenged death among the simpler peoples has always been a fact of overwhelming gravity. This has been true regardless of the variance in the idealization of revenge.

---

[20] Church, *op. cit.*, p. 113.

[21] *Ibid.*, p. 246.

[22] Swanton, "Social Conditions, Beliefs, and Linguistic Relationships of the Tlingit Indians," p. 449.

[23] Karsten, *op. cit.*, p. 2.

No-retreat societies would have been incomprehensible to the Melanesians. They valued their lives highly and lost them as seldom as possible. This fact alone would have made them poor soldiers. A few Polynesians felt the same way, although the presence of war gods, of special paradises for slain warriors, suppressed this feeling. Death-contempt in Polynesia has been linked with strong feelings of tribalism or nationality. It was not so linked on the American Great Plains, where tribalism was weak or absent, but it was also common in the African kingdoms where strong tribalism existed. Therefore no generalization can be made from death contempt alone.

Buck reports that warriors were capable of vowing their deaths on Mangaia. Here such attitudes were linked with a well-developed war god theology. The high-born noble Tiora did not shrink when informed by the war priests that their god demanded his sacrificial death at the enemy's hands. He went against the foe alone and they obligingly killed him, unaware that his immolation was intended to accomplish their own defeat.[24] Melanesia could produce no Tiroa, Horatius at the Bridge, or Arnold von Winkelried.

The fact that formalized death-contempt existed in several areas of Eurasia is not surprising. The recklessness of the northern berserk man has already been noted, while there is at least a legend that among the early Slavs a deadly game was sometimes played merely to while away the long nights. Among a group of warriors sitting around the drinking table, one would make a bet that he could cut himself free from the hangman's noose with his saber. His companions would cover the bet, tie a rope to a beam, and noose it to the man's neck while he stood on the table. His bare saber was then given to him and the table removed. He was then suspended to all intents as if he were being executed, save that his hands were not tied. He would then try to hack himself free from the strangling cord. If he succeeded, he won the wager. If he did not, he lost his property—and his life.

Caesar reported a condition among the Aquitanians which resembled the no-retreat idea and institution of war-friendship noticed elsewhere. They had a society of elite fighters salled *solidurii,* or "bound-by-duty." These men were war-friends, enjoying all benefits with their comrades but sharing their misfortunes, even to death. If

[24] Buck, *op. cit.,* p. 49.

one of their fellows met calamity, they all shared it on the spot. If they could not do this, they committed suicide[25]

None of the foregoing statements must be interpreted as pretending that certain areas were above fear. But fear can be inhibited, and no military society has lacked devices for doing so. Other values have been set higher than that of life, or the life value itself may not have reached a development as strong as our own.

Nowhere has the element of fear become more apparent than in nonliterate man's military preparational ceremonies. The multitude of dances and other pre-combat rites were devices to insure the proper glandular activity enabling warriors to walk into probable death. Of such value were the multitude of charms, amulets, war bundles, and so forth, which supposedly guaranteed victory for "our" side, took a supernatural advantage of the enemy, and influenced the outcome of the fight by means other than skill, prowess, equipment, or merit. As has already been pointed out, magic may be tactical.

Even such well-organized societies as the Cherokee sought invulnerability by elaborate formulae before setting out on an expedition.[26] A man, feeling himself invulnerable and sure of success, could afford to be brave, daring, and valiant, so such mass mutual incitement might actually have had value in the field.[27] The Osage, for example, were a peaceful people but, like others, were forced by circumstances to fight both offensively and defensively. At such times the warriors did not pretend to rely solely on their own strength, but "cried without ceasing for divine aid" against the foe.[28] It was the first duty of a war party to select a man to call upon *wakando*. It was he who won, if victory was achieved, and all honors went to him.

The Winnebago, too, like the peaceful Osage and the ancient Israelites, sought to inhibit fear by reliance on the supernatural. War was their honor-path, the avenue to social prestige, and the means of satisfying strong emotional needs. Given this great importance, prayers for success in war were the most important ones. Indeed, war prayers were also included in most of the ceremonies of peace.[29]

---

[25] Caesar, *op. cit.*, iii. 22.

[26] James Mooney, "The Sacred Formulae of the Cherokees," *Annual Report* 7, Bureau of American Ethnology (Washington: 1885-1886), pp. 388f.

[27] Kroeber, *op. cit.*, p. 844.

[28] La Flesche, *The Osage Tribe: Rite of the Chiefs*, p. 49.

[29] Paul Radin, *The Winnebago Tribe*, Annual Report 37, Bureau of American Ethnology (Washington: 1915-1916), p. 156.

Radin points out the valuation of human life to the Winnebago in a very realistic manner. It is not surprising that war should have been surrounded by ceremonial and tabu, for life was at stake, and to an economically precarious community, the life of every laborer was precious. The chief of the Thunderbirds, therefore, exercised a restraining influence in the public interest, demanding an accounting from everyone who left on a war party. He sought to prevent anyone from endangering himself unnecessarily. If the foolhardy endangered others, they had to face the kin of their comrades like any other wrongdoers. Neither was anyone permitted to head a large party unless he could acquire a special blessing from the supernaturals regarding every detail of the campaign.

Men may vary from place to place in their estimation of their own lives, but life is about all that the individual knows he owns. Hence, many fear-inhibiting ceremonies have been observed even in fierce Africa. The primitive warrior's wish for a sure thing was apparent in the sacrifices offered in Nigeria before the warrior's departure. The priest rubbed each man with magic leaves to render him invisible. Then an animal was slain, and as it died, the priest called the roll of the famous enemy warriors, hoping thereby to call their souls to him, leaving their owners spiritless and hence helpless in the coming battle.[30] The Nigerian warriors then drank fresh goat's blood to gain new vigor and valor. To guard against his own friends, each recruit put a few drops of his blood into a bowl of palm wine from which all drank with mighty oaths to the god to abstain from treachery.[31]

Such works have not been confined to simple Nigeria. When the Zulu king proclaimed a war, the first thing the soldier did was to go to his own cattle kraal where his ancestral spirits dwelled to fortify himself with magic. Kidd reports that "So many are the various modes of doctoring the army that one despairs of reducing them to anything like order." The warriors drank emetics and purgatives. The shamans worked magic over bits of enemy property. They performed rites whereby the warriors become invisible and invulnerable and their weapons unseen. Warriors ate lion heart, tiger blood, and such things to gain sagacity, ferocity, agility, and other military virtues. An ox was then thrown with bare hands and its shoulder cut

---

[30] Talbot, *Life in Southern Nigeria*, p. 233.
[31] *Ibid.*, p. 244.

out alive, which the shaman cooked with a "sickening mess" which the soldiers had to eat. A man was killed if he had to spit out this foul morsel, for he had thus given strength to the enemy. The shaman then made incisions in the men's flesh and rubbed the medicated beef into the wounds. The tortured ox was chased about until dead, and the longer his agony endured, the more unfortunate the enemy. The ox was then roasted and the ancestral spirits were invoked for war-aid. Indeed, many natives thought that the real battle was between the spirit ranks in the air above the earthly fight. While the chief himself had to be doctored, he really stayed at home to manipulate the spirits in the manner of a priest-king.

Omens were inspected, and if favorable, the warriors were painted and sent forth, but unfavorable omens would cause the priests and shamans to postpone the expedition. The warriors "fight with the most marvelous bravery when they are assured by their doctors that success is certain," but they "lose heart quickly in a forlorn hope. They are either stupidly and magnificently brave or ridiculously timid and fearful."[32]

Kidd's comment is obviously unsympathetic, but the modicum of truth therein has more than once given the white man the victory over the nonliterate warrior when the estimate of the tactical situation indicated otherwise.

Despite fetish and shaman, defeat sometimes comes to every army. What, then, of the faith in the magic? The same excuse is given which all of us have heard in freshman physics when the laboratory demonstrator has failed to produce the textbook result. It is easy, as in Nigeria, to claim some inadvertent breach in the law, or the intervention of superior enemy magic.[33]

We have observed that courage has been a rare quality in the western Pacific. Only rarely did a warrior stand out as personally brave. The Papuan was an assassin, not a soldier.[34] Seeing that the attitudes of bravery in New Guinea and Melanesia have not been particularly strong, much attention has been paid to such things as war dances, or rather to fear-inhibiting ceremonies. Such squabblers would not enter a fight if the chances were not entirely in their favor. Fear replaced fury in an even fight, and they were at their best with

---

[32] Kidd, *op. cit.*, p. 309.

[33] Talbot, *Life in Southern Nigeria*, p. 234.

[34] Abel, *op. cit.*, p. 130.

their foe a captive tied to a tree.[35] The Kiwai practiced many rites to affect the enemy adversely from a distance, especially to make him so preoccupied with women that he would fall easy prey, making extensive use of the genitalia of their own women to secure this. They had a long list of omens to be read before starting, a common enough practice. Many tabus fell on the stay-at-homes as well: the old women had to keep good fires burning in the men's house; the whole village had to keep quiet lest the enemy hear a noise from afar and be warned. The women could do only necessary work, therefore, and had to abstain from eating the flesh of any shy animal. The wife could not mourn her absent husband, and had to refrain from adultery lest he die in battle.

Another Zulu-like element was observable in the Loyalty Group where the shamans likewise attempted to insure victory by preparing a magic broth by a secret formula. They poured some of the mixture in a hole and retired to see if a lizard would come and taste it, though they abhorred lizards under other circumstances. They were delighted if a reptile obliged. Being thus reassured of the magical efficacy of the brew, the warriors gulped it down, thinking that they had their enemies where they wanted them.[36]

The characteristic men's lodge of Melanesia was important in such fear-inhibiting work. Brown says of New Britain that all the victory-insurance rites were held in the club houses. He says parenthetically that he never met a brave man in New Britain.[37]

The men of New Britain had a war god who insured victory if uninjured cuscus, harmless local marsupials, were roasted alive and eaten. One of the party would be killed if any of the little animals were dead or injured before being put on the fire. And so the feast continued, invoking the aid of the god, blaming him for their warlike idea, and putting it up to him to make them successful. The weapons were then blessed at his shrine.

Perhaps the more courageous Polynesians did not make so much of fear-inhibiting devices, but they did use them. The dances held in Samoa before battles were just the ordinary ones, but each village had a characteristic war song. The priests invoked the war gods of the various villages for success, protection, and courage for the war-

[35] Landtman, *op. cit.*, pp. 149, 153, 155.

[36] Hadfield, *op. cit.*, p. 174.

[37] Brown, *op. cit.*, p. 153.

riors, especially addressing themselves to the war-powerful Cuttle Fish. Each warrior then confessed his transgressions, made what restitution he could, and was shriven by the priests with coconut milk lustration. The warrior who did not confess would be killed.

Firm belief in a hereafter made the Germans contemptuous of death. A similar indoctrination also led the Celts to do deeds of valor. Caesar, speaking of the Gallic Druids, said that they taught the metempsychosis of souls as their cardinal doctrine, so that, fear of death being removed, the warriors could be incited to great valor.[38] The Valhalla myth of the old Teutons was a fear-inhibiting idea too well known to need recounting here. Many things were worse than death in their minds, such as failing to protect one's chief or king. For a liegeman to lay down his life in defense of his leader was a boon surpassing all others.

Courage was not lacking in barbarian north Europe, but it was sometimes intermixed with cowardice in the same manner that later was to mystify the European in viewing the conduct of the American Indian and Zulu. Agricola's remarks about the Britons being superstitiously reckless at times and cowardly at others has a familiar ring.[39]

Parenthetically, almost all the Roman writers remarked on the evils of acculturation in destroying the courage of the barbarians. Caesar says that the Nervii were aware of this and strove, like some other nonliterate tribes, to maintain themselves free from enfeebling and corrupting Roman vices.[40]

While the men of Northern Europe were brave, they had the same need of fear-inhibiting ceremonies as any other warrior. After all, death is both so painful and so very final that even brave men must be soothed into accepting it, or made to feel that they are invincible. Caesar was once surprised that Ariovistus did not strike hard at him to win a decisive victory, but upon questioning the prisoners, he discovered that the German matrons, whose duty it was to foretell victory by lot and divination, had declared the heavens unpropitious and warned the king not to fight before the new moon.[41]

---

38 Caesar, *op. cit.*, vi. 14.
39 Tacitus, *Agricola,* 11.
40 Caesar, *op. cit.*, ii. 15.
41 *Ibid.*, i. 50.

Tacitus described the fear-inhibiting ceremonial of the Germans. Archeology shows that the Hercules epos had diffused to the northwest before the Romans arrived. The Germans said that the demigod had appeared to them and taught them to sing hymns to him on the eve of battle. They likewise had a peculiar war-cry, and the leading men could predict the outcome of the approaching battle by the way the warriors performed this shouting rite.[42] Tacitus likewise said that Germans divine the outcome of battle by ordeal. One favorite method was to capture somehow a member of the prospective enemy group and pit him against one of their own champions, refraining from battle if the stranger won.[43] Fear could be repressed by entering only those battles the favorable outcome of which was assured. Tacitus recorded the fear-inhibiting nature of the human sacrifice of a member of the we-group, as well as the presence of certain victory-insuring palladia. The Germans would not tolerate so much as a disciplinary blow from their commanders but submitted to death if the war divinity demanded it. The priests also carried "certain fetishes . . . and emblems into battle to insure success."[44]

More than one battle between two nonliterate groups, or between a nonliterate group and civilized men has come to an abrupt end because the shamans or someone else suspected unfavorable magic. Justin characteristically relates that a coalition of Celts under a petty chief named Catumandus attacked the Greek colony of Marseilles in about 400 B. C., but were frightened away by some magico-religious omen.[45]

Attitudes toward the enemy and his life have been as variable as those toward the lives of members of the we-group, ranging from sympathy for captives to torture. Prisoner torture has been common enough. The eastern portion of the United States was noted for it. Simple abuse during the victory dance was common throughout the west. Some western Indians, such as the Wyandot, would adopt prisoners at times and kill them ruthlessly at others.[46]

It is hard to generalize about the Plains and other western tribes. The Plains-Cree subjected prisoners to a sort of semi-slavery in which

---

[42] Tacitus, *Germania,* 3.
[43] *Ibid.,* 10.
[44] *Ibid.,* 7.
[45] Justin, in Hubert, *op. cit.,* p. 301.
[46] J. W. Powell, "Wyandot Government," *Annual Report 1,* Bureau of American Ethnology (Washington: 1879-1886), pp. 59-69.

the lives of the men were in constant danger, while the persons of the women were at the disposal of their captors. They had, however, a horror of captive torture.[47] The life of an enemy refugee was perfectly safe in an Osage village provided he had eaten Osage food. The Omaha did not kill captives but kept them until the end of the war. At the conclusion of hostilities they could remain with the Omaha permanently if they chose, and could have the same role and status as a born Omaha, although they were not formally adopted. The Omaha were notoriously cruel to the wounded enemy, though, and enjoyed chopping them to pieces in sight of their friends, throwing bits after the retreating foe, who raged appropriately.[48]

The enemy in South America could only be an enemy. The Carib considered every human who could not speak their dialect a person marked for slaughter.

Both chivalrous and hateful attitudes toward the enemy existed in Eurasia. Granted that all conflict follows certain rules, extreme consideration toward an enemy either because of chivalry or international law seemed most marked among the early Hindus. But they discovered the disutility of this attitude against unchivalrous enemies, such as the Nagas who relied on tactical magic, or the Rakshashas who relied on ambush and the principle of surprise. The unchivalrous Pisachas also made the terrain more difficult by scattering thorns and dotting it with underground obstacles like modern tank traps. The Dasya chief Namuchi loosed hordes of lovely women on the Arya troops with orders to seduce them. In the end the Arya reverted to pre-chivalric methods of warfare, including poisoned arrows.[49]

All this aside, the *Vedas* did show over the long period during which they were written a slow development of chivalry and attitudes of fair play in warfare. With the development and elaboration of tactical principles, they relied more and more on truly military methods, abandoning the stupid slaughter of savages, and passed out of the realm of this study and into civilization. Indeed, as early as the Battle of the Ten Kings, Aryan tactics and strategy were well-developed and one Eurasiatic people, perhaps the first in the world, ceased to be primitive warriors. True, it is hard to exaggerate the loathing

[47] Skinner, *Political Organization, Cults, and Ceremonies of the Plains-Ojibway and Plains-Cree, passim.*

[48] Dorsey, "Siouan Sociology," p. 332.

[49] *Rig Veda*, vi. 15, 75.

with which they viewed the Dasya enemy whom they robbed. The race difference provided adequate symbolization, social distance, and motive for hate. They ascribed all sorts of low practices to them and called them many vile names in the Sodom and Gomorrah fashion. While such attitudes may not be admirable, they have not been the monopoly of savage warriors.

We have been led to think that disregard for enemy life and his feelings are characteristic of warfare, but this is not nesessarily so. The gentle Papago considered an enemy life precious and its destruction a murder, even though committed by a Papago warrior in legitimate war. A Papago man who had killed an enemy was unclean and dangerous, and the ordeal of purification necessary to readmit him to society was even more severe than the hardships of the warpath. He had to expiate for the murder of the hated Apache for sixteen days, four periods of four days each. He had no comforts. He was allowed no more bedding and warmth than he had on the warpath. He was isolated from his fellows. It was tabu for him to see fire, to scratch himself, and so on. He was attended by a man who brought him a little food each day and supervised his exercise. His hair had to be worn long as if he were in mourning. Finally, he was allowed to clean up and join a dance, which was very rigorous. The Papago wounded were also thought to have received Apache contamination and were forced to purify themselves for four days.[50]

Sympathy for the enemy was not universal in America. The Jibaro intertribal wars had no idea of expiation or balancing a life for a life, for these people fought only for extermination. The hated tribe had to be annihilated without regard for sex or age, along with its livestock, so that no potential avenger should survive.[51] Yet the Jibaro killer also had to go through a lengthy and troublesome purification rite, but presumably from different motives than those of the Papago. This is not clear, however. A killer could not enter his own house until his captured head was prepared. He wore no paint or adornment and had to dress as a penitent.[52] Even his wife and daughter had to be purified partly because of their close relationship and partly because they had touched his blood-polluted clothes and person.[53]

---

[50] Densmore, *Papago Music,* pp. 187f.
[51] Karsten, *op. cit.,* p. 16.
[52] *Ibid.,* p. 35.
[53] *Ibid.,* p. 37.

These purification rites were not admittedly conscience-cleansers, however, but they were motivated by fear of the enemy spirit thirsting for revenge, which might be the same thing.[54]

The bloody Zulu are estimated to have killed easily a million men in the wars of Chaka. They militarized the BaThonga and persuaded them to accompany their career of slaughter. But note that while the killer of enemies attained great glory, he also acquired great danger. The killer was subject to the persecution of the *nuru* of his victim's vengeful spirit. *Nuru* might haunt him into insanity, might make his eyes swell, might instill such blood-lust into him that he would fall upon his own family with his assegai. The victorious slayer therefore had to receive magical medication to purge him of *nuru*.[55]

An Ibo warrior, after decapitating an enemy, licked some of the blood from the knife in order to become identified with the slain, thereby becoming immune from attack by the ghost. After the peace he therefore could feast in the enemy's village, and even drink wine from the victim's palms without spiritual danger. Indeed, after the blood-licking the spirit of the slain might become reincarnated as the slayer's son, and hence become an ally.[56]

Scraps of an enemy were no more an unmixed blessing among some Africans than they were among the Papago. Neither, as has been observed, was his death. His magic was still potent, his revenge something to fear. The Nigerian warrior was glad to return home after the peace ceremony carrying many heads, but he had to bathe in every stream he came to *en route* and anoint himself with medicine "to stay the avenging power of the blood which was shed." Otherwise the man might not enter his house or approach any of his wives.[57]

The brave Zulu freed themselves with even greater difficulty from death-contamination. The slayer first had to stab the fallen enemy through the bowels lest the unreleased spirit drive him insane. He then removed his victim's loin cloth and substituted it for his own until his purification. He carried the death-dealing assegai point downward instead of in the usual horizontal position. He could not mingle in normal society nor partake of *amasi*. He had potentially con-

---

[54] *Ibid.*, p. 39.
[55] Junod, *op. cit.*, pp. 477ff.
[56] Meek, *op. cit.*, p. 242.
[57] Talbot, *Life in Southern Nigeria*, p. 242.

tracted a disease called *iZembe* which would cause dysentery, kidney disorders, and finally insanity unless purified with herbs and shamanism. He had to live on the veld with those of his kind, wearing a sprig of wild asparagus in his hair. There he was respectfully treated and well fed by the rest of the community. This residence on the veld might be for quite a while, for the slayer had to find a female of a tribe other than his own or, *faute de mieux*, a boy, and have intercourse with her, or him. This woman did not contract *iZembe* herself but passed it on to the next man with whom she cohabited. The killer had to submit to many charms before entering his own kraal and taking up normal life. Even so, all his subsequent life he was forced to abstain from the milk of any cow whose calf has not yet sprouted horns, from the annual first-fruits of the season, or beer made from new grain, unless he had fortified himself with charms each time.[58]

Why this revulsion against man-killing? Why such rites even among fierce people? Why also the retreat from blood-revulsion to such beautiful and esoteric religious ceremonialism as the Pawnee Hako?

Not all Africans had such obvious blood-guilt as the murderous Zulu although among other peoples it often only had less patent expression. The Dahomeans, for example, had no apparent fear of killing an ordinary enemy, for they were mass-destructive people, but they feared to kill the king of a conquered people lest his magic and his gods work against them. He was kept in splendid captivity surrounded by plenty of choice women until he died naturally.

The Papuans looked upon their enemies as a type of game. But since this was so for the enemy as a whole, the hatred toward a particular individual could be greatly mollified in spite of all their spleen-venting attitudes. If a warrior observed a friend on the other side whom he wished spared, he would hold his bow in front of the man or mark him with betel spittle, and be sure these signs would be respected.[59]

The attitude toward the feminine element in the enemy population was universally mild in Polynesia. In Melanesia an enemy was an enemy regardless of sex, and was therefore marked for slaughter. Ivens reports an exception to this in the Southeast Solomons where

[58] Krige, *op. cit.*, p. 276.
[59] Landtman, *op. cit.*, p. 159.

war was considered man's business and women were allowed to visit to and fro in Polynesian fashion.[60]

The Polynesians were capable of the most intense hatred toward the enemy's male fighting effectives. Yet they often showed them the most intense ceremonial courtesy before the action began. Brown gives an interesting description of the Samoans he knew. The combat lines would meet and address each other with formality as great chiefs and warriors, and present each other with food in an excess of courtesy. One side would ask the other if it wished to fight that day or postpone the action. The other would reply that "It is not for us to speak of such things in the presence of chiefs and warriors such as you." The most polite words in the language were used, and the most gentlemanly caution was exercised by each side to keep from seeming to dictate to the other. Once the fight was joined, however, the Samoans meant to kill and all chivalry was dropped, the language bandied between the lines becoming very scurrilous.[61]

Gallantry paid the Maori poorly when they tried it with modern British troops. They played the game more fairly than fair in the European concept. They were amazed when the British shot the people whom they sent from the palisades for water, for was not water necessary? When British ammunition ran low they waited for them to bring up supplies, for why fight a man on uneven terms?[62]

Let us repeat. There has existed a dread of taking enemy life, a feeling that if the life of a member of the we-group was precious, so was that of a member of the other-group. Fear of death-contamination has demanded expiation or purification among many folk. The blood-dread or fear of the vengeful spirit of the slain enemy – and they probably are the same – has been apparent in black Oceania. In Papua, according to Riley, captured skulls themselves first had to be washed. Then the head preparateur had to purify himself by bathing in salt water, taking great care to cleanse his teeth, nostrils, and mouth. When washed the men were supplied with a quantity of perfumed leaves.[63]

Landtman describes the following Papuan method of freeing the warrior from blood stain. The slayer took a long stem of a certain

[60] Walter G. Ivens, *Melanesians of the Southeast Solomon Islands* (London: K. Paul, Trench, Trubner, 1927), p. 300.

[61] Brown, *op. cit.*, pp. 166f.

[62] Del Mar, *op. cit.*, p. 153.

[63] Riley, *op. cit.*, p. 270.

creeping plant and slit it at both ends. Stepping into the sea or swamp, he passed the slit creeper over his head and body to the waist. Turning toward the shore, he completed the slit in the vine, threw both parts behind him, and kicked some water, and apparently the evil, backward with his foot.[64]

Even in Polynesia, where hate was a thoroughgoing affair and where the art of war had a considerable development, a killer had to be purified by a priest after battle and to wash himself thoroughly. In New Zealand he was not permitted to enter his own enclosure until his was done, after the South African way of thought.

Peace, then, seems to be the normal situation in the minds of even warlike peoples. War and killing push men into some kind of marginality which is at least uncomfortable, for there seems to be a basic fear of blood contamination, an essential dread of human murder. If man did not consider human killing something out of the ordinary, why has there been such common fear of the enemy dead, the idea of contamination of even a prestigeful warrior of the we-group? Does the blood of even righteously punished Cain cry up from the ground as well as that of virtuous Abel? In spite of ethnocentrism, of hatred for foreign ways, of a justifiable desire for the property of the other-group, of the implication of simian ancestry to other tribes, yet the cry of Shylock, that the other-group members have the same anatomy, the same emotions as we, cannot be downed except by the conscience-cleansing ceremonies which civilization has denied us. Nonliterate man has relied on ancient and powerful ceremonial sanctions, while civilization prefers mental hospitals. We have seen that the channelling of frustration into hatred toward the enemy is good for the internal harmony of the we-group, but the enemy is human, too. Humanity is capable of ambivalent attitudes toward its enemies.

[64] Landtman, *op. cit.*, p. 160.

CHAPTER 12

War and the Organization of Society

WHILE CIVILIZATION HAS USED MATERIAL TOOLS TO MASTER THE PHYSical environment, few will deny that organization, leadership, and administration in group endeavor are necessary for success. Disorganization and unorganization limit success. Psychologists and social scientists know that because men differ in capacities and interests, they also differ in the roles they must play in society's organized division of labor and in the statuses which accompany these roles. All societies are formally or informally characterized by stratification in role and status. There is no need to discuss this fact in detail, for it is the theme of many elementary treatises.

An inspection of primitive military behavior reveals little to controvert this general theory. Organization with clear-cut command functions brings success in war just as it does in economics, politics, or any other field of social endeavor. Because warfare is a life and death matter this organization must become so definite and exacting that it is called discipline. Foregoing chapters have said that the lack of tactical operations made primitive war "primitive." In the end, this means nothing more or less than saying that the non-civilized fighter is no soldier, his warfare is not war, and his butchering is futile and primitive because his operations lack organization and because he has developed the functons of leadership and command so poorly.

Successful organization and management in the peaceful walks of life and in martial affairs have a rough parallel development. Cooperative hunting and fishing will require organization and direction and are ordinarily good training schools for organized warfare with a developed command element. Men have more to eat when they cooperate under direction in extracting nature's gifts from her, and they likewise are more successful against their human enemies. Yet the parallel is only a rough one. Cultural lags play a large part in military history and prehistory. Martial activity is fraught with emotion, and social behavior on the emotional plane relies heavily on tradition. Men in danger look to the old men for advice, and old warriors and generals tend to fight the battles of the past.

When civilized man first began visiting the "savages" he almost invariably wrote of their social systems in terms of the one from which he had come. Most social aggregates were called kingdoms and their head men denominated kings. Later explorers called almost every social group a "tribe," whether they might have been viewing kinship organizations, associations, local bands, groups of friends, hunting parties, religious bodies, or monarchical states as formalized as that of Bourbon France. Hence the term "tribe" has practically no meaning, for the socio-political organizations of nonliterate men are too complex and varied to come under any such simple term. The term here means nothing more nor less than a group of persons who collectively permit some sort of social relation and authority, weak or strong, among each other and collectively deny any authority on the part of an outside person or group of persons. This definition is of necessity weak and inclusive, embracing the constitutional government of the United States as well as a small band of hunting Bushmen in the Kalahari desert of South Africa.

Tribal cohesion and political authority are most important in any discussion of war. Without both of them, but few men could be put and maintained in the field, but slight control exercised over them when there, and but meager results expected from their activity.

Some societies such as the Jibaro, have completely lacked tribal organization and common political authority.[1] Each Jibaro family father was and is by theory master of the house, its only master, and there is no chief in peace times. The Jibaro do not even have a specific term for a chief.[2] The forests and river courses of tropical South America where they live are inhabited by similar men of implacable ferocity which, combined with the inhospitable climate and unproductive character of the land, make this the only region of the New World still inhabited by real Indians. The typical fight in this area is really the feud, which being a family matter, is a category of its own outside a military discussion. Nevertheless, the families of one community are upon occasion capable of gathering together and making

[1] Karsten, *op. cit.*, p. 1.

[2] *Ibid.*, p. 7.

war upon another community. The tactical chapters showed that, and surely the great Carib invasion must have been accompanied by something resembling true war. People such as these could hardly be expected to go to war under a commander and to obey his orders. But what is expectable does not invariably occur, and these tribes perceived the utility of the command institution better than some others, the Eskimo, for example.

The California Indians had a somewhat more closely knit political society than the familial Jibaro. Most Californians were at least organized into bands, local groups, or villages which cut across kinship lines. The village was generally the basic socio-political unit, and the tribe as a larger unit typically did not exist. The Mohave, however, constituted a sharp contrast to the typical people, for with them the tribe was all and the local settlement unimportant. They thought of themselves as a national entity living in a specific territory which was regarded as an emotional value.[3] Consequently they were led by chiefs: a head chief of hereditary of vague authority, a war chief in whom most of the emotional attitudes were centered, a chief of entertainments, and a shaman. The last three acquired office through supernatural experiences.[4] The Mohave are mentioned with the typical Californians to provide contrast. Of the more typical people it has been said that:

> No distinction or principle exists in the native mind between murder and war. It is rather clear that all so-called wars were only feuds that happened to involve large groups of kinsmen, several such groups or unrelated fellow townsmen of the original participants. Whoever was not drawn into a war was careful to remain neutral as in a private quarrel.[5]

The foregoing remarks describe the Yurok. Most Californians were absolutely nonmilitary; they possessed next to none of the traits requisite for the military horizon, a condition which would have taxed their all but nonexistent social organization too much. Their societies made no provision for collective political action. When a terrier bites a spaniel, the other spaniels, *as spaniels,* do not enter the fight, and the Californians felt the same way.

Both the South American Forest and general California patterns were really nontribal, simple, and primitive, and neither area con-

[3] Kroeber, *op. cit.,* p. 727.
[4] *Ibid.,* p. 745.
[5] *Ibid.,* p. 49.

tained many good warriors. The preceding chapter discussed the Jibaro feeling toward their enemies, which exterminative attitude alone made them into something resembling soldiers. It was not merely coincidental, by contrast, that the Mohave had ideas of territoriality and also achieved more military success than did the typical California groups.

Africa is a continent which has generally been characterized by strong social organization, although this has not been true for the whole continent. Some people had a poor political or extra-kinship concept of the tribe as a whole, the Pygmies being a case in point. The Bushman of the Kalahari desert did indeed get together once a year to talk things over, but the clan was far more important with them than was the tribe, which was most shadowy. There have been people even in the royalist Sudan with practically no tribal concept. The natives of Mongalla, the southern-most province of the Anglo-Egyptian Sudan, for example, had no word for "tribe," and apparently possessed only a vague concept of the "tribe-as-a-whole."[6]

One certain test of lack of adequate military organization — that is, adequate from modern standards — is a sense of tribalism which will prevent fighting inside the we-group. We have just discussed people with little of this sense. The we-group to such people was some kin organization. Such extended families have had little or no hesitancy in attacking other sibs which were of the same cultural, linguistic, or even social group, large if weak in structure.

The Eurasiatic Chuckchee illustrate a transitional condition. The old Siberian tribes generally fought with other tribes but were not above a little intra-tribal scuffling. The various branches of the Chuckchee still distrust each other and have occasional fights.[7] This is reminiscent of the Crow of Montana, who generally fought an outside group as a whole but could have reasonably lethal struggles between the constituent clans. The distrust of the River Crow for the Mountain Crow is still noticeable.

Most Melanesians were to all intents a tribeless and a warless people. The kin group with them was the important social unit, and war does not flourish where the sib is too strong. Such strong kin feeling and military efficiency are almost antonyms. Where kinship

[6] Leonard F. Nalder, ed., *A Tribal Survey of Mongalla Province* (London: Oxford University Press, 1937), p. 18.

[7] Bogoraz, *op. cit.*, p. 657.

lines cut across those of village, tribe, or other group, and kinship takes precedence, there is little place for real war. The tradition exists in Melanesian Lenarkel that a man would not shoot at his sister's husband if he were a member of the other side in battle.[8] Much of Melanesia had so little concept of the political tribe, of social grouping beyond the immediate kin, that intra-village fighting was very uncommon. Some groups acknowledged a shadowy central authority, but a chief who had so little sense of tribal cohesion that he would buy off raiders by giving them heads from his own people, as in the Banks Islands, could hardly be expected to be an efficient commander.

The Melanesian tribelessness was sometimes reduced by one great social control institution, the secret association. Thus, if a chief had much power on islands where the secret lodge was dominant, he might speak with authority in his capacity as head of the lodge, not as chief *per se*. In tropical West Africa the secret society seemed to bolster up the rising central authority, but this was hardly true in Melanesia. It did not act as a king-maker and was a drag on the development of adequate patterns of command, not the reverse.

The linkage between war and the rest of the social pattern is always interesting, although there are few general statements to be made for mankind as a whole. Perhaps the most important of these made possible by this study is that while intense in-group feeling or nationalism has made better and tactically more efficient wars, tribelessness has not meant lack of bloodshed. Perhaps the concept of the state, such as west and northeast Africa has known, is necessary for true war properly so-called. The corollary is not true, however, that the rise of the state brought more wars into the world, nor is there reason to think that the abolition of the national state would mean the abolition of institutionalized slaughter. This study has shown that people with but little social cohesion, little concept of those political attitudes which produce and maintain the state, have killed off just as large a percentage of their populations as have the warlike, well-knit groups.

If the behavior of subpolitical people is any criterion, abolition of the strong tribe or state might indeed mean the abolition of effective war on a grand scale, but it would also mean abolition of the longer periods of peace and larger areas of peace which the strong state affords. Where there is no war- or peace-declaring authority, there

[8] Humphreys, *op. cit.*, p. 49.

is no peace at all. Brown reports, for example, that there were no regularly organized wars in New Britain but that each independent village was in constant and perpetual fear of the next similarly independent village. Indeed, continual killing inside the village between hostile families and their allies was socially acceptable.[9]

The existence of the strong, far-flung tribe or state provides peace over wider territories, then, even though the fewer wars fought by them are more intense. Family quarrels which go as far as man-killing call into action the police power of the central authority in large, closely organized societies.

The spread of central authority over territory and population has not always been accomplished by force and coercion. The alliance for war, or confederations such as that of the Iroquois, sometimes has been purely voluntary. The military alliance was an important trait in Samoan sociology. A district would often wait for months until it could align its allies before embarking on war. The Samoan council of allies determined affairs of policy, which was strength, but each group fought under its own leaders, which was weakness.[10] Nothing brought Greece so much together as the military alliance against the Persians. External war as well as conquest, then, can knit tribes together and thus increase the area of peace.

A condition intermediate between tribeless localism and adequate central authority in America existed among such peoples as the Teton-Dakota on the Plains and the Plateau Flathead. Such tribes admitted tribal authority for some affairs of life, and likewise submitted to tribal war controls of certain kinds. In addition to these, many social affairs were dominated by the family, band, or voluntary group. They likewise had tribal war parties instead of those organized around the extended family. The Teton planned a tribal war party in a council of chiefs, and these plans apparently were well conceived and executed. Yet it must be admitted that among such people the anarchical uncontrolled, individually organized war party was typical. Their not-too-distant neighbors, the Omaha, likewise had a sense of nationalism. For this reason, they thought that defensive war was more honorable than offensive, and a man who acquired war honors in defending women and property was ranked higher than he who achieved his honors in offense. These attitudes are understandable among people

[9] Brown, *op. cit.*, pp. 152f.
[10] *Ibid.*, p. 169.

who had mastered agriculture and had, in comparison with most Plains hunters, a sense of a well-knit social order.[11]

There was considerable variation in tribal sentiment and effective institutions in the Southeast Woodland area. There were monarchical civil states which succeeded in war, such as the Natchez, and those whose military success was as limited as the authority of their social control devices, such as the Choctaw. One eye witness said of the latter,

> This nation is governed by a head chief whose power is absolute only so far as he knows how to make use of his authority, but as disobedience is not punished among them, and they do not usually do what is requested of them, except when they want to, it may be said that it is an ill-disciplined government.[12]

While most southerners failed to achieve monarchical organization, yet the idea of tribal solidarity was far from absent. When a foreigner killed a Georgia Cusabo, for example, a tribal council was called. If no one appeared to defend the aggressor, an embassy was sent to the foreign group to demand satisfaction in the name of all the Cusabo. Should such people be disposed to peace, their council weighed the merits of the case and, if finding their tribesman guilty, had him executed without warning him. Otherwise the Cusabo organized a war party of the slain man's kin which kept the field until it had killed the exact number of men they had lost. They then sent the enemy a token of their satisfaction.[13] Bossu said that the Choctaw thought poorly of a leader who lost any men even though victorious. This made the chiefs too tender regarding losses and forced them to take minimum risks through the use of ambuscades, topography, skill in scouting, care in avoiding ambush, and the dawn attack.[14] The Choctaw may have disappointed Bossu, but the tactical chapters showed that they could make war of a sort.

The most important point of contrast between America and Africa was the greater power and authority of the group on the latter continent. When African kings went forth to war, their subjects went

[11] Fletcher and La Flesche, *op. cit.*, p. 431.

[12] Anonymous French Memoir, in Swanton, *Source Material for the Social and Ceremonial Life of the Choctaw Indians*, p. 90.

[13] Alexander Hewat, *Historical Account of the Rise and Progress of the Colonies of South Carolina and Georgia* (London: A. Donaldson, 1790), cited in Swanton, *Early History of the Creek Indians and Their Neighbors*, p. 77.

[14] Bossu, in Swanton, *Source Material for the Social and Ceremonial Life of the Choctaw Indians*, p. 163.

along. No one could pick and choose the campaign he liked, stay at home when he would, plead a bad dream, or some other anarchical foolishness. Such a man would have been cut to ribbons in most African societies. Of course this strong social control machinery has not been observable all over the continent, as noted in the opening of this chapter; but tribal weakness, the situation of the marginal Africans, has not been typical of the continent. The kingdoms of the Sudan, the Congo drainage and, far more, the harsh and authoritative kingdoms of East and South Africa are the most typical. Admitted that the Zulu kingdom was of late origin, at least in its final extreme form, yet the seed must have fallen on fertile soil, for the Ama-Zulu embraced gladly an authoritative, totalitarian military state. At the end of the typical preparatory shamanizing, the warriors danced, brandished their weapons, and screamed at the chief their intentions of victory. They shouted their pledges that he might do as he pleased with their lives. possessions, and kraals if they failed. They were serious in pledging whole villages to the chief that they would win, and their chief was serious in accepting this oath.[15]

This devotion to the nation and its head was spread by the Zulu to other folk, such as the nearby Thonga, who readily accepted the idea of national authority. Their preparatory rites were national, not personal as in America. The chief, the central cell of their social organism, was threatened, hence all warriors responded to the call to surround and protect him. Individual courage was whipped up in their un-American war dance, but the rites were for the preservation of the group and in honor of its chief.[16]

According to legend, nationalistic ideas were implanted in the lake region of Africa by white men from the north typified by the culture-hero Kintu, who probably was a symbol of the Hamite invasion. The Sahara was a barrier to the diffusion of materials, but it served as a channel for ideas. It is a point of no importance that the Negro perhaps obtained some ideas of organization by diffusion, but it is important that he received them. The American Indians outside the great focal areas had no barriers like the Sahara between them and civilization, yet they were in the majority incapable of absorbing ideas of authoritative social control.

---

[15] Kidd, *op. cit.*, p. 307.

[16] Junod, *op., cit.*, p. 76.

To be sure, the African Negro did not allow himself to be regimented in all places without protest, but who would? The western Ibo did not evolve the kingship and when it was imported to them it was the occasion of civil wars.[17] By contrast, the Dahomeans had a real royal bureaucracy in peace *and* war. Consequently their enlistment, supply, command, etc., were formal, efficient, and nonprimitive.[18]

Study shows that one cannot speak in general regarding the social organization and military practices of all the South Pacific areas: Polynesia, Melanesia, Micronesia, and Indonesia. Indonesia, of course, lies so close to the mainland of Asia that the dominant cultures are marginal Asiatic and not insular, so will not be discussed at all. The real point lies in the fact that one must not overstress the concept of isolation. Many if not most of the coastal peoples of Oceania accepted the sea as a challenge, not a barrier. They were the most successful blue water voyagers of all nonliterate men, surpassing, indeed, civilized Europe, Asia, and Africa until the Renaissance voyages of discovery began.

The opinion among competent ethnologists is that the Polynesians, at least, came from some place in the Orient at a date of no great antiquity and that somewhere, somehow, sometimes, they may well have been in contact with peoples near the centers of ancient civilization, which might explain their superior social and military organization.

All Melanesian war, in contrast, has been primitive, but this primitivity must be explained sociologically, not geographically. Betel chewing diffused into hither Melanesia from the west but civilized tactics did not. Some Polynesian war was hardly primitive. Most, though not all, Polynesians were as successful as the Achaean Greeks as portrayed by Homer, while some of the better organized tribes could have crushed the well-greaved heroes.

It must be kept in mind that war is, in Oceania as elsewhere, an essential part of the societal complex, perhaps of one its strongest links, and certainly one of its clearest reflectors. The relationship of efficient social organization in the arts of peace and in the arts of group conflict is almost absolute, whether one is speaking of civilization or subcivilization. Successful war depends upon team work and

[17] Meek, *op. cit.*, p. 113.
[18] Herskovits, *op. cit.*, II, p. 70.

consensus, both of which require command and discipline. Command and discipline, furthermore, can eventually be no more than symbols of something deeper and more real than they themselves. Which was the cart and which the horse is not a question easily answered for all peoples. But Polynesia had great nobles and effective, workable social stratification based upon sensible division of the social task. Melanesia had none of these things beyond the most rudimentary need. In Polynesia there were tabued kings and war lords descended from the gods. In Melanesia custom was king. Polynesia had commanders and approached the military threshold. Melanesia contained such childish warriors that one would have to come to the simplest parts of Pre-Columbian America or the very darkest Africa to find their equal in folly. This does not mean that Melanesians were not as happy as Polynesians, but it does mean that Polynesian teamwork could have and did defeat Melanesian tribelessness whenever the two came in contact.

One fact which marked the tribes of barbarian Europe as approaching civilized standards was their social organization which could easily be put to military purposes. Almost all of them had rudimentary states wherein a type of king ruled, sometimes hedged about by a council of nobles or elders, sometimes not. In this they differed but little from those rudimentary kingdoms of Africa. Others had such strong chieftainships that they could put up effective resistance against the early imperialists of the classical empires. After all, archeology shows that these tribes had been receiving waves of cultural influence from the civilized eastern Mediterranean for a very long period before they entered the historical arena. One must go to Central Asia, or even to the north of that in search of the truly primitive.

The kinship groups did not have to be destroyed if they were used wisely. Tacitus revealed that the traditional sib organization of the Germans, disciplined, subordinated, and welded into working order by the higher political authority, was one of the sources of Teutonic strength. Tactical units were bound together by the emotional value set on blood ties. This gave them strong incentive to courageous action.[19] There is no doubt but that the abolition of sibs can go too far. The British still enroll their territorial regiments from the same areas and give them local names. Men of old friendship and kin ties, led by their ordinary social leaders, make a formidable team.

[19] Tacitus, *Germania*, vii. *passim*.

The United States practice of forming regiments without regard for local feeling, the National Guard excepted, overlooks a source of military *esprit*.

The interaction of social organization and war need not be one-sided. War may affect the social organization as well as the reverse. The presence of an able and warlike enemy may have an effect upon the nonmilitary, economic, and social institutions which might never have taken place in a regime of peace. In another place the Pima opinion has been cited that the presence of the warlike Apache, raiding as they did from weekly to monthly, forced upon them their sexual division of labor. The presence of an aggresive enemy necessitated the service of the men on permanent war footing so that the fields had to be tilled by women. The effect of war on the Pima was most striking. Neither the Spaniard nor the Mexican could cope with the Apache, so the Pima were left to their own devices. They therefore concentrated their tilled fields instead of leaving them widespread. They perfected a system of defense and engaged in sham battles to test and perfect it. A system of runners was instituted to bring assistance. Physical training was incumbent on all males. Indeed, all their social life became regulated with reference to possible Apache attacks, and eventually all their arts, myths, and religion became tinged with the war tension. Russell makes the interesting comment that, "the Pimas were building up a war cult that in time might have led them from the lethargic state in which the natural environment tended to fit them."[20] Such instances clearly show that geographic determinism cannot tell the whole story of warfare or social practice.

A similar tradition exists among the Osage. According to their legends, the military branch of the government passed through two stages. They claim that originally their social organization was very chaotic, but under the impact of war they perceived the utility of setting up orderly social controls. The first stage was marked by giving the control of war to one sib, which carried with it internal authority to suppress disorder. This sib had the sole right to initiate military action, therefore, and to punish internal strife. Unfortunately, it became so overburdened with war ceremonial that prompt action was out of the question, which led to the second step. The war ceremonial was stringently reorganized so that the war sib could act

[20] Russell, *op. cit.*, p. 204.

with speed in an emergency. It was furthermore seen wise to permit the other groups to organize war parties under certain circumstances.[21]

The transition of a democratic people to a monarchical one has taken place under historically observable conditions. It is reported that the Miskito of Central America were at one time quite democratic except during war, when the council of elders appointed a war chief from among the distinguished men. Later under the pressure of continued war, and with British inspiration and protection, the Miskito war chief rose to the position of a king. He began holding large areas which he governed by village chiefs. Did warfare become more efficient under the new arrangement? Apparently it did. With the kingship, Miskito rule spread over the Sumu, Paya, and Rama.[22]

Attention is merely called to this parallel. There is no need to do more with readers historically trained to appreciate the rise of European kingdoms, civil states, feudal institutions, and dictatorships.

Theorists in the past have often ascribed to war and conquest the chief role in the formation of the state and civil society. Later writers have been doubtful of such simple explanations and have considered other methods of attaining civilized conditions. Since there have been but few regions with the long record of Egypt, as related in such works as Moret's *From Tribe to Empire,* it must be admitted that that rise from a kin society to the civil state cannot be described for the world as a whole.

The comparative ethnography and tradition of Indian America tend to show that strong military patterns *followed* the strengthening of the social controls into rudimentary political bodies or states. The American evidence, cloudy as it is, does not bear out the military determinists without important exceptions. In Africa one finds a different situation. The military determinists could find one convincing text book situation after another. On that continent war produced many though not all of the states. That this situation was caused by the greater and more complicated mass migrations and invasions of that continent is most possible. But why should this happen in Africa more than it did in America? Or is it that we do not have adequate knowledge of what happened in America?

---

[21] La Flesche, *The Osage Tribe: Rite of the Chiefs,* pp. 65f.

[22] Conzemius, *op. cit.,* pp. 82ff.

The situation is rather clear in the southwestern Sudan. A numerous, hardworking population with a relatively high culture lived in that area. As noted, work in favorable environments produces results in stored-up food which is a temptation to hungry people from less favored regions. When the starved barbarians assailed the southwestern United States corn-growers, those people simply quit, which is one of the important reasons why the pueblo area shrank and shrank. Not so in fighting Africa! The threat of defeat united many communities in defense of their lives and property. Widespread war-chieftainships and confederacies arose which survived into peace times. When outside aggressions welded wide territories into defensive organizations, this added strength was used to the detriment of some still independent peoples.

Further south, where the forests were too dense for large scale operations, the people remained separate and martially incompetent except in the west Bantu kingdoms, such as those of Congo, Bushongo, and others.

Constant contact with enemy peoples in an open country did not produce civil governments on the American Great Plains. In that region agriculture was too poorly developed, and only a few tribes made an effort or remembered how to grow corn. There was little to defend. The concept of territoriality was therefore too weakly developed among them. By contrast, the open country of the grain-growing Sudan permitted the formation of the civil state after the people had been hammered and welded by war. It is a fertile region without forests, marshes, or rivers terrible enough to interfere with military communications. In such areas as Ibo, and others to the south, the lines of communication were too cut up for the formation of such strong states as the Sudanic empire of Bornu.

Parenthetically, the influence of Islam in the formation of kingdoms and empires on the Gold, Ivory, and Slave Coasts must not be overestimated. The Arab and Mohammedan invasions and missionary wars had strong influence, but the rise of some strong states, Bornu and the Fulani for example, antedated either the birth of the Prophet or the importance of his faith.

The west African kingdoms before Islam's rise to power were examples of the turned worm, as in the case of the Iroquois in America. Founded for defense, they almost always became aggressive. Defense taught them the elements of true war, which elements could in turn be used to take other people's property by capture or tribute. Binger said that as soon as any Negro chief could command twenty thousand soldiers he dreamed of empire. His standard of living rose and, as he had no budget, he had to hunt slaves to make up his deficit.[23]

America might have had another story to tell if the southwestern pueblo-building tribes had possessed the politico-military acumen of the Fulani. Both were beset by hungry men, but war, government, and confederation fitted the cultural pattern of the one and not the other. Felt need is not always sufficient to call forth invention, or even the acceptance of devices which other people have invented. Culture and social life do not work that automatically. One need not turn to such humble peoples as Bushmen, Pygmies, and Hottentots. All Negroes did not have or use the capacity to form military states for their own survival. There were many folks among them whose patterns permitted an undisciplined, untrained, worthless warrior class who loved war well enough but could no more develop or accept real war or war-chieftainship than could the Plains *coup*-counters. But as evidence of the untrustworthiness of unilateral theories of social development, witness the intersectional fights in Mongalla. External threats in this region had no unifying effect. The Moru did not unite to repel the Zande menace, and the Lugbari failed to unite against the Kawa incursions. The expectable process did not take place.[24]

Lack of diffusional opportunities does not account for such failure, for the Moru were instructed by Zande efficiency. Just what part individual and tribal attitudes play in military development is no better understood than in other phases of social history. No doubt the Zulu had some effective organization before the rise of the military geniuses Dingiswayo and Chaka, but under them they achieved a social effectiveness in all realms and a proficiency in military techniques and organization, in particular, which left little to be desired. Their history and character in the Nineteenth Century were admittedly molded by their military system, before which all other walks of life had to yield precedence, but to what extent was their adaptation of adequate war patterns governed by their character?[25]

[23] Louis G. Binger, *Du Niger au Golfe de Guinee* (Paris: Hatchette, 1892), I, p. 502.

[24] Nalder, *op. cit.*, p. 18.

[25] Krige, *op. cit.*, p. 261.

Zulu government and Zulu war were indeed adequate. The Zulu rise to power was not caused by new weapons but an improved method, in part, of handling one considered obsolete. Let us pause once more to stress the principle that war, true war, is a matter of social organization, not of material culture or weapons. Zulu war represents a cultural thrust by a non-material culture, and not the more common cultural lag so often observed.

The Zulu spread their ideas of royal and military power to many peoples in South Africa. Not all of them, however, abandoned the clan for the royal principle quite as wholeheartedly as the Zulu. The Thonga, for example, retained many features of the old kinship society. Indeed, that which had gone before formed a good foundation for the later condition. The old clan chief traditionally acquired his position because of a magical and spiritual character derived from his sacred ancestor. While this laid upon him a vast tabu system, it was not enough to emasculate his power of administration, so that the new Zulu idea could constitute an effective overlay. The fusion of the two, the old and the new, formed an absolutist state, a well-organized government with good laws and courts and a keen sense of justice. The last of these South African military empires was destroyed in 1895-1896 by the Portuguese victory over Gungunyana at Mandlakazi.

The story of the state supported by arms can also be told for Dahomey. "Of the forces which contributed to the stability of the monarchy, the army was of first importance."[26] The Dahomeans evidently overdid the thing, for Burton says that the population of the kingdom was not one third what the natural resources should have supported. The annual withdrawal of both sexes from industry to indulge in the slaving wars, the horrible sacrifices of the "Customs" at the capital, the conscription of so many women into the king's army of virgin Amazons, and the not infrequent disastrous defeats held the population in check.[27]

Sociology was made to conform to the war patterns in several places in Melanesia. In the Northwest Solomons, for example, a man had to support his fellow clansmen in war. One of the chief causes for acculturation and the breakup of the clan spirit in this area has been the

---

[26] Herskovits, *op. cit.*, I, p. 70.
[27] Burton, *op. cit.*, II, pp. 155f.

peace which the white man has enforced. The clan no longer has a real job.[28]

A conformation of the social pattern to war needs, reminiscent of our own history, has been clearly apparent in Polynesia. Mangaian sociology shows traces of two opposing forces, an older group of settlers who wished the society to be characterized by rank and title in hereditary succession, and a newer group who wished it to be based on physical force and war. Buck says that succession to title and property was strongly influenced by this conflict, and that success in war was the concept which was increasing in importance.[29]

Such people, organized into a caste society with divine chiefs, were capable of invading, occupying, and subjecting no mean areas of territory. The leader of a successful war party could gain the temporal lordship over all Mangaia, setting up the power of a military dictator which overshadowed that of any tabued hereditary lord. The latter could only become a *roi faineant,* occupied with sacred things. The real or military chieftainship was confirmed or changed with each battle. If the dictator chose to abdicate in favor of another, he became the military right hand of the new temporal lord.[30]

Another sociological effect of abruptly altering the war pattern can be seen in Samoa. Brown thinks the long and continual wars kept the population down. Exposure in trench or fort, battle casualties, food scarcity during war, the separation of sexes for the duration, together with the very few marriages which could be consummated while the men were in the field checked any real increase in numbers.[31] Brown might also have mentioned that abortion and infanticide prevailed in Samoa. Thus war kept population down, and peace should have increased it. However, the peace-making European did not bring an increase in Polynesian population, strangely enough, but depopulation. It cannot be positively stated that this situation was caused by the introduction of a new culture which upset the old ways and caused men to cease to be proud and life-loving, as Pitt-Rivers thinks. Yet there is an element of truth in what Brown says, and we have seen that social organization of any kind is based on the underlying population.

---

28 Blackwood, *op. cit.,* p. 33.
29 Buck, *op. cit.,* p. 84.
30 *Ibid.,* p. 35.
31 Brown, *op. cit.,* p. 173.

The concept of society organized on a territorial basis has been mentioned as one of the marks of civil society in contrast with consanguineous society. This has always had a marked effect on a tribe's military patterns. There is a rough correlation between this trait and true war which, however, has been far from automatic. The South American Indians as a whole, for example, had a keener sense of territoriality than did tribes of no more cultural complexity on the northern continent. The Brazilian littoral was so valuable because of the good things the sea yielded that there was incessant Indian war for it during the Sixteenth Century. But, for the most part, the primitive warrior has been more concerned with his kin than his land.

The appreciation of this concept in Africa was remarkably stronger than in America. Whether as herders of domestic animals, or as farmers, or both, the Negroes had a higher valuation of economic land as a supporting agency than simple hunters and gatherers ever could have had. The Indian apparently devolved his agriculture in America, and an effective domesticator of animals he never became, save in the alpaca area. The reverence which the Negro has for the soil, the deification of the mythical lords of the soil, is most impressive. There have been no Negro groups of any importance without appreciation of gardening, farming, and herding. This, unfortunately, cannot be said of the Indian. He worked under a cultural handicap and, if these pages compare him unfavorably with the African as a warrior, one must keep this extenuating circumstance in mind.

Furthermore, African Negroes, almost as a whole, came into knowledge of the metallurgical arts very early in their cultural history. Since in the history of our own people iron came later than copper-bronze metallurgy, it is a fair premise that copper-bronze smithing has been more obvious than iron metallurgy. It is then possible to make a really unfavorable comparison of the Indian with the Negro. The latter early appreciated and utilized the less obvious metal, while the former, excepting the Peruvians, could not grasp the virtues of copper except in the most rudimentary fashion.

The point to be noticed is that active agriculture and herding not only have provided the economic basis (and cause) of effective warfare but, linked with metals, have been the great builders of the state. They have contained the seeds of the destruction of kin societies and the building of civil governments. That civil society has always made more effective war than could a sib or kin society should be obvious.

It has been said, perhaps too loosely, that America was a democratic continent while Africa was the continent of the kings. There is some validity in this, for north of Mexico and in most of South America, Indian social groups considered themselves peoples rather than countries. It was quite different in Africa. There were kingdoms which considered the tribal area of greater importance than the blood tie. Few American Indians would have had the emotional reaction of the Bantu BaThonga when it became known that their territory was invaded. Anyone could and did give the hue and cry once a hostile foot touched the land. The women fled and the men hastened to the capital.[32] It is not meant that the Indian had no concept of territoriality. The concept, however, was pale in comparison to the African one, and this must be taken as one explanation for the Indian's inferiority as a soldier.

The importance of closely integrated and efficiently functioning socio-political institutions has been strikingly demonstrated in the power or lack of power to declare states of war or peace. To be sure, many people think that the universal state of all persons below literate levels has been one of war. This hardly squares with the facts. Many tribes in varying states of culture considered war the unusual, so unusual that it required some formal act of declaration. It is impossible to say that this idea correlates with either the very simple or the complicated cultures. It has been evident in all degrees of cultural development. Perhaps no simpler or more wretched people existed in either of the Americas than the inhabitants of Tierra del Fuego. They were also accustomed to bitter and long standing feuds. Nevertheless, one Captain Low, quoted by Cooper, says that the West Patagonians made a rude image of a man with long red teeth and with a neck halter of hide. Around this they stuck spears, arrows and clubs. This they set up as a declaration of war. A similar method was used by the Auracanians.[33]

Among the somewhat more developed Plains-Ojibway, war was declared by the soldier society, the *okitcita*, who, upon sufficient

[32] Junod, *op. cit.*, p. 455.

[33] John M. Cooper, *Analytical and Critical Bibliography of the Tribes of Tierra del Fugo and Adjacent Territory*, Bulletin 63, Bureau of American Ethnology (Washington: 1917), p. 154.

injury, sent tobacco by a runner to each band or camp. The enemy was not informed. The ceremonial included only friendly bands, and was never more than semi-public, or semi-private, for their warfare never got beyond such a condition.[34]

When the somewhat better organized but yet simple Canadian Algonkians went to war, they sent as a messenger to the people they intended to attack a slave formerly captured from that people, bearing an axe with a handle painted red and black.[35] The Huron sent a black wampum belt to the enemy-to-be.

The royal Natchez lagged little behind the level which civil and civilized states had achieved a few years ago. They declared war by leaving a "hieroglyph" picture in enemy territory to announce their intention of attacking at a certain phase of the moon.[36] The anything-but-royal Pomo behaved similarly. This, to be sure, destroyed the surprise element, which may be why modern nations have lost their manners.

If a tribe with a concept of nationalism lived in contiguity with one which had little or none, the primitivity of the latter was immediately apparent. An instance of this was seen in the continual wars between the Plateau Salishan Flathead and the Plains Blackfoot. The former had a fair concept of nationality. The hereditary high chief alone had the power of declaring war and peace, aided by his council. The Blackfoot idea was not so strong. No man or body of men could bind the tribe, or for that matter, authoritatively commit one band. The Flathead wished the right to pass east of the Rockies to hunt bison on the Great Plain, while the Blackfoot, lacking adequate vegetable food, wished to wander into the Flathead valleys in the spring to gather bitter root and camas. Upon many occasions the Flathead thought they had concluded a valid treaty with all the Blackfoot to wander onto the Plains, only to find themselves assailed by Piegan bands whom they considered friendly. Very naturally they would then attack the first Blackfoot band which came onto their bitter root flats as treaty breakers, although it might be the same band with which they originally had negotiated. The fact that the Flathead had an

---

[34] Skinner, *Political Organization, Cults, and Ceremonies of the Plains-Ojibway and Plains-Cree,* pp. 490f.

[35] Lahontan, in Garrick Mallery, *Picture-Writing of the American Indians,* Annual Report 10, Bureau of American Ethnology (Washington: 1880-1889), p. 358.

[36] *Ibid.,* pp. 358, 362.

authority which could commit the nation and the Blackfoot did not was the source of bitter warfare over several centuries.[37]

In Africa this power has varied with the other powers of the kingship. Many kingdoms have expected the king to take counsel with his local chiefs. Just who these chiefs were and just what was their source of authority has an important bearing. If they were survivors of a formerly important sib system, that was one thing. If they were the appointees and therefore creatures of the king, that was another. This latter was the most common situation among the strong South African monarchies. Such principalities never were feudal in the European sense, so there never was some Duke of Burgundy or Earl of Warwick to set his will against that of the king. This is not saying that the king was in all cases absolute, for some tribes not only had officials who were king-appointers but also who were king-deposers. Foreign relations were, however, always the royal prerogative wherever monarchy existed. The African kings were seldom field commanders themselves, so the right to declare war and peace was an important part of the war complex in their estimation.

The methods, or lack of method, and forms of declaring war and peace have been more manifold in Africa than those found in America. Strangely enough, there has been some tendency for the formalities to decline as the power of a central government has risen. The kings have been the realists, not the democrats.

The politically retarded Nigerians, for example, threw away the principle of surprise for reasons of state. When one town wished to fight another, it informed the enemy by two messengers who laid some powder, shot, and caps on a plantain leaf upon the road near the enemy town. Except among the northeastern Ibibio, who gave no warning, the fighting started at the boundary on a day agreed upon by both sides. The peace declaration was almost Californian in its formality. When one side wearied, it sent to the enemy one of its own men or a neutral friend dressed in palm leaves and white bast, carrying peppers in his hand. If the proposal was accepted, both sides met at the boundary and sacrificed a goat, a dog, and sometimes a cow. A neutral chief sometimes divided a palm leaf among the parties. Talbot says the neighboring Oronn celebrated

[37] Harry H. Turney-High, "Cooking Camas and Bitter Root," *American Anthropologist,* XXXVI, n.s. 1933, p. 263.

peace by implanting a sacrificial goat's head on a stake upon which a dog had been impaled through the jaws to die slowly. Eggs were then placed on "medicine" leaves and sprinkled with goat's blood. The chief men then crushed all this together with their hands and smeared their erstwhile foes' faces with the mixture, expressing the wish that they will see each other's blood no more. They then divided the goat's cooked flesh and other food, and sang, danced, ate and drank in joy at the peace.[38]

In contrast, the highly organized kingdom of Dahomey did not take the enemy into its confidence. The king formally declared war, at which ceremonial he and his functionaries performed elaborate dances, but the enemy was not informed since the Dahomean army relied on surprise.

The Papuans in Oceania considered peace declaration women's work. If peace was desired, a couple of men went with their wives to the hostile village. The presence of the women indicated the end sought, so the rights of embassy were respected. The suit for peace was almost always accepted, and the men thereupon broke each other's beheading knives and exchanged arm guards. At night the hosts had relations with their guests' women, "and that is the real object of the visit." In a few days the erstwhile hosts returned the visit and brought some of their wives for their former foes to enjoy.[39]

The more chiefly Solomon Islanders were not quite so informal about peace-making as the Papuans, but the end and the means were largely the same. When one side had enough war they would inform the enemy of the fact and ask for one of their chiefly daughters as a bride for one of their own chiefs. If all went well the fighting ceased and the side which sued for peace brought a large bride price for the young woman.[40] These people, like many others, had an economic attitude toward peace declaration as well as a sexual one. The war ceased when one side had enough. Valuable presents were exchanged to make matters right, sometimes without regard for the rights of the quarrel or the number of the slain on either side, which latter element was both un-American and un-African.[41]

---

[38] Talbot, *Life in Southern Nigeria*, pp. 241f.
[39] Landtman, *op. cit.*, p. 165.
[40] Ivens, *op. cit.*, p. 310.
[41] *Ibid.*, p. 304.

Melanesian peace declarations had little idea of honor. Miss Powdermaker records an instance when the people of Tagam village were afraid of those of Lesu. The Tagam people fled to a neighboring community and the Lesu folk plundered their fields. Tiring of this, they sent a message saying that they wanted no more war and persuaded the Tagam folk to return. This they did, and the first ceremonials of peace were held, but Lesu had no intention of honoring its word and murdered the chief of Tagam as soon as possible. When the Tagam people were about to run away again the men of Lesu protested that they really meant it this time, that the real object of the war had been the chief's life, and the peace ceremonies were repeated and respected.[42]

The signal for peace in the New Hebrides seems to have been fronds of palm carried between the combatants.[43] The Loyalty Islanders were so formal in their declarations that one suspects Polynesian influence, for they never undertook war without observing a strict diplomatic etiquette, no matter how serious the quarrel. The two chiefs negotiated for possible peace by three messengers whose persons were as sacred as Greek or mediaeval heralds. Diplomatic representations were not broken off and war begun until peace efforts were made and each chief duly notified. After peace had been declared the victorious chief sent his adversary a present to show that all ill feeling was over, which the defeated chief received with all protestations of good will. Enmity smouldered, however, and the defeated chief could be expected to reinstitute the war as soon as he felt himself strong enough.[44]

The Polynesian Mangaian were a thoroughly political people. While they occasionally indulged in a surprise attack, for the most part the great formality of their social pattern demanded that an aggrieved chief formally challenge another to war. Peace likewise had to be formally declared by announcement on the peace drums and a human sacrifice to the war god. In other words, these people recognized war and peace as definite social statuses and observed the shift from one to the other by specific rites of passage. Such civilized attitudes developed in conjunction with the rest of the social pattern. Surprise attack and "treachery" had been common there

[42] Powdermaker, *op. cit.*, pp. 42f.
[43] Humphreys, *op. cit.*, p. 59.
[44] Hadfield, *op. cit.*, pp. 169f.

before the rise of the temporal lordship mentioned before. After that event it became customary for a group aspiring to power to render formal declaration of a state of war to its opponent and his allies. The neutral social groups had the role of furnishing the human sacrifices needed for declaring peace.[45]

War in Samoa was proclaimed formally only to members of the we-group. Heralds were sent from the capital town to subordinate ones and allied capitals, whereupon warriors and councillors converged on the capital. The prospective enemy found out about it as best he could, usually through observation of warlike preparations or the murder of some member of his group.[46]

The Metal Age Eurasiatics likewise exhibited an efficient social authority to declare peace and war. The rudimentary states which came into being with the Metal Ages could behave effectively in this regard. Primitivity such as observed elsewhere, with the usual exchange of gifts and ceremonial meals, existed among the Siberians. The following refers to the war-weariness of the Siberian Chuckchee and the Eskimo-Aleut peoples of St. Lawrence Island. The islanders, whose massacre was mentioned in the tactical discussion, eventually sought revenge with considerable success, but the next summer they sought peace, their honor having been vindicated. This was acceptable to the Chuckchee, and an exchange of fine presents took place. The transferral of a shaman hostage exactly evened the score and removed the *casus belli,* the gifts clinched the matter, and the gerontarchs were satisfied. One more war was concluded.[47]

Europe and Asia contribute little that was novel regarding the interrelationship of the social pattern and that for war. These patterns operated in functional dependence, and changes in the one were apt to produce changes in the other. Defects in sociological coherence likewise produced military incapacity. The Thracians, say the old writers, could easily have threatened Greece, but their intense localistic attitudes prevented them. This relatively small category is thought once to have had as many as fifty "tribes," and Strabo knew of as many as twenty-two in his time. Herodotus called them the most powerful people in the world, barring the Hindus, and repeated the opinion that they would have been invincible if they had been

[45] Buck, *op. cit.,* p. 158.
[46] Brown, *op. cit.,* p. 164.
[47] Bogoraz, *op. cit.,* p. 657.

able to effect internal unity. They could never accomplish this, and "herein therefore consists their weakness."[48]

The allied field of tactical organization has been revealed very indifferently by the field reports. Perhaps this is due to the small size of most nonliterate war parties, for in many ways organization is a function of size. This is not entirely true, for two men going about any job efficiently should have their work organized.

The size of the better African military groups alone required organization, which was forthcoming. It is said that the Dahomey state could muster fifty thousand men without difficulty during the height of its power, so its army was therefore divided into three echelons.[49] The first division consisted of three thousand fierce females; the second consisted of residents of the capital including the palace guard; the third was a levy of the male population of the nation. Each local chief had his own force which was mustered into national service at the outbreak of hostilities. The older eyewitnesses were astounded at the regularity of the Dahomean formations with their units, officers, and standards.[50] Forbes said the regular army amounted to twelve thousand fighters, of whom five thousand were Amazons. In any event, Dahomey could muster a fair-sized army even by European standards.[51] These troops are said to have been uniformed after a fashion.[52]

The Dahomean army was primarily organized into left and right wings, each with its own commander, the right wing being the larger. These appear to have resembled brigades or divisions. Under the two commanders were officials whose functions were like those of modern field officers, while beneath them were units and commanders resembling modern companies and their commanders. These companies, according to Herskovits, had their own uniforms and names, and apparently had different weapons of specialized function.[53]

When King Chaka came to power in Zululand he immediately set about organizing the Zulu mass, using the traditional age-sets or

---

[48] Herodotus, v. 3.

[49] Frederick E. Forbes, *Dahomey and Dahomeans* (London: Longmans, Brown, Green, Longmans, 1851), I, p. 14.

[50] William Snelgrave, *A New Account of Some Parts of Guinea and the Slave Trade* (London: J. J. and P. Knapton, 1734), in Herskovits, *op. cit.*, II, p. 80.

[51] Forbes, I, pp. 14f, in Herskovits, *op. cit.*, II, p. 81.

[52] *Ibid.*, II, p. 56.

[53] Herskovits, *op. cit.*, II, p. 82.

"circumcision guilds" as a base. These were seldom large enough to serve his military purposes, so he altered them into regiments.[54] The need of organization is apparent when one considers that Chaka kept a force of one hundred thousand men under arms, one half of which was on constant call.[55] The South African regiment was about the size of a modern infantry battalion. The essential tables of organization were worked out by Dingiswayo, Chaka's royal mentor in Mthethwaland.

A tool is a good tool only if the skill exists for its use. Similarly, all the good tactical principles imaginable are vitiated if the command and administrative functions necessary for their employment are lacking. The importance of organization in Eurasiatic war was particularly well illustrated by the rise of Genghis Khan and his Mongols. These people were once no more than ordinary Turko-Tartar pastoral nomads, indulging in the pettiest tactical operations or subtactical raiding. Genghis rose to power by two means: luck and organization. Actually, luck rarely favors a man for long. Often what the vanquished think is the victor's luck is his power of organization, his ability to be prepared for any emergency. Genghis really owed his success to the second factor, his enormous capacity for organization and his tireless vitality in seeing that his wishes were carried out. He rose from a petty chief to a world power, and he did it by absorbing other petty chiefs and putting his fighting force under simple though effective tables of organization.

It was also to adequate military organization that the invading Aryas could attribute their conquest of India. These people were governed by a military aristocracy, under whom they defeated the Dravidians and others who lacked it. The Brahmans unfortunately showed a gradual shift in attitude from a strong military spirit to an otherworldliness, from commander to priest, so that when the European powers decided to take over India there was no really effective resistance. The Brahmans could not pray the French and British rulers out of India, and the spirit of the Kshatriya caste of warriors and rulers was broken.

War, therefore, is not unique among the various social activities. Success in that type of group behavior requires organization and cooperation, as it does in all else. Economics has long taught that lack

[54] Krige, *op. cit.*, p. 261.
[55] Kidd, *op. cit.*, p. 290.

of division of labor, or poor specialization of function and coordination of effort, characterize backward economic systems which result in a small production for consumption. An economy so based is obviously primitive. This is no less true in warfare. One may legitimately speak of certain peoples as practicing primitive war, because they had too little specialization of troops, division of labor and function, too little coordination and command to fight more effectively.

The tactical discussion showed that specialized troops have been most rare among nonliterate societies. This fact alone would keep the bulk of nonliterate fighters in the category of the primitive. Such Jacks-of-all-arms and masters-of-none have offered too small a range of opportunity. They have not offered enough spread for men of different capacities and temperaments to perform functions for which they were best fitted. This type of fighting did not permit the commander to emerge, nor did it need him. It prevented the stratification through differentiation of function and ability wherein a coordinator, director, commander might be superordinated. The tactical discussion said that nonliterate forces taken afield were ordinarily small, the time consumed by their campaigns minute, their type of war in turn requiring little specialization and, therefore, little team work. Since team work is the essence of effective tactics, most nonliterate fighters were poor tacticians, and hence poor soldiers.

It has been stated by some theorists that the civil state, royal or democratic, invariably evolved from the power of some military commander to overawe the commonalty. That this has happened often enough is well known, but there is more to the story. Civil society and orderly government require discipline, and this discipline has sometimes come from nonmilitary sources. It may have sprung from disciplined economic cooperation or it might have had religious inspiration. In America the rudimentary civil chief was often a peace chief, just as forbidden to shed blood as the pope was forbidden to command the troops of the papal states in the field. In this division of labor between a war chief and a peace chief there existed possibilities of progress through specialization and professionalization. It is folly, however, to expect that the two powers would develop efficiency at the same rate of speed. The field literature is full of instances of the peace chieftainship having acquired effectiveness while the war chieftainship remained in the hands of some counter of *coup*, some merely brave and distinguished individual fighter; for a personally brave and able man is not necessarily a good commander for that reason alone. In Napoleon and Lord Nelson there was too much of the physical and perhaps the temperamental weakling for either to have been a good Plains *coup* counter, who had to be an extremely brave and able fighter in personal combat. They were good enough to be great captains among the highly civilized French and British, but the Creek or Coeur d'Alene would have never made them war chiefs. Indeed, the fact that a man is a good and brave individual fighter may temperamentally unfit him for command. He may be too much of an individual to have a group concept strong enough to coordinate and lead a mass.

The discussion of the relation of civil society to effective war may be dropped with this statement. Many of the slayers of consanguine society have been identified: the Nile flood, economic food production, commerce, secret societies, the division of labor and specialization inherent in Bronze Age metallurgy, new gods, and many others. But there is certainly one which has been consistently neglected. This is the rise of the army with officers. The sib society and the Tables of Organization are almost antithetical.

Afterword

The Survival and Revival of Primitive War

IT WAS IN THE THIRD DECADE OF THIS CENTURY THAT IT OCCURRED TO ME that the behavioral scientists, including myself, knew too little about war to be very helpful in discussing peace, except to deplore the former. This attitude is changing rather rapidly now, but I speak of the 1930s. And so, in an effort to analyze that kind of war here called primitive as basic, I began the library research which produced this book. Since then the United States has been involved in three major wars about which innumerable books have been published, but neither the wars nor these volumes seem to me to have impinged upon the validity of this book.

Research reveals that adequately logistic, competently strategic. and completely tactical warfare is the external force arm of the political state, a threshold which only a minority of the world's social systems had achieved by the opening of this century. The combat methods of systems that have neither invented nor accepted civil government from without are revealed as primitive war. It may now be stated as an axiom that subpolitical systems of social control practice primitive war, while those with even a naive state have developed those tactical principles which most military theorists consider true without regard to time or place. This is no place to review the contents of this book, but it should be mentioned that primitive war is fought without political goals, and usually without economic ones as well, without central control of the fighting forces, and with virtually no discipline or command. The primitive warriors' fighting methods, or tactics and strategy, are related to the foregoing, and yet, the readers of this book and similar ones may discern an echo of these obsolete methods in our own news media.

The ethnologist can watch his television and, upon occasion, walk his own streets, and see in the confrontation something very reminiscent of the Australian aborigine's method of making himself unpleasant to an out-group, about the simplest expression of armed hostility known to man. The aborigines came together, formed some kind of a battle line, then tried to out-scream, out-insult, and out-threaten each other, the meanwhile hurling missiles at relatively safe ranges. It is true that sometimes one or more contestants were maimed, and even killed, but this was incidental, almost accidental, to the action. In such a fatal case, both sides ordinarily dispersed, if they had not done so before out of boredom. What did they accomplish? Well, they enunciated their valor, their civic virtue, and they registered a "protest" against the harshness of Australian life, which they were incapable of ameliorating. The Australian confrontation, as is so much of primitive war, was a tension-release device and no more.

The temptation here is to observe that primitive war still lives in such behavior. Indeed, the anthropologist's historian friend points out to him that there is little new here. The so-called Boston Massacre was an eighteenth-century confrontation with authority wherein a black man, one Crispus Attucks, was killed by overreaction on the part of the police power. And then there was a band of students, frustrated by the existence of an establishment, which rampaged along the wharves and destroyed a large amount of tea which did not belong to them. Was this merely Australian tension release on the rococo Harvard campus? Is it only primitive war when the screen brings such Australian behavior into the living room from Tokyo, to the United States, by way of Paris? The aboriginal technique is there, but there have been additions.

Again, the anthropologist's mind reverts to Melanesia, Indonesia, and the drainage basins of the Amazon and Orinoco Rivers in South America, and there he sees men lying in wait to kill *any* member of an out-group, the more defenseless the safer. An enemy skull is valuable, be it of an able man, or an old woman, or even a child. Is this akin to modern terrorism? Is this slaying, often with torture, only a revival of warfare in its most primitive kind, a type of man-questing not far removed from the hunt for game animals? It is true that the activities of the eighteenth-century Sons of Liberty, the nineteenth-century Ku Klux Klan, the Irish Republican Army, the East African Mau Mau, the Algerians against colonial France, the quite efficient Viet Cong, and El Fatah, at the moment of writing, are all highly reminiscent of headhunting in the tropical rain forests. Like the nonliterates, the modern terrorist specializes in attacking the harmless individual rather than the armed forces of his enemy. Indeed, his target is ordinarily the members of the population most like himself So one asks again, is this only a revival of very primitive war? The temptation is to answer affirmatively, but it is best pushed aside, at least for the moment.

The author's generation of ethnologists, trained as so many of us were on the American Great Plains, might think it sees something more than vaguely familiar in the daily newsprint. Fight as a part-time occupation, join a war party only when you want to, submit to no one's real command and discipline, hit and run, avoid real battle, kill and destroy, and never give up, but just go away covered with valor and tell about the coups you counted. Unlike the terrorist and headhunter, the primitive warrior on the Plains nominated the enemy's fighting man as the prime but not only target. And so does the modern guerilla. Is the modern petty warrior a revival of the primitive one?

We know that the American revolutionary cause was once lost in South Carolina; and in the minds of most South Carolinians, it was good riddance. The poor farmer detested wealthy, slave-owning coastal planters such as Francis Marion, and considered the Revolution a rich man's war and a poor man's fight. The coonskin cap element of the west, now that the port of Charleston was open, could again make a living acting as middlemen between the Indians and the ships bound for Europe. The prosperous exporters crowded the office of Cornwallis seeking permits to do business as usual, and the noble earl charmed them all. He did not charm the guerrillas Thomas Sumter and Francis Marion. It may be that the former, who drank whiskey in quantity, was too unintelligent to know that the war was lost. Besides, he prospered too much in his role as a land pirate to give up that source of profit. Marion, though, was brilliant, even if he thought vinegar the proper beverage for a fighting man. Even the French diplomat to the Continentals, Vergennes, suggested that the eastern seaboard be permanently divided into crown colonies to the south, and an independent nation to the north. Later United States policy permits such division for others — East and West Germany, North and South Viet Nam, North and South Korea — but abhors dichotomy for itself. It was intolerable to Sumter and Marion, and their cause was eventually won.

The Americans in a relatively few years saw as able a general as Ulysses Simpson Grant doubt that he could wage conventional war in the Shenandoah Valley because of the operations of that able guerrilla, John Singleton Mosby. That was the grandparental, or great grandparental generation, but in our own day we have witnessed the humiliation of one of France's few capable generals, de Lattre de Tassigny, seemingly by Pathet Lao guerrillas, and the tarnishing of the professional reputations of Generals Westmoreland and Abrams by the Viet Cong. Ah, says the anthropologist, did not Crazy Horse do the same thing to George Armstrong Custer? Does not the modern guerrilla fight like the valiant Teton, Oglala, Brule, Assiniboine, Blackfoot, Apache, and Navaho? Is he not a revival or survival of the primitive warrior? Not really, and the modern guerrilla can no more gather around himself the aura of invincibility than his predecessors.

Who is now living on reservations, and not very happily?

No guerrilla force, no matter how able, has ever won against the conventional troops of a civil state. The plain of history is covered with the bones of those who tried: Saracen raiders, Vikings, Magyars, and in our own day the Lhota Naga hill tribes who sickened but did not conquer the new army of independent India. Fierce, dedicated, and capable as they were, the Boers, the Moros, and the Huks lived eventually with a foreign flag over them. Even the great textbook writer, Che Guevara, is dead. There is a fundamental reason for this, and it should not be difficult either to state or to understand.

This book says in more than one place that successful warfare is a matter of social organization, not of superior weapons. All the great military theorists have said this, and so have all the great captains. To regard the superiority of weapons as the crucial consideration is a civilian attitude easily controverted. Of course, weapons have their part; of course, there is an inherent unity of material and nonmaterial culture. This is not the point under discussion. State-building people have conquered those organized on a tribal, or kinship, basis because they were better organized. The Roman weaponry was somewhat better, but not much, than that of the Gauls. What carried the eagles to the Rhine was, as the standards themselves proclaimed, SPQR, *Senatus Populusque Romanus*, the Senate and the people of Rome. The Gauls, even the Belgae who Caesar said were the bravest, could not organize a sufficiently adequate government, nor could they form a legion. It is useless to point out that Crazy Horse defeated Custer at the Big Horn because the better rifles were fraudulently in Indian hands. Custer defeated himself before a shot was fired — and every tactician knows this. That the British eventually bought Gatling guns from the Americans and defeated the South African Zulu is not in point, either. The British had whipped a large part of the world with the weapons they had before this, and besides, the men of Kings Dingiswayo and Chaka were not primitive warriors but first-class soldiers in every sense. The key invention is that of the state, that is, civil in contrast with kin-based social control. Civil government is the dividing line, the threshold, the horizon between that which is civilized and that which is not. Only the state can raise large armies. It alone can discipline and train men into soldiers rather than warriors.

Only government can command, not request, and can punish those who do not feel like fighting that day. The state and craft specialization also go hand in hand, and only craft specialists can provide the superior weaponry in quantity for armies. Only the polity can tax to provide these arms as needed, and can afford to take men from productive labor and train them. The political state has also invented one more crucial trait, the civilian. And so, the nonliterate warriors are primitive by default, not design. If their organization was not as good as they could make it, it was as good as they did make it. The primitive warrior was without the backing of an organized, structured government. He was unwilling to submit to discipline, and incapable or impatient of obeying definite command. He discovered only the tactical principles inherent in animal hunting. He sought goals, beyond the protection of the local village, too involved in social climbing and personality reinforcement. He was too immediately concerned with the engagement just ahead to plan campaigns instead of battles. He was, therefore, unable to think in terms of strategic plans and unwilling or unable to exploit a victory to the total subjugation of the enemy's fighting and noncombatant forces. And just as important as any of these, he was so concerned with the immediate combat of two opposing groups in definite and immediate confrontation that he was unable to recognize the existence of noncombatants — or civilians, if one will — on whose state of mind the ultimate decision so often rests. So therefore these fighting men remained what are called primitive warriors in this book.

We must now ask, are the fighters mentioned in the beginning of this essay — confronters, terrorists, and guerrillas — really primitive warriors? Viewing their activities, are we really seeing survivals and revivals? As far as subtactical techniques, simplicity of armaments, and almost savage logistics are concerned, they are as primitive as any Plains Dakota who ever painted his face, but the resemblance stops right there. Their goals are civilized even if their means are not. The anthropologist had better not reminisce too much. He is looking into the future, not the past.

One can undoubtedly make too much of confrontationism. No doubt many of the Harvard youths went to the Boston Tea Party as a lark, or as tension release from the rather dreadful living conditions of eighteenth-century students and the necessity of parsing Greek verbs, but no doubt there was another element present. The confronters outnumbered the small British infantry patrol and could have overwhelmed them. The old government-issue "Brown Bess" musket was slow to reload, and the unit could have been rushed while doing so, the two opposing lines being so close together in space. The military police patrol fired after warning the mob to quit throwing rocks and disperse, and the Boston Massacre provided folklore for the approaching revolution, and a martyred black man. From this beginning, forces developed compelling General Gage to abandon Boston. One is also informed that much of the student protest demonstrations throughout the civilized world, the Soviet Union and its allies excepted, is for release from nonpolitical tensions, but the civilized motive of fomenting civil war and revolution must be present in a hard-core, organized minority. Of course the Bostonians fled, and so would the modern confronters if fired upon seriously. The Soviet army in Budapest clearly demonstrated that rock-throwing students cannot fight tanks and machine guns. The confronter's role is not to fight regular troops, but to demonstrate a protest, to reveal the weakness of the political state, and to win over many an innocent and ambivalent bystander by exhibiting a few broken crowns. The fighting techniques may be Australoid, but the motive is civilized and sophisticated.

This sophistication is even more pronounced in terrorism. The methods may be those of a Papuan headhunter, but the aim is the alienation of the uncommited, the clarifying of issues, and the polarizing of sentiment for, or against, the cause. The motive is revolutionary but, as the nineteenth-century Ku Klux Klan demonstrated, terrorism can be counterrevolutionary and might become so again. It is not sporadic political murder such as those which ranged in the West from William Rufus of England and Henry IV of France, through Lincoln and Huey Long, to the Kennedys. Indeed, while the movement might start, as in Papua, with the murder of a prominent person as something of a declaration of war, it specializes in killing, maiming, and torturing the defenseless. It, unlike the assassinations of political leaders which were not followed through by similar acts, is constant pressure against a weak polity aiming to diminish its will to continue the fight, frightening the public into accepting a peace on terrorists' terms, and providing the folklore of martyrdom for apprehended and executed terrorists.

The tropical rain belt terrorist is unorganized, untrained, and either works alone or with very few. The modern terrorist is highly trained, strictly disciplined, and part of a far-flung apparatus. He is as dedicated to a political cause as any soldier. This is, of course, the terrorist's strength, but it can be a weakness for the side which employs him. As the membership with weak stomachs tends to drop out of the movement, a dedicated hard core is left which accepts discipline and orders only from its own. There is an element of political compromise in civilized war and, often, in civil war. The terrorist apparatus may turn on its central authority if it shows signs of departing from the extremist position for which it has given up so much. Again, as Jomo Kenyatta discovered after he had detribalized, demoralized, and remoralized his Mau Mau by conditioning them to atrociousness below all but Jibaro or Papuan ethical standards, it is difficult to recondition some terrorists into peaceful, productive citizens once the cause is won. Perhaps the Russian Bolsheviks showed more foresight. They used the anarchist terrorists until victory was assured, then completely eliminated them.

Far from recognizing the terrorist as a legitimate combatant, his opposition considers him a felon and treats him as such. The confronter, for that matter, is considered a petty misdemeanant if he merely screams insults and throws rocks, but a felon if his missiles destroy property or life. The guerrilla, however, has a grudging recognition in the law of war. His target is the isolated, presumably vulnerable small units of his enemy's conventional army. He is fighting for a recognized government, or one which seeks this status. As such, he is legally something of a soldier, and is often given prisoner of war status if captured. He may be armed no better than a Sioux, and have to live on the country like one, but unlike his primitive counterpart, he is disciplined and dedicated to a cause rather than his own glory, and in this he loses his primitivity.

As we have noted, the guerrilla's chance of success against enemy troops of any quality is almost nil. If, by contrast, his cause provides him with a conventional army, even a small one, to act as his pivot of maneuver, he can sometimes accomplish remarkable victories. Sumter and Marion would eventually have been eliminated by Tarleton. Their doom was sealed, it seemed, but the Continental Congress sent south its able field commander, Nathanael Greene, and the irregular warfare combined with the fine continental line regiments harried Lord Cornwallis to his ultimate defeat. Granted that Napoleon's army in Spain was of fair quality, and it could hardly have been better than fair, it almost certainly would have won eventually against the petty warrior which gave this type of warfare its name. Wellington arrived, however, and with guerrilla help, completely defeated the French. As a matter of fact, the duke did too well. Instead of acting as a pivot of maneuver for the guerrillas and allowing them to complete their almost accomplished task of demoralization, he drove the French forces out of Spain, and not only permitted them but forced them to concentrate, regroup, and continue to be a menace to his cause.

The great guerrilla, Lawrence of Arabia, saw this Wellingtonian error and did not repeat it in World War I. He and his Arab partisans kept up their demoralizing pressure on the Turk, but waited for the arrival of the last first-class commander of regular horse calvary, Lord Allenby. The two of them settled the Turkish problem for many a year. Guerrilla Mosby and the regular Confererate calvary of McCausland did much to postpone the decline of Jubal Early, but the latter's army was small and neglected. The Confederate irregular Ashby, instead of being the harassing force for Braxton Bragg, went off on his own to invade Ohio and was destroyed — as could have been predicted. Quantrill did not deign to join the regular force of General Price in the invasion of Missouri where he could have been useful.

In recent years, in spite of some opinion to the contrary, it was not the Pathet Lao partisans who threw the French out of Indochina, but the competent regulars of General Giap. Not long afterward, the Viet Cong demonstrated that they could not defeat the Americans under Westmoreland. Acting later as the harassing arm of the same Giap and his North Vietnamese regulars, they have proved that primitive tactics, or lack of them, backed by a strong conventional force, can be very annoying.

Our conclusion, then, is that while the fighting methods of primitive war have proved useful to some modern political states, it is doubtful if they represent a survival. They are in part revivals, but it is doubtful if the confronters, terrorists, and guerrillas know this.

A great distinction between primitive and true (or civilized) war implicit, but not emphasized, in this book is the sociologic invention of the civilian as separate from the fighting forces. Primitive warriors made no such distinction, nor could they. Old man, woman, or child, an enemy was an enemy and met a fate worthy of the name. A Melanesian sea raid was happy to bring home a female captive to torture, roast alive, and cannibalize, and that is only an extreme example. Civilization, one of whose meanings is craft specialization and class distinctions, introduced that of the noncombatant public. This does not mean that the citizens of a captured city always fared well. The humane idea did not occur to the Greeks, but the Romans gradually realized that a conquered people was a source of tax income, of sequestration of consumption goods, and, since the Romans' technological ambition exceeded their ability to harness natural energy, of slaves needed for their mighty works. Yet, after the conquest of Gaul, it dawned on them that an empire could be built upon the willing service of formerly independent people. These should be won over, as the Celtic and Greek peoples eventually were, to form those Gallo-Roman and Byzantine civilizations which served as the bastions against barbarism for so long.

Some idea of chivalry towards the captives trickled through the knightly intelligence with the revival of civilization in the Middle Ages. It was never perfectly observed, but it was there. The collapse of humane morals, called the Renaissance, returned the civilian to his victim status. One loathes to read of the sack of Rome by the troops of the Emperor Charles V even today. Interestingly enough, the Renaissance cavalry was not allowed within a fallen city for a share of booty and beauty until the infantry was surfeited. The footmen had done the dirty work of trenching and countertrenching. This bloodbath proved too much for western man; and once more, from the dawn of international law and civilian rights with the publication of *De Jure Belli ac Pacis* by Hugo Grotius, through the Geneva Conventions, to the American expenditure of billions on the economic rehabilitation of conquered enemies, the idea arose that war is made between two hostile governments, and that the civilian has a legal right to his person and property. Yet there are those of us who have seen the shambles of Coventry left by the *Luftwaffe,* and have helped drag the bodies of children from the rubble of London. We have seen Düren in Germany leveled to the ground by the United States Eighth Bomber Command, and living Japanese can tell you of Hiroshima and Nagasaki. Is this a return to primitive war? I think not.

If "limited war" refers to conflict with the enemy's armed forces alone, and if "unlimited war" marks all his manpower and resources for destruction, then "total war" is aimed at the whole of his population, all of his property, and his entire potential. Thus, the generals and princes of the baroque and rococo limited wars invited the pampered civilians to be spectators of *la guerre en dentelles,* that lacy, professional battle parade. The princes wanted the affection of potentially conquered civilians as taxpayers and producers, and the generals did not want them to scorch the earth before and behind them. From this viewpoint onward there was an irregular progress towards the foundation of the Civil Affiairs–Military Government Corps by the United States Army with the specific mission of helping the enemy civil population recover and be prosperous. Of course the founding of CAMG was to protect our own rear from civilian starvation, pestilence, and civil disorder, but the idea of protecting, rehabilitating, and converting the civilian was also there. Now the guerrilla, fierce as he is, has the same motives. He seeks to pamper the civilian public not only to subvert it from the side of legitimacy but to use it as a mask to conceal himself from the vengeance of the enemy's conventional forces. The guerrilla has to be able to blend in with the civil population when not fighting. He needs supporters among the noncombatants wherein he can swim like a fish, as Chairman Mao said. All theorists, from the Romans, to Mao, Guevara, and the Americans Hamlett and Yarborough have emphasized this.

And yet the shadow of total war once more hovers over us all. Is this a revival of the concepts of primitive war? One ought not think so. The primitive warrior butchered the civilians because he was incapable of conceptualizing such a status. Modern war against the unarmed civilian is the deliberate decision of that civil government which the primitive warrior did not have. Furthermore, it might be salutary to see that total war was not invented by the Germans and Japanese. It had its seed bed in North America in the eighteenth century as a sibling of democratic war and its offspring, the mass-man army.

One is tempted to consider all civil wars as total wars, but he remembers that several Roman wars of a civil type were only political power grabs whose leaders wanted the Italian population to be safe, prosperous, productive, and taxable. If civil war is also revolutionary in nature, however, there can be no pampered spectators, no innocent bystanders. This has been mentioned before, but the American revolutionists were very harsh to colonial loyalists and simple farmers who merely wanted to be left alone. Of course, whenever and wherever the "Tories" got around to organizing, as in the Carolina Waxhaw country, they returned this love with interest. If one wishes to read about what happened to loyalist women and children, in particular, the monographs are available. Later Ulysses Simpson Grant ordered General David Hunter to make all valleys south of the Baltimore and Ohio Railroad a "desert as high up as possible." And it was Grant who ordered his troops to "eatout Virginia clear and clean . . . so that crows flying over it for the balance of this season will have to carry their provender with them." That women and children starved or had their homes burned over their heads was not a military consideration.[1] Yet it was not Grant who invented total war. He and his generals, Hunter excepted, were in private life the kindest and gentlest of men, and surely William Tecumseh Sherman was. These generals were responsible soldiers, and they had but one political head and commander in chief. Abraham Lincoln dodged the issue in writing (and who would not?), but it is an old principle of command that authority may be

[1]One must be fair. Violence begets violence, and in reprisal, the bitter General McCausland, paid a visit to Chambersburg, Pennsylvania, which is still remembered there.

delegated downward, but responsibility cannot be. Lincoln's famous cavalry leader, Philip Sheridan, an observer in the Franco-Prussian War, sat one night at Prince Bismarck's dinner table, and heard his host half apologize for the rough treatment dealt a French village. The hero of Winchester set the tone for the future by replying, "The people must be left nothing but their eyes to weep over the war."[2]

The confronter and terrorist recognize the status of the civilian and capitalize on his ambivalence, perhaps his sense of guilt for things as they are, and his self-protective wish to be on the winning side. These almost primitive, but surely theatrical, warriors stage performances with a strong missionary aspect. The guerrilla, too, cannot survive without civilian help. The prosecution of total war, however, rests on the cold, unemotional decision of a political government. It is not theatrical nor missionary. It is conquest naked and raw, and we all live under the shadow of its possibility.

Here are some hard facts which we of the civilian public must face before anyone goes further. Every reader is a beneficiary of past wars, primitive or civilized, and each one of us is a victim. This is valid for every American, and others, no matter how much of a minority his ethnic group may be. Now who wants to call quits? Practically everybody does, it seems. All the great military powers proclaim their longing for peace, permanent peace, which is somewhat reminiscent of the Iroquois League, the most efficient pre-Columbian fighting machine north of the Rio Grande. It called itself The Great League to Enforce Peace.

The military is the external force arm of civil government, and the purpose of the public armed forces is to make war. All such wars are defensive, according to the politicians and chiefs of state. The last one to speak otherwise was Frederick the Great of Prussia, who said, "My armies are on the march. My generals are victorious, and my professors are figuring out the causes of this war." Can we modern professors figure how we may have the benefits of stable, orderly government without its hitherto inevitable dysfunction of war? Dear readers and colleagues, you do not need me to tell you that the hour is late.

---

[2]Charles Francis Adams, *Studies Military and Diplomatic, 1775-1865,* 1911, p. 287.

Bibliography

The following list contains only the works actually cited in the text.

Abel, Charles W., *Savage Life in New Guinea*, London: London Missionary Society, 1902.

Adair, James, *The History of the American Indians*, London: E. and C. Dilly, 1775.

Appianus of Alexandria, *Roman History*.

Armstrong, Wallace E., *Rossel Island*, Cambridge: Cambridge University Press, 1928.

Avienus, Rufus Festus, *Ora Maritima*.

Basden, George T., *Among the Ibos of Nigeria*, Philadelphia: Lippincott, 1921.

Bateson, Gregory, *Naven*, Cambridge: Cambridge University Press, 1936.

Beech, Mervyn W. H., *The Suk*, Oxford: Oxford University Press, 1911.

Belloc, Hilaire, *Poitiers*, London: 1913.

Binger, Louis G., *Du Niger au Golfe de Guinee*, Paris: Hatchette, 1892.

Blackwood, Beatrice, *Both Sides of Buka Passage*, Oxford: Oxford University Press, 1935.

Boas, Franz, *Tsimshian Mythology*, Annual Report 31, Bureau of American Ethnology, Washington: 1909-1910.

Bogoraz, Waldemar, "The Chuckchee-Social Organization," *American Museum of Natural History Memoirs*, vol. 11, part III, New York: 1904-1909.

Bossu, Jean B., *Nouveaux Voyages aux Indes Occidentales*, 2 vols., Paris: Le Jay, 1768.

Brackenbury, Sir Henry, *The Ashanti War*, Edinburgh and London: W. Blackwood, 1874.

Brewster, Adolph B., *The Hill Tribes of Fiji,* Philadelphia: Lippincott, 1922.

Bromilow, William E., *Twenty Years Among Primitive Papuans,* London: Epworth Press, 1929.

Brown, George, *Melanesians and Polynesians,* London: Macmillan, 1910.

Brown, John T., *Among Bantu Nomads (Bechuana),* Philadelphia: Lippincott, 1926.

Brown, M. J., *Historical Ballad Poetry of Ireland,* New York: Benziger Brothers, 1912.

Buck, Peter H., *Samoan Material Culture,* Honolulu: Bernice P. Bishop Museum, 1930.

———, *Mangaian Society,* Honolulu: Bernice P. Bishop Museum, 1934

Bunzel, Ruth L., "Introduction to Zuni Ceremonialism," *Annual Report 47,* Bureau of American Ethnology, Washington: 1929-1930.

Burton, Sir Richard F., *A Mission to Gelele, King of Dahomey,* New York: Scribners, 1893.

———, *The Lake Regions of Central Africa,* New York: Harpers, 1864.

Bushnell, David I., *Burials of the Algonquian, Siouan, and Caddaoan Tribes West of the Mississippi,* Bulletin 83, Bureau of American Ethnology, Washington: 1927.

Caesar, Caius Julius, *The Gallic War.*

Childe, V. Gordon, *The Dawn of European Civilization,* London: Kegan Paul, 1939.

Church, George E., *Aborigines of South America,* edited by Clement R. Markham, London: Chapman and Hall, 1912.

Clapperton, Hugh. *Journal of the Second Expedition Into the Interior of Africa,* London: J. Murray, 1829.

Codrington, Robert H., *The Melanesians,* Oxford: Clarendon Press, 1891.

Conzemius, Eduard, *Ethnographical Survey of the Miskito and Sumu Indians of Honduras and Nicaragua,* Bulletin 106, Bureau of American Ethnology, Washington: 1932.

Cook, Albert S., and Tinker, Chauncey B., *Selected Translations from Old English Poetry,* Boston: Ginn, 1902.

Coombe, Florence, *Islands of Enchantment,* London: Macmillan, 1911.

Cooper, John M., *Analytical and Critical Bibliography of the Tribes of Tierra del Fuego and Adjacent Territory,* Bulletin 63, Bureau of American Ethnology, Washington: 1917.

Cureau, Adolph L., *Savage Man in Central Africa,* translated by E. Andrews, London: T. F. Unwin, 1915.

Czaplicka, Marie A., *Aboriginal Siberia,* Oxford: Clarendon Press, 1914.

Dean, Wallace, *Fijian Society,* London: Macmillan, 1921.

Del Mar, Frances, *A Year Among the Maoris,* London: E. Benn, 1924.

Denig, E. T., "Indian Tribes of the Upper Missouri," edited by J. N. B. Hewitt, *Annual Report 46,* Bureau of American Ethnology, Washington: 1928-1929.

Densmore, Frances, *Chippewa Customs,* Bulletin 86, Bureau of American Ethnology, Washington: 1929.

———, *Chippewa Music,* Bulletin 53, Bureau of American Ethnology, Washington: 1913.

———, *Mandan and Hitdatsa Music,* Bulletin 80, Bureau of American Ethnology, Washington: 1923.

———, *Papago Music,* Bulletin 90, Bureau of American Ethnology, Washington: 1929.

———, *Teton Sioux Music,* Bulletin 61, Bureau of American Ethnology, Washington: 1918.

———, *Yuman and Yaqui Music,* Bulletin 110, Bureau of American Ethnology, Washington: 1923.

DeVries, David P., *Voyages from Holland to America,* translated by Henry C. Murphy, New York: Billin and Brothers, 1853.

Dio, Cassius, *Roman History.*

Dornan, S. S., *Pygmies and Bushmen of the Kalahari,* London: Seeley, Service, 1925.

Dorsey, James O., "A Study of Siouan Cults," *Annual Report 11,* Bureau of American Ethnology, Washington: 1889-1890.

———, "Omaha Sociology," *Annual Report 3,* Bureau of American Ethnology, Washington: 1881-1882.

———, "Siouan Sociology," *Annual Report 15,* Bureau of American Ethnology, Washington: 1893-1894.

———, *Traditions of the Skidi Pawnee,* Memoirs, American Folk-Lore Society, Vol. VIII, Menasha 1904.

Duncan, John, *Travels in Western Africa,* London: R. Bentley, 1847.

Dutt, Romesh C., translator, *The Mahabharata,* London: Macmillan, 1899.

———, *The Ramayana,* New York: Dutton, 1910.

Ellis, Alfred B., *The Ewe Speaking Peoples,* London: Chapman and Hall, 1894.

———, *The Tshi Speaking Peoples,* London: Chapman and Hall, 1887.

———, *The Yoruba Speaking Peoples,* London: Chapman and Hall, 1894.

Ferguson, W. S., "The Zulus and the Spartans: A Comparison of their Military Systems," *Varia Africana,* II, Harvard African Series, Cambridge (Massachusetts): Harvard University Press, 1918.

Fewkes, Jesse W., "Hopi Katchinas," *Annual Report 21,* Bureau of American Ethnology, Washington: 1899-1900.

Firth, Raymond W., *Primitive Economics of the New Zealand Maori,* New York: Routledge, 1929.

Fletcher, Alice C., and La Flesche, Francis, *The Omaha Tribe,* Annual Report 27, Bureau of American Ethnology, Washington: 1905-1906.

Forbes, Frederick E., *Dahomey and the Dahomeans,* London: Longmans, Brown, Green, and Longmans, 1851.

Fortune, Reo F., *The Sorcerers of Dobu,* New York: Dutton, 1932.

Gifford, Edward W., *The Kamia of Imperial Valley,* Bulletin 97, Bureau of American Ethnology, Washington: 1931.

Gilbert, Vivian, *The Romance of the Last Crusade,* New York: D. Appleton, 1923.

Goddard, Pliny E., *Jicarilla Apache Texts,* Anthropological Papers, American Museum of Natural History, vol. VIII, New York: 1911.

Hadfield, Emma, *Among Natives of the Loyalty Group,* London: Macmillan, 1920.

Hawkins, Sir John, *A True Declaration of the Troublesome Voyage of M. John Haukins,* London: 1569.

Herodotus, *History.*

Herskovits, Melville J., *Dahomey,* 2 vols., New York: Augustin, 1938.

———, and Frances S., *An Outline of Dahomean Religious Belief,* Memoir 41, American Anthropological Association, Menasha: 1933.

Hewat, Alexander, *Historical Account of the Rise and Progress of the Colonies of South Carolina and Georgia,* London: A. Donaldson, 1790.

Hilton-Simpson, Melville W., *Land and Peoples of the Kasai,* Chicago: McClurg, 1911.

Hinde, Sidney L., *The Last of the Masai,* London: W. Heineman, 1901.

Hobley, Charles W., *Bantu Beliefs and Magic,* London: H. F. and G. Witherby, 1922.

Hoernle, Agnes W., "The Social Organization of the Name Hottentots of Southwest Africa," *American Anthropologist,* vol. 27, 1925.

Hollander, Lee M., editor and translator, *Old Norse Poems: The Most Important Non-Skaldic Verse Not Included in the Poetic Edda,* New York: Columbia University Press, 1936.

Hollis, Sir Alfred C., *The Masai,* Oxford: Clarendon Press, 1905.

Hubert, Henri, *The Rise of the Celts,* translated by M. W. Dobie, New York: Knopf, 1934.

Humphreys, Clarence B., *The Southern New Hebrides,* Cambridge; Cambridge University Press, 1926.

Hunt, George T., *The Wars of the Iroquois: A Study in Intertribal Trade Relations,* Madison: University of Wisconsin Press, 1940.

Ivens, Walter G., *Melanesians of the Southeast Solomon Islands,* London: Kegan Paul, Trench, Trubner, 1927.

Jenness, Diamond, and Ballantyne, Andrew, *The Northern D'Entrecasteaux,* Oxford: Clarendon Press, 1920.

Johnston, Sir Harry H., *The Uganda Protectorate,* London: Hutchinson, 1902.

Junod, Henri A., *The Life of a South African Tribe,* 2nd ed., Neuchatel: 1927.

Karsten, Rafael, *Blood Revenge, War, and Victory Feasts Among the Jibaro Indians of Eastern Ecuador,* Bulletin 79, Bureau of American Ethnology, Washington: 1923.

Kidd, Dudley, *The Essential Kaffir,* London: Macmillan, 1904.

Kidder, Alfred V., *An Introduction to the Study of Southwestern Archaelogy,* Papers of the Southwestern Expedition, No. 1, Department of Archaelogy, Phillips Academy, Andover, Massachusetts, New Haven: Yale University Press, 1924.

Krause, F., "Sling Contrivances for Projectile Weapons," *Annual Report,* Smithsonian Institution, Washington: 1904.

Kroeber, Alfred L., *Handbook of the Indians of California,* Bulletin 78, Bureau of American Ethnology, Washington: 1923.

Krige, Eileen J., *The Social System of the Zulus,* London: Longmans Green, 1936.

La Flesche, Francis, *The Osage Tribe: Rite of the Chiefs: Sayings of Ancient Men,* Annual Report 36, Bureau of American Ethnology, Washington: 1914-1915.

———, *The Osage Tribe: Rite of Vigil,* Annual Report 39, Bureau of American Ethnology, Washington: 1917-1928.

———, *The Osage Tribe: Rite of Wa-xo-be,* Annual Report 45, Bureau of American Ethnology, Washington: 1927-1928.

Landtman, Gunnar, *The Kiwai Papuans of British New Guinea,* London: Macmillan, 1927.

Le Moyne, Jacques de Morgue, *Narrative,* translated from the Latin of De Bry, Boston: J. R. Osgood, 1875.

Linderman, Frank, *American,* New York: World Book Company, 1930.
———, *Red Mother,* New York: John Day, 1932.

Livy, Titus, *The History of Rome.*

Lowie, Robert H., *The Assiniboine,* Anthropological Papers, American Museum of Natural History, vol. 4, part 1, New York: 1909.

———, *The Crow Indians,* New York: Farrar and Rinehart, 1935.

———, *Dances and Societies of the Plains Shoshone,* Anthropological Papers, American Museum of Natural History, vol. 11, part 10, New York: 1915.

———, *The Material Culture of the Crow Indians,* Anthropological Papers, American Museum of Natural History, vol. 23, part 3, New York: 1922.

———, *Plains Indian Age-Societies: Historical and Comparative Summary,* Anthropological Papers, American Museum of Natural History, vol. 11, part 8, New York: 1916.

———, *Societies of the Arikara Indians,* Anthropological Papers, American Museum of Natural History, vol. 11, part 8, New York: 1915.

———, *Societies of the Kiowa,* Anthropological Papers, American Museum of Natural History, vol. 11, part 11, New York: 1916.

Macleod, Olive, *Chiefs and Cities of Central Africa,* Edinburgh and London: W. Blackwood, 1912.

Malinowski, Bronislav, *Argonauts of the Western Pacific,* New York: E. P. Dutton, 1922.

Mallery, Garrick, *Picture-Writing of the American Indians,* Annual Report 10, Bureau of American Ethnology, Washington: 1888-1889.

McGee, W. J., *The Seri Indians,* Annual Report 17, Bureau of American Ethnology, Washington: 1895-1896.

Mead, Margaret, *Social Organization of Manua,* Honolulu, Bernice P. Bishop Museum, 1930.

Meek, Charles K., *Law and Authority in a Nigerian Tribe, a Study in Indirect Rule,* London: Oxford University Press, 1937.

Meyer, Kuno, *Miscellenea Hibernica,* Urbana: University of Illinois Press, 1917.

Mooney, James, *Myths of the Cherokee,* Annual Report 19, Bureau of American Ethnology, Washington: 1897-1898.

———, "The Calendar History of the Kiowa," *Annual Report 17,* Bureau of American Ethnology, Washington: 1895-1896.

———, "The Ghost-Dance Religion and the Sioux Outbreak of 1890," *Annual Report 14,* Bureau of American Ethnology, Washington: 1892-1893.

———, "The Sacred Formulae of the Cherokee," *Annual Report 7,* Bureau of American Ethnology, Washington: 1885-1886.

Morley, Sylvanus, *An Introduction to the Study of Maya Hieroglyphs,* Bulletin 57, Bureau of American Ethnology, Washington: 1885-1886.

Murdock, George P., "The Organization of Inca Society," *Scientific Monthly,* March, 1934.

Nalder, Leonard F., editor, *A Tribal Survey of Mongalla Province,* London: Oxford University Press, 1937.

Nelson, Edward W., "The Eskimo About Bering Strait," *Annual Report 18,* Bureau of American Ethnology, part 1, Washington: 1896-1897.

Ogden, Sir G. *The Basutos,* New York: 1910.

Polo, Marco, *The Book,* translated by H. Yules, London: 1903.

Powdermaker, Hortense, *Life in Lesu,* New York: W. W. Norton, 1933.

Powell, J. W., "Wyandot Government," *Annual Report 1,* Bureau of American Ethnology, Washington: 1879-1886.

Radin, Paul, *The Winnebago Tribe,* Annual Report 37, Bureau of American Ethnology, Washington: 1915-1916.

Rattray, Robert S., *Ashanti,* Oxford: Clarendon Press, 1923.

———, *Ashanti Law and Constitution,* Oxford: Clarendon Press, 1929.

Rhys, Sir John, *Celtic Britain,* New York: E. and J. B. Young, 1882.

The Rig Veda

Riley, E. Baxter, *Among Papuan Headhunters,* Philadelphia: Lippincott, 1925.

Romans, *Natural History of East and West Florida,* New York: 1775.

Roscoe, John, *The Bagesu,* Cambridge: Cambridge University Press, 1924.

Roscoe, John, *The Banyankole,* Cambridge: Cambridge University Press, 1924.

Roth, Walter E., *An Introductory Study of the Arts, Crafts, and Customs of the Guiana Indians,* Annual Report 38, Bureau of American Ethnology, Washington: 1916-1917.

Routledge, William S., and Katherine, *With the Akikuyu of British East Africa,* London: Longmans Green, 1910.

Russell, Frank, "The Pima Indians," *Annual Report 26,* Bureau of American Ethnology, Washington: 1904-1905.

Sarasin, F., *Ethnologie der Neu-Calendonier und Loyalty Insulander,* Munich: 1929.

Schebesta, Paul, *Among Congo Pygmies,* London: Hutchinson, 1933.

Skinner, Alanson B., *Notes on the Eastern Cree and the Northern Saulteaux,* Anthropological Papers, American Museum of Natural History, vol. 9, New York: 1911.

———, *Political Organization, Cults, and Ceremonies of the Plains-Ojibway and Plains-Cree Indians,* Anthropological Papers, American Museum of Natural History, vol. 11, part 6, New York: 1914.

———, *Social Life and Ceremonial Bundles of the Menomini Indians,* Anthropological Papers, American Museum of Natural History, vol. 13, part 1, New York: 1913.

———, *Societies of the Iowa, Kansa, and Ponca Indians,* Anthropological Papers, American Museum of Natural History, vol. 11, part 9, New York: 1915.

Smith, Edwain W., *The Golden Stool,* London: Holborn House, 1926.

Snelgrave, William A., *A New Account of Some Parts of Guinea and the Slave Trade*, London: J. J. and P. Knapton, 1734.

Spaulding, Oliver L., Nickerson, Hoffman, and Wright, John W., *Warfare*, New York: Harcourt Brace, 1925.

Speiser, Felix, *Two Years with the Natives of the Western Pacific*, London: Mills and Boon, 1913.

Sturluson, Snorri, *The Heimskringla*, translated by W. Morris and E. Magnusson, 4 vols., London: 1893.

Swanton, John R., "Creek Social Organization and Uses," *Annual Report 42*, Bureau of American Ethnology, Washington, 1924-1925.

———, *Early History of the Creek Indians and their Neighbors*, Bulletin, 73, Bureau of American Ethnology, Washington: 1922.

———, "Religious Beliefs and Medical Practices of the Creek Indians," *Annual Report 42*, Bureau of American Ethnology, Washington: 1924-1925.

———, "Social Conditions, Beliefs, and Linguistic Relationships of the Tlingit Indians," *Annual Report 26*, Bureau of American Ethnology, Washington: 1904-1905.

———, *Source Material for the Social and Ceremonial Life of the Choctaw Indians*, Bulletin 103, Bureau of American Ethnology, Washington: 1931.

Tacitus, Cornelius, *Agricola*.
———, *Germania*.

Tactics and Technique of Cavalry, 6th edition, Washington and Harrisburg: Military Service Publishing Company, 1935.

Talbot, Percy A., *In the Shadow of the Bush*, London: Macmillan, 1912.

———, *Life in Southern Nigeria*, London: Macmillan, 1923.

———, *The Peoples of Southern Nigeria*, 4 vols., London: Oxford University Press, 1926.

Teit, James A., "The Salishan Tribes of the Western Plateau," edited by Franz Boas, *Annual Report 45*, Bureau of American Ethnology, Washington: 1927-1928.

Thomas, Northcote W., *Anthropological Report on Sierre Leone,* London: Harrison and Son, 1916.

Thomson, Sir Basil H., *The Fijians: A Study of the Decay of Custom,* London: W. Heineman, 1908.

Torday, Emil, *On the Trail of the Bushongo,* Philadelphia: Lippincott, 1925.

Turney-High, Harry H., "Cooking Camas and Bitter Root," *American Anthropologist,* vol. 35, n.s., 1933.

———, *Ethnography of the Kutenai,* Memoir 56, American Anthropological Association, Menasha: 1941.

———, *The Flathead Indians of Montana,* Memoir 48, American Anthropological Association: Menasha: 1937.

Underhill, Ruth, *The Autobiography of a Papago Woman,* Memoir 46, American Anthropological Association, Menasha: 1936.

Verendrye, Le Chevalier de la, *Journal,* Report on Canadian Archives 1889, Ottawa: 1890.

Weeks, John H., *Among Congo Cannibals,* Philadelphia: Lippincott, 1913.

———, *Among the Primitive BaKongo,* Philadelphia: Lippincott, 1914.

White, Leslie A., "The Acoma Indians," *Annual Report 47,* Bureau of American Ethnology, Washington: 1929-1930.

Williamson, Robert W., *The Ways of the South Sea Savage,* Philadelphia: Lippincott, 1914.

Wissler, Clark, *The American Indian,* 3rd edition, New York: Oxford University Press, 1938.

———, *The Blackfoot,* Annual Archaeological Report for 1905, Toronto: 1906.

———, *The Indians of Greater New York and the Lower Hudson,* Anthropological Papers, American Museum of Natural History, vol. 3, New York: 1909.

———, *Material Culture of the Blackfoot Indians,* Anthropological Papers, American Museum of Natural History, vol. 5, part 1, New York: 1910.

———, *Social Life of the Blackfoot Indians,* Anthropological Papers, American Museum of Natural History, vol. 7, part 1, New York: 1911.

———, *Societies and Ceremonial Associations of the Oglala Division of the Teton-Dakota,* Anthropological Papers, American Museum of Natural History, vol. 11, part 1, New York: 1912.

INDEX

INDEX

INDEX

INDEX

INDEX

INDEX

INDEX

INDEX

INDEX

INDEX

INDEX